Praise for *Ignited*

"Managers of the world, rejoice. There is finally a book for you. Vince's book contains some of the best advice you'll ever get on getting the best out of people and enduring the constant stress that comes with managing human beings. Simple, easy to use, and inspiring. If you manage people, buy one. If you manage managers, buy a box. In a world of leadership books that may or may not apply to your situation—this book will hit you in the bull's-eye."

—Tim Sanders, author of *Love Is the Killer App:
How To Win Business and Influence Friends*
and former Chief Solutions Officer at Yahoo!

"*Ignited* is a groundbreaking leadership book that if followed will unleash any organizations most underutilized resource—Middle Managers. Too long neglected and too often abused, Vince Thompson lays out how to maximize these managers' untapped potential, and it is HUGE! If you need results and need an energized management team, *Ignited* is the only book you need to read."

—Chester Elton, co-author of the New York Times
best-selling *Invisible Employee*

"Leading from the middle has always been a tough job. In today's rapidly changing environment, it's even harder. With *Ignited*, Thompson takes managers right to the heart of their roles and shows them how they are uniquely positioned to energize their companies. Ignited promises more power, more purpose, and more success and really delivers."

—Linda A. Livingstone, Ph.D., Dean,
The Graziadio School of Business and Management,
Pepperdine University

"What will make your career hot—or not—is whether you can inspire a burning desire for change and growth in the people around you. Vince Thompson shows how to do this to get the success you deserve."

—Keith Ferrazzi, best-selling author of *Never Eat Alone*,
CEO of Ferrazzi Greenlight

"Thompson's the real deal and his book on management stands out like none other. I'm recommending it to my team and encourage you to take his purpose-filled advice and truly be Ignited!"

—**Alan Cohen, CMO TV Guide**

"Anyone trying to navigate the treacherous shoals of today's middle management dilemma without this book does so at his or her own peril. Vince Thompson spells out in delicious detail how to stand apart from the crowd and actually get things done"

—**Granville Toogood, executive coach and author of**
The Articulate Executive—Learn to Look, Act and Sound like a Leader

"*Ignited* is just superb. Rich with terrific insights into the managers' dilemmas, this book delivers on the promise for managers to become "Ignited", energized and passionate in their work. One of the experiences and recommendations so resonated with the current situation my friend is in that I pointed it out to him and now he's reading the book as well! I'm certain I'll be recommending this book for years to come."

—**Jan Sola, Ph.D., Associate Director, Executive Development Center, Leavey School of Business, Santa Clara University**

"If you want to get to the top, you've got to make meaningful contributions. With *Ignited*, Thompson provides a framework for purposeful and powerful action."

—**Jeffrey Fox, best selling author of *How to Become CEO and How to Get to the Top: Business Lessons Learned at the Dinner Table***

"Thanks to Vince Thompson, we're reminded that we, managers in the middle, are not alone! With entertaining anecdotes, real life examples, and solid research, you'll find *Ignited* really connects. You'll laugh, you'll cry, and if you follow the advice you'll find yourself managing your career rather than being managed by it. This wonderful book is a must read for anyone in management."

—**Lisa Tichadou, Sales Training Manager, Employee Development, Los Angeles Times**

IGNITED

IGNITED

MANAGERS!
LIGHT UP YOUR COMPANY
AND CAREER

For More Power, More Purpose,
And More Success

VINCE THOMPSON

An Imprint of PEARSON EDUCATION
Upper Saddle River, NJ • New York • London • San Francisco • Toronto • Sydney
Tokyo • Singapore • Hong Kong • Cape Town • Madrid
Paris • Milan • Munich • Amsterdam

www.ftpress.com

Vice President, Editor-in-Chief: Tim Moore
Acquisitions Editor: Paula Sinnott, Jennifer Simon
Editorial Assistant: Susie Abraham
Development Editor: Russ Hall
Associate Editor-in-Chief and Director of Marketing: Amy Neidlinger
Publicist: Amy Fandrei
Marketing Coordinator: Megan Colvin
Cover Designer: Chuti Prasertsith
Managing Editor: Gina Kanouse
Project Editor: Terra Dalton
Copy Editor: Lisa Thibault
Indexer: Erika Millen
Compositor: codeMantra
Manufacturing Buyer: Dan Uhrig
Proofreader: Page One Editing, Inc.

FT Press offers excellent discounts on this book when ordered in quantity for bulk purchases or special sales. For more information, please contact U.S. Corporate and Government Sales, 1-800-382-3419, corpsales@pearsontechgroup.com. For sales outside the U.S., please contact International Sales at international@pearsoned.com.

Pearson Education LTD.
Pearson Education Australia PTY, Limited.
Pearson Education Singapore, Pte. Ltd.
Pearson Education North Asia, Ltd.
Pearson Education Canada, Ltd.
Pearson Educatión de Mexico, S.A. de C.V.
Pearson Education—Japan
Pearson Education Malaysia, Pte. Ltd.

Library of Congress Cataloging-in-Publication Data

Thompson, Vincent S., 1963-
    Ignited : managers, light up your company and career for more power, more purpose, and more success / Vincent S. Thompson.
        p. cm.
    Includes bibliographical references and index.
    ISBN 0-13-149248-9 (hardback : alk. paper)   1. Industrial management.   I. Title.
HD31.T523 2007
658.4'09--dc22   2006019566

Dedication

To Jackie, the love of my life, who makes it all seem possible.

CONTENTS

Part III

ACKNOWLEDGMENTS

A t the height of the social change defining the Sixties, someone asked the Grateful Dead's Jerry Garcia a simple question: Why? Jerry responded by saying, "Somebody had to do something, and it's just incredibly pathetic that it had to be us."

I can't repeat Jerry's line without laughing. Any of us who have felt the call of duty can certainly relate. As a manager, I spent far too many hours hoping a great and powerful force would hit the Restart button and create a world for managers where things made sense and business could be and mean all that we wanted it to. With that day not appearing to have been scheduled in my Outlook calendar, it was time to try and do what I could.

Having heard and believed that a good idea does not care who it belongs to, I gave myself the room to explore and began looking at my own Manager's Universe for answers. What I found almost instantly was a passionate and thoughtful community who shared the vision and would give tirelessly to the realization of this work.

The initial validation and trigger for the publishing deal came from my dear friend and mentor Jason Jennings, whose phenomenal success as an author and speaker is a true testament to the power of his passion to give and help others. Jason listened to the premise of Ignited, added key insights, and connected me with Tim Moore and Paula Sinnott at Pearson's FT Press. Tim and Paula challenged me to go deeper in my thinking and then guided me into a book deal with them supported by the power of their company, one of the world's leading publishers.

Soon after, a research team was born. Susannah Kim, a Pepperdine MBA student joined, along with Attila Szucs who led much of the early research effort. As a former telecom manager in Hungary and an Accenture consultant, Attila had come to Los Angeles to finish his own MBA and went deep into the history of management and management practices for this book. Near the conclusion of this first year of research, we were joined by Brian Solon who, with a JD/MBA, budding musical career, and passion for business books, had just finished as the lead researcher on Jason Jenning's bestselling *Think Big, Act Small*. Brian challenged our existing research, took us even deeper, and helped with the outline, early editing, and wordsmithing. We were also fortunate to have Nick Morgan, founder of Public Words and editor of the *Harvard Management Communication Letter*, as an early guide in the book's structure. Nick's partner Nikki Smith-Morgan played a key role as well. In order to administer our survey of managers and connect with the community, we needed a great Web site, and we were thrilled when Tim Sanders set us up with Jack Wu of ScreamStream. Jack not only designed a great site (www.BeIgnited.com), but also powered up his own network to help with our cause.

As you may imagine, all of this effort was rather challenging given that during most of the work I was employed full time as a sales manager. Our research team met on Saturdays, and my managers at AOL were incredibly supportive of me using my white space during the weekdays when needed to work on *Ignited*. When it came time to draft the early pages, they even allowed me a flex schedule during a four-month period that provided many weekdays for writing. It would be hard to overestimate what that support has meant for this project, and with thanks that'll last a lifetime, I'd like to acknowledge Kathy Kayse, the talented Michael Barrett and Mike Kelly, who together turned our ad unit at AOL into a real business while at the same time making it a great place to work.

A few chapters into the early work, something really wonderful happened. We were able to attract Karl Weber to the project. Karl, the former managing director of Times Business (then a division of Random House) and a best-selling author himself, joined to help take the work up a notch with better prose and additional insights. We might never have had the chance to work with someone of Karl's prestige, but he believed that the stories needed to be told, and soon Karl was my partner in this. I'm so thankful for Karl, who taught me a lot and dimensionalized the work in ways far beyond what we could have imagined in the start. Karl is a great writer and a great friend.

With the pages rolling in, Russ Hall, our development editor from FT Press, was there to keep us on track and challenge us to provide insights on every page. As a successful writer and Texan, Russ used great anecdotes that entertained us and at the same time nailed the points. Upon completion of the first draft, Paula Sinnott decided to spend more time with her newborn, and Jennifer Simon took over her passion, while adding her own unique and powerful perspective. Jennifer, along with Pearson's Associate Editor-in-Chief and Director of Marketing Amy Neidlinger, spent an extraordinary amount of time nurturing our message, helping us connect deeper to our themes, and guiding our efforts through the journey from idea to marketplace. Their expertise, professionalism, and true care is so appreciated. As Managing Editor, Gina Kanouse and her team, including Terra Dalton and Dan Knott, made our words a book; Chuti Prasertsith gave us a cover that really popped.

Along the way I also had lots of great help from my wonderful and sharp assistant Tina Trankiem, marketing assistants Adam Fox and David Schlosberg, and our witty transcriber Lynn Colomello. I also benefited greatly from the sanity checks provided to me daily by the AOL Media Networks Team in Los Angeles, who kept me thinking, kept me motivated, and always made me feel part of something bigger. On the public relations front, Amy Fandrei from Pearson partnered with Pam Lontos and Chris Hollis of PR/PR to evangelize our message to traditional and online media. Our marketing manager on *Ignited*, Kenneth Gillett, tapped the expertise of his firm, Target Marketing, and expanded our marketing universe in really exciting and fun ways. Kenneth has built a business by really over-delivering, and we're thankful for that.

The support from other authors that I've admired was humbling; Tim Sanders, Keith Ferrazzi, Larry Haughton, Chester Elton, and Keith Rosen all were there for me and offered their help as needed.

I'd also like to thank our book review team: managers Sue Burger from AOL, Grant Eppler from Heinz, Gary Cormier from Brass Ring, and Brad Simmons from Experian. Their insights, as well as those who are profiled within this book and the survey respondents who gave elaborate detail, provided additional insights that really helped shape the solutions put forth.

I must also take time to thank those who took my early morning and late evening calls and played a key role in the book's content. They are my board of advisors. These folks kept me sane, inspired me, and have been there through whatever life brings: Pat Shaughnessy, Mary Furlong, Charlie Warner, Mark Chassman, Byron Elton, Dave Hoover, Shawn Campbell, Jon Furie, Jeff Gordon, and Marc Sternberg—you mean the world to me. Of course, there's my lifelong board, my parents. My beloved father, Wade Thompson, who unfortunately passed away before our book's launch, was there throughout the book's development and always believed so strongly in taking a stand. My mother, Joan Miller Thompson, the original salesperson and cheerleader in our family, is, as you read this, most likely in some bookstore sneaking copies of this book from the back shelf to the end aisle display.

Finally, thanks to Dilbert and the cast of the television show "The Office." These characters, while making me laugh, regularly demonstrated the pathetic state of management and fueled the frustration and discontent that led me to action and ignited the team of warriors who joined me. Let's hope a day comes when their comedy is based on the past, not the present.

ABOUT THE AUTHOR

Vince Thompson, principal at Middleshift Consulting, works with Internet companies to design world-class online marketing solutions and build sales organizations. His clients include Napster, StarStyle.com and Break.com.

Thompson has spent fifteen years as a manager leading teams in challenging industries and hotbeds for learning: first in restaurants, then in television stations, and now in the Internet business.

He spent seven years as Regional Vice President of Sales for America Online. There, he designed AOL's sales training organization, managed teams in San Francisco, Los Angeles, Chicago, and Dulles, VA; and served as Regional Vice President of AOL's Southwestern Region, where his teams led AOL's West Coast Entertainment and Auto relationships.

He is a featured expert in the Quantum Sales Training Series, has spoken widely on online advertising, and has contributed to the Iowa Press textbook *Media Selling*.

Thompson holds an undergraduate degree in Communications from the University of Southern California's Annenberg School of Communications, and an MBA from Pepperdine University. He lives in Los Angeles, California with his wife and two daughters. To join Vince and the community of Ignited Managers, as well as receive special content and tools, sign up now at www.BeIgnited.com.

INTRODUCTION: LIVING IN QUAKE COUNTRY

Is This You?

Do you have a boss who's not the CEO? Do you have direct reports? Does their success depend on you and your success depend on them?

Welcome to The Middle—perhaps the most crucial location in the world of business. The Middle is more often defined by the questions surrounding it than by the value it creates.

On any day of the week and sometimes weekends, your job in The Middle is tough. Add to that the familiar challenges you face outside of work—the pressures of family life, a kid who needs help with math, a dog that wants to play catch, the new diet to start, eldercare, prescriptions, finances, 401(k)s and 529(b)s. More to do at work. More to do outside of work. You feel trapped by the confines of time.

To cope with the new realities, you work eight hours a week more than your parents did and sleep two hours less a night than your grandparents. (It's not your imagination—we have the survey figures to prove it.) Everyone is looking for ways to save time, collapse time, expand time. Those who can't do it sacrifice sleep, to the detriment of their health. Otherwise, they increasingly fall behind.

Is this you?

If so, you're not alone. There are 5.4 million managers leading teams in more than 30,000 U.S. firms. They spend each day pressured from above and below, searching for the answers that matter.

But for too many managers the existing answers fall far short. In a national survey of middle managers (Fall 2005), Accenture found that the level of satisfaction that managers reported with their companies had collapsed from 67 percent in 2004 to 48 percent in 2005. In a more recent Accenture survey (Fall 2006) that included managers in the United Kingdom, France, Germany, Spain, and Australia, the numbers remained unchanged. Managers are at risk and the output of this collapse is reflected in their actions. According to Accenture, 58 percent of U.S. managers are open to changing jobs and 30 percent are currently looking to make a change. In other words, more than half of the managers leading teams today are ready to walk out the door—leaving their teams, their companies, and for some, if necessary, their homes and communities, behind in hopes of making a fresh start elsewhere.

This came as shocking news to some business leaders. But many managers had seen it building for years—years in which managers in The Middle have been displaced by technology, de-positioned by consultants, handcuffed by red tape, distracted by mergers, spoofed in the media, and denigrated as low-value bureaucrats. No wonder so many managers lost their way and (worse) lost their desire.

Is this you? If so, welcome to Quake Country.

Quake Country

Today's managers no longer live on safe, high ground. Instead, they live in Quake Country, where the land has been eroded, squeezed, and shifted like the ground surrounding the San Andreas fault. It's a place where, as one manager told us, "It seems as if every time I get some forward momentum, the ground falls out from under me."

In Quake Country, technology, competition, innovation, and social change are all in a continuous state of hyperdrive. No wonder the business shocks are coming with greater frequency than ever before. We see the effects each morning in *The Wall Street Journal*, with some companies seemingly springing to prominence overnight, while others are pushed into irrelevance just as fast.

Look at my own business: the world of media, information, and entertainment. In just the past five years, the music business has been changed forever by file-sharing, Internet radio, ring tones, subscription services, and the iPod. Netflix revolutionized the movie rental landscape. Then, just as Blockbuster and Wal-Mart adopt the new rental model, the prospect of releasing theatrical motion pictures online the same day and date as theaters suddenly alters the playing field again. With DVRs, video online, and user-generated content, what will happen to commercials and the future of advertising? No one knows.

The same sense of uncertainty permeates almost every industry. What about manufacturing—will it all migrate to low-wage sweatshops in the developing nations of Latin America, Asia, and Africa? What about healthcare—where's the solution to the looming crisis of 45 million uninsured and soaring health-care premiums that threaten to bankrupt big employers? What about the service economy, the supposed replacement for the old industrial economy—will software development and financial management and customer relations all be outsourced to India, Singapore, and Malaysia? What about banking and finance, roiled by deregulation and wave upon wave of mergers and acquisitions—which of yesterday's great firms will still be standing three years from today? Who knows?

Quake Country is a land of perpetual change. A place where companies merge, morph, rise, and fall at an ever-accelerating pace—where the only thing certain about the latest management buzz phrases—from "failing fast," "coopetition," and "cannibalization" to "process commoditization," "productive friction," and "social networking"—is that they will be replaced by new ones tomorrow, each change leaving the essential business problems unresolved.

On the level of CEO firings, corporate bankruptcies, class action suits, and antitrust actions, the news media follow the action ·intensely, almost obsessively. But what they rarely discuss is the life within these troubled companies. How are the people in The Middle dealing with the changes? How are they accomplishing the work of their companies? How are their lives being distorted, their families dislocated, their careers disrupted? Most important, what can they do to survive, even thrive, in the midst of corporate chaos?

Life in Quake Country can be deeply scary. The fact that this reality is rarely spoken about outside the office of the career counselor or psychotherapist doesn't help matters.

Sorry, We Seem to Have a Bad Connection

In Quake Country, corporate strategies are changing faster than ever. They have to. The threats and opportunities are coming faster, and the board of directors and the big investors want answers. So the suits on executive row (where every floor is carpeted, every wall paneled, every lunch catered, every voice hushed) scramble with their consultants to serve up the Strategy du Jour, hoping the latest idea will impress the analysts on Wall Street and placate the pension managers and mutual funds.

Unfortunately, at any given time most of the workforce is unaware of, or disconnected from, the corporate goals. A recent poll of almost 8,000 full-time employees by Harris Interactive offers the following sobering facts:

- Fully one-third of workers feel they are at a dead-end in their current jobs, and 42 percent say they are "trying to cope with feelings of burnout."

- Only 37 percent believe that their "top management displays integrity and morality."

- Only 29 percent say that their "top management is committed to advancing the skills of employees."

- Fewer than half say they "really care about the fate of this organization."[1]

Burnout. Cynicism. Disconnection. How fun can this be?

---

[1] "Many U.S. Employees Have Negative Attitudes To Their Jobs, Employers and Top Managers." *The Harris Poll* #38, May 6, 2005. Harris Interactive. Available online at http://www.harrisinteractive.com/harris_poll/index.asp?PID=568.

It's also a proven recipe for corporate failure. After all, the key to success in any large organization is connecting the dots, plugging people into something they can believe in and giving them a clear and meaningful way to contribute. The faster and better this is done, the faster companies reach their goals and poise for the next leap forward.

Managers in The Middle are the connective tissue in their organizations. Only they have the ground-level expertise required for success, the links to people above and below them in the corporate structure, the insights into customer needs, competitive realities, and the organization's strengths and weaknesses. As Quy Nguyen Huy put it in the *Harvard Business Review*, "A new executive's fresh ideas don't have a prayer of succeeding unless they are married with the operating skills, vast networks, and credibility of veteran middle managers."[2] Sadly, this is a truth that many companies have forgotten. They roll out new strategies without taking the time to consult with or even inform the people who hold the key to their success . . . the women and men in The Middle.

The research for this book involved an extensive online survey and more than 100 in-depth interviews with managers in a range of industries from companies like Bank of America, Gateway, ABC, Nordstrom, Harrah's, Intel, Rawlings, and Airbus. This research underscores the troubling facts about how disconnected managers feel from the companies they work for.

Sixty-five percent of the managers surveyed feel squeezed rather than empowered by their roles. They talk about unclear lines of authority within their organizations, constant turf battles that no one dares to mediate, and frequent encroachments into their relationships with their teams, which diminish their roles and erode the trust they've worked so hard to build. Forty-five percent have problems navigating big ideas through their organizations—each one an opportunity lost through sheer organizational inertia, confusion, and dysfunction.

The symptoms of corporate disconnection described by the interviewees are numerous:

---

2 Quy Nguyen Huy, "In Praise of Middle Managers." Harvard Business Review, September 2002, page 72.

- Goals that don't align, policies that conflict, and contradictory interpretations of company priorities.

- HR policies that offend and impede employees rather than support and encourage them.

- Arduous reporting requirements that reflect a lack of trust rather than any real need for information.

- Corporate mergers, acquisitions, divestitures, and reorganizations that produce no value while consuming vast amounts of employee energy.

- Turf wars between company fiefdoms whose chieftains concentrate more on protecting their prerogatives than on advancing corporate goals.

- Great efforts made and success achieved without recognition.

Most managers caught in The Middle paint a dismal picture of their current roles and the struggles they must wage every day.

So Why Do We Do This?

If life in The Middle is so stressful, frustrating, unrewarding, confusing, and depressing, why does anyone live there? Why not drop out of the corporate grind and try to make a go of it as an entrepreneur, a schoolteacher, a carpenter, a shopkeeper, or a nurse?

Many people *have* dropped out. The ranks of the self-employed have grown enormously in recent years. For some, self-employment is an ideal solution. When you run your own shop, the only rules are the ones you establish. There are no time-sucking meetings, no paperwork, no command-and-control hierarchy. All the value you create goes to your benefit, or that of your family. For someone with the right personality and business skills, the freelance way is liberating and rewarding.

But not everyone has that temperament. It's true that self-employment has no red tape, no petty rules, no restrictions on your freedom. It also has no economic safety net, no colleagues with whom to share problems and triumphs, no financial or managerial resources to fall back on, no health insurance or paid vacation or pension plan. For millions of people who *like* working closely with other people every day and *enjoy* the benefits of being part of a large and powerful organization, life within a corporation could be deeply satisfying... except it isn't.

For most managers, the motivation to remain inside the company is pretty simple, really. *They want to make a difference.* Our interviews and surveys confirmed just that. Managers are hand raisers. They want to participate, gain new responsibilities, make their companies better, and make a positive difference in the lives of the people around them.

For such people, dropping out is not the answer. Changing jobs may not be the answer, either. In many cases, those who do change jobs find themselves trading one unpleasant reality for another equally discouraging one—and worse, may even find themselves achieving far less success.

In 1980, Harvard professor John Kotter shattered some myths about management in his groundbreaking book *The General Managers.* Kotter argued—contrary to popular belief—that managers need a great deal of specialized information and skill in order to be successful. Thus, according to Kotter, the best managers don't reach their highest degrees of competency until they've been in their jobs for six to ten years. The familiar assumption that someone with good management skills can rapidly and easily move between companies or even between industries is simply not true. The expertise of a veteran manager is fundamentally *not* portable.

We're not saying managers shouldn't seek new opportunities. But managers who shift jobs should be running *to* something, not *away* from something.

Ignited is about a better solution—a way to stay within the corporation and begin making the kind of real difference we want to make, taking back our businesses, careers, and lives in the process.

Getting Ignited

It really is up to us—the managers in The Middle—to make the changes we know are necessary. And despite the many negatives about today's workplace that we've already listed, there are signs that *now* may be a time when the opportunity to make massive changes in the world of work is greater than ever before.

What are the indications that we may be on the verge of a dramatic shift in the nature of life in The Middle—for the better? Here are a few:

- *Demographic change.* As the Baby Boomers approach 60 and prepare to retire, there will be a vacuum of leadership at the top. The vacuum will be exacerbated by the exodus of managers who abandon corporate life for the entrepreneur's or freelancer's road. (Hence an estimate by *BusinessWeek* that some 24 percent of all middle management positions will be vacant in the next few years.) Tomorrow's leadership positions are going to be filled by managers of today who can figure out how best to prepare themselves for the opportunities ahead.

- *The increasing complexity of the business world.* As business becomes increasingly globalized, outsourced, and technology-driven, the complexity of everyday management challenges grows. Companies must rely on managers in The Middle to carry out their corporate strategies, which are often based on complicated networking relationships among manufacturers, marketers, distributors, and customers in many countries around the world. This means that the sophistication and skill of the managers in The Middle are more important than ever—giving those managers greater leverage and bargaining power than they've previously enjoyed.

- *Growing corporate flexibility.* One positive result of the reengineering movement of the 1990s was the smashing of the old military-style corporate hierarchy, with its rigid job ladders and pay scales. And with the failure of delayering has come a new appreciation of the importance of managers in The Middle—and a growing recognition that companies must attract and reward them. In the future, compensation packages will be customized and personalized; for the best managers, standard pay scales will not apply.

- *The demand for reinvention.* In a world of ever-accelerating change, old business models are becoming obsolete more quickly than ever. Pressure from new technologies, new competitors, new customer requirements, and new social and demographic circumstances are forcing great companies, from GE and General Motors to IBM, Kodak and Disney, to rethink their tried-and-true ways of doing business. No one is immune. Even eBay is working to reinvent. And when a company does reinvent, making a successful transition from one business model to the next, who is it that generally takes the lead? It's the managers in The Middle—those who understand the context of their environment (internal and external) and are prepared to take over when the entrepreneurial insights that fueled the first phase of growth are exhausted.

There's a real window of opportunity here for managers in The Middle to seize the power, purpose, and success they deserve. And if they do this right, the benefits will flow to their companies as well. A new, *genuinely* empowered generation of managers can steer their companies off the paths that have led so many into scandals, unnecessary layoffs, catastrophic misreadings of the market, and other disasters. They can bring about a creative renaissance of American business, a time of renewed profitability, shared value, and productivity that will benefit everyone in the country.

This combination of changes is a perfect platform for *Ignition*—the coming rebirth of purpose and power that managers in The Middle can experience if they choose to make it happen.

It's time for another "greatest generation." Let it be Us.

The Fulcrum

Imagine corporate vision on one side and the company's front-line contributors and customers on the other. The manager resides between them at a critical point where leverage and energy come together. This is the *fulcrum*, the power base from which the manager operates.

For too long, too many managers have allowed their fulcrum to fall below the two sides, becoming much less valuable in the process. They failed to rise up and satisfy the intense pressure exerted by corporate vision on one side and the needs of the front-line workers and customers on the other. They spent their days tackling immediate tasks rather than broader strategic challenges, and thereby failed to harness all of their potential power. They let opposing forces de-position them.

The most successful managers' fulcrum point flexes to a place *above* the corporate vision and front-line/customer sides. These managers enjoy the respect and support of both their leaders and their followers. They are also perceived by their peers as the best people with which to partner. Their elevation of the fulcrum point to its highest possible level represents the power of being ignited at its best (see Figure I-1).

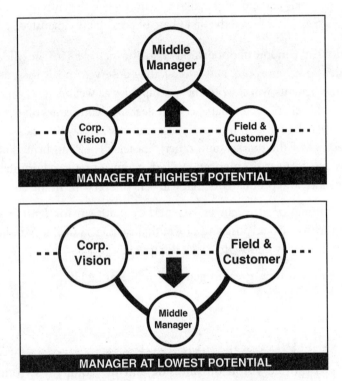

Figure I–1 The manager's shifting fulcrum.

Getting Ignited

In this book, we'll be laying out clear and practical steps that will deliver you more power, more purpose, and more success starting today. We recognize the realities that you must deal with every day as a manager in The Middle—limited power, restrictive corporate policies, financial constraints—and will offer concrete ideas about how to overcome the negatives and even (sometimes) transform them into positives.

We also recognize that your goals in life are not identical to the goals of your company—that life in The Middle is, in part, about balancing your personal needs with the often draconian demands of the corporate system. For most managers, a time comes (sooner or later) when the two things simply *can't* be happily balanced any longer—when their incompatibility is such that a parting of the ways is necessary. We'll look at this reality and offer our best advice about how to make those turning points work for you, not against you.

If all this sounds appealing, you've picked up the right book. Here's a road map of what to expect as we travel the following pages together.

Part I, "Get More Power," offers some basic tools for improving the thinking and behavior of managers in The Middle. If you are a seasoned and emotionally intelligent manager, these principles will speak loudly to you. Much of what you've learned from your most successful managerial experiences will be reinforced; lessons you may have missed or forgotten somewhere along the way will be provided; familiar wisdom will be offered with a new twist that (we hope) will make it more valuable and practical than ever before.

If you're just getting settled in as a manager, we hope that this section will really propel you forward. We've seen the ideas in Part I enable first-year managers to achieve third-year levels of performance. We wish the same for you.

Part II, "Get More Purpose," is about seven Ignition Points that are keys to the unique value that managers in The Middle can create. As we've noted, those in The Middle are uniquely positioned to transform broad corporate strategies into concrete programs that produce profits; to transform grand visions into specific actions that improve companies and attract customers; and to transform collections of well-meaning but uninvolved and unmotivated employees into a unified force for creativity and productivity that produces financial and personal rewards for everyone. The Ignition Points are the tools you must understand and use to make these changes happen.

Finally, Part III, "Get More Success," is about making a life even as you are making a living. Business success is wonderful and important, but achieving balance among the things that really matter is even more essential to ultimate happiness. It's not always easy, especially for managers struggling to survive life in today's corporate Quake Country. In these chapters, we'll offer insights about finding your own balance, however you define it.

Intrigued? Excited? Great—let's start getting ignited together.

BASE CAMP:
THE IGNITED QUIZ

Before we go any further, take a moment to reflect on a few simple questions. The purpose of the Ignited Quiz is help you understand where you are today in your career and establish a baseline that can be used to measure the value this book delivers you. For each of the following statements, select the level to which you agree or disagree.

THE IGNITED QUIZ

1. In my job, I know the people (both inside and outside my company) who I need in order to get things done.

Strongly agree	Agree	Neither agree nor disagree	Disagree	Strongly disagree

2. I know where my relationships stand with the people I count on and I know how to increase the value of those relationships.

Strongly agree	Agree	Neither agree nor disagree	Disagree	Strongly disagree

3. I'm confident that I have aligned our corporate goals with those of my team members and we're getting the performance we need.

Strongly agree	Agree	Neither agree nor disagree	Disagree	Strongly disagree

4. I feel capable of motivating my team with or without a clear corporate vision or in times of great change.

Strongly agree	Agree	Neither agree nor disagree	Disagree	Strongly disagree

5. I'm confident in my ability to tackle disconnects, areas of slippage, and competing agendas by selling through a plan for success that has buy-in and commitment.

Strongly agree	Agree	Neither agree nor disagree	Disagree	Strongly disagree

6. I have access to the key people at the highest levels of my company, whose input, approval, and support are crucial to my effectiveness on the job.

Strongly agree	Agree	Neither agree nor disagree	Disagree	Strongly disagree

7. I understand how to use my knowledge of vendors and customers to create innovation within my company and drive our strategic agenda.

Strongly agree	Agree	Neither agree nor disagree	Disagree	Strongly disagree

8. I am excited about my role as a manager in The Middle of my company and about what I can contribute to the success of the business.

Strongly agree	Agree	Neither agree nor disagree	Disagree	Strongly disagree

9. I have a mentor inside the company who helps me navigate the political, social, and business challenges I face.

Strongly agree	Agree	Neither agree nor disagree	Disagree	Strongly disagree

10. I have a personal system or method for organizing my time and energy that enables me to achieve balance in my life and to focus on the right things.

Strongly agree	Agree	Neither agree nor disagree	Disagree	Strongly disagree

Count the number of "Strongly agree" and "Agree" answers you chose. Then find your own level from among these options:

- *8-10 "Strongly agree" and "Agree" answers:* Congratulations! If your answers have been honest and accurate, you are probably among the most effective and empowered managers in The Middle in your company.

  We suggest you focus on the one or two statements for which you may *not* have been able to offer an "Agree" answer, and read the relevant chapters of the book that will help you improve those specific skills. Then pass this book along to those colleagues who need it more than you do. (You know who they are.)

- *5-7 "Strongly agree" and "Agree" answers:* You're like most managers—effective in some ways, struggling in others.

  Make a note of those statements for which you could not choose an "Agree" answer. These are areas of personal development on which you need to focus. While you read the rest of this book (as you should), pay close attention to those topics that will help you address your own areas of vulnerability. By the time you finish *Ignited*, you should have the tools you need to turn every answer on the quiz into a positive one.

- *0-4 "Strongly agree" and "Agree" answers:* You're probably among the millions of managers who are daydreaming about changing jobs or dropping out of the corporate system altogether. That *may* be the right choice for you—but more likely, you simply need to develop the skills and insights needed to make your job in The Middle more satisfying, rewarding, and effective than it is today.

Work your way through the pages of *Ignited*. Think through each of the mental exercises and experiments we recommend. Try applying the ideas on your job. Then revisit the quiz. We'll bet that the number of "Agree" answers you're able to choose will have shot up—along with your on-the-job morale.

PART I

GET MORE POWER

1

ACTION WITH TRACTION

Banging Pots

The time: Almost 25 years ago. It was my second day at a new summer job, working in the kitchen of a local diner. The dish tank was hot and humid. Behind me sat a row of plastic trays filled with greasy dishes. In front, a busboy was sliding another tray onto the table, slopping dirty dishwater onto my new tennis shoes and the soggy rubber mats below. After three-and-a-half hours of scrubbing plates and glasses, my hands were sore, my shirt soaked with dishwater, and my hair matted to my forehead. I leaned against the stainless steel table for a minute to catch my breath.

With a bang of the swinging door, Rusty, our cowboy cook, came flying around the corner, a cast iron burner in each hand. "What's up, boy? I didn't hear any noise, so I thought you weren't working. Take these things and degrease 'em. And lemme give you a word of advice. You wanna take a break, you better bang some pots. You better sound busy. No noise from the dish tank means work ain't getting done... you got it?"

I had just learned one of my first lessons in business: *Look busy. Act busy. Sound busy. And if you're not accomplishing anything, at least bang some pots.*

Flash forward. I'm selling TV ad time in a cubicle at a large firm on mid-Wilshire in Los Angeles. I am one more person in a sea of blue blazers (standard apparel for assistants with aspiration). We knew it was a competition: One of us would be getting the promotion. Which one? The one who paid the dues and looked the part. The one who *looked busy.*

Of course, this conflicts with the things we're taught in training programs on time management and productivity, and with the slogans tossed around in the latest books on leadership:

> "Don't work hard, work smart!"

> "Collapse time!"

> "Achieve balance!"

> "Focus like a laser on what's essential!"

All of these ideas sound good... but how do we do it?

How do we "collapse time" when, after answering our last six voicemail messages we find that nine more have piled up in the mailbox? How do we "achieve balance" when our company is behind the eight ball and struggling to launch that quarter-saving new product ahead of schedule? What happens when there's a changing of the guard? What happens when sales are off? What do those in the executive suite want and expect?

We all know the real answer. They want to see activity. They want production reports, sales reports, and marketing reports. They want to hear phones ringing, keyboards clicking, printers buzzing. They take comfort in knowing we're doing all we can. They want to hear the sound of banging pots.

The pressure to join the potbangers is intense. It's one of the big reasons that sensible concepts like job-sharing and telecommuting have taken so long to catch on in most corporations: "I can't work at home. If the boss doesn't see me in the office, he'll think I'm not working." Being productive is less important than being *seen* to be productive. But we all know, deep inside, that the noise from our banging is ultimately meaningless. We long to trade the treadmill of endless, ineffectual *action* for the lasting value of traction.

Traction is when our efforts in the workplace make a genuine, measurable, and lasting difference... when the things we try to do *get* done and *stay* done.

Most managers achieve traction, but usually in the form of sporadic breakthroughs that lurch them forward, then leave them to sit, exhausted, until they can build energy, purpose, and focus once again. It's better than nothing. Our goal is to gain *real* traction, traction that cuts deeper with every move, which carves a path and carries momentum into the future.

In order to achieve this level of traction, we must create and nurture an environment for ourselves and our team members where traction is second nature. It starts with our bosses, their goals, their needs, and our alignment with them. With alignment attained, we can employ a host of tools to keep us on the path to the traction we desire.

In the pages that follow, you'll consider the concept of Management Value Added, a powerful tool for setting your course. You'll explore the difference between traction and slippage, and how to build a portfolio of projects that stick rather than slip. Building upon these concepts, you'll look at achieving group traction and offer some new ideas for ensuring follow-through.

The Problem with Time Management

If you've been living in the corporate world for some time, you've probably attended a training session where one of the exercises was to conduct a "time spent" analysis in order to increase your efficiency. You cracked open your calendar, reviewed how you spent your time for the past week, and identified black holes that were wasting your energy. Maybe you even went so far as to break your activities into categories, separating the "urgent" things from the "important" things and both of these from the "insignificant" things.

Time management studies like these can be interesting, but the findings are almost always the same. Virtually every manager who works through the exercises discovers that he or she is spending too much time on "putting out fires"—dealing with the daily dramas and emergencies around the office—and not enough time thinking and planning for long-term projects that really matter. E-mails, instant messages, phone calls, and that guy from Purchasing who drops in "just for a second" and chews the fat for 45 minutes undo our best-laid plans—not to mention the endless, interminable, usually pointless meetings.

We know all this. Why doesn't it ever change?

The problem lies in our approach. Time management programs usually focus on your personal productivity, analyzing how you choose to spend your time. This is all fine and dandy, but it misses one essential truth: In an organization that's devoted to banging pots, *you better bang pots or have a damn good reason for not banging them.*

That's why, after the PowerPoint presentation had ended and the trainer went home, you fell back into your old, unproductive rhythms—not because you didn't agree with the time management expert's analysis, but because you returned to normal life in the world of The Middle... which means doing what you think your boss wants you to do. Bang! Bang! Bang!

Managing Your Managers

In order to take back your time, your life, and your career, you need to make a new *kind* of change in your approach to self-management. You must step into the realm of *managing your managers* and thereby altering their expectations related to your time. The goal is to achieve complete alignment between *what your bosses want (and perhaps need) you to do* and *what you believe you really should do.*

In the same way that you coordinate the schedule in your PDA and your laptop with the one in your desktop computer, you need to continually coordinate with your bosses to ensure that you are clear, on track, and working from the same plan.

All of this starts with having a happy and supportive boss. And that means a successful boss. Your boss *has* to be successful. For if he is not, his failure may cast a negative light on everyone on his team. Many potentially great careers have been stalled, not because of the effort of the individual, but because of a boss who failed to make an impact, who failed to demonstrate his own value and the value of those on his team.

The first step in managing your manager is to move beyond your own needs to examine your bosses' needs. Sounds reasonable—but understanding those needs and figuring out what to do to meet them isn't usually straightforward. In fact, it's a challenge in itself, requiring a whole new set of skills most people have never thought about.

Needs Explicit and Needs Implicit

Let's start by dispelling a common misunderstanding. Lots of people in business assume that "meeting the boss's needs" means doing exactly what the boss wants them to do—accepting the boss's vision and direction wholesale. Wrong! This assumption is simple-minded and inaccurate. It leads to managers in The Middle focusing on aligning their lips with their boss's backsides rather than meeting anyone's *actual* needs.

Real "managing upward" demands a more serious and subtle analysis of human needs, which starts with the realization that needs come in two forms—*explicit* needs and *implicit* needs.

Explicit needs are easier to understand. They may be stated in the strategic plan promulgated by the company or the division, or they may be announced by your boss whenever the team gets together for the usual pep talk/torture session. They may sound something like this:

- "We need to expand our business internationally."

- "We need to create a shipping policy that will save us some money and keep the administrative assistants from running around the office like decapitated chickens every afternoon at 4 p.m. when the FedEx guy makes his last pickup."

- "We need to commerce-enable our Web site before Amazon.com decides to start selling the same kinds of widgets we sell and drives us out of business."

- "We need to hire two more designers, fast, so we'll have a prayer of getting the fall product line into the stores sometime this year."

Explicit needs are the kinds of things that make it into the lists of goals you write every year at objective-setting time. They're the things you tell people you're working on when they ask. They tend to be the things you are proud of accomplishing (if and when you happen to accomplish one of them).

Implicit needs are more subtle. People don't talk about them. Sometimes they're not even aware of them. Most of the time they are things that people would deny if confronted with them. They sound like this:

- "Make me look good in front of my boss so that when he gets kicked upstairs he'll recommend me for his job."

- "Help me demonstrate my creativity by coming up with some ideas for next year's marketing campaign that I can tweak a little and show off at the next divisional conference as if they were mine."

- "Help me feel more like a leader and less like the kid who was always picked last in the schoolyard basketball games."

- "Figure out some way to keep the department running when I'm not around so I can go on vacation for ten days in a row without having to call the office every two hours to make sure the damned place isn't on fire."

While explicit needs tend to run a linear path, implicit needs tend be random, triggered by emotion and circumstance. But don't think of them as flighty and certainly not as insignificant. They are ever-present, tenacious, and can overrule the explicit needs with a swiftness and power that can be awe-inspiring.

It's a fun exercise to sit down with a sheet of paper and try listing your boss's implicit needs. It's also deadly serious. From the first day you meet your new boss through the last day you work together, you need to devote a portion of your time and energy to scoping out his or her implicit needs and defining them with as much precision as possible. Then measure whatever you do against those needs. (Your boss certainly will.)

One implicit need that virtually every boss has (and therefore belongs on the to-do list of every ignited manager) is the need for *confidence*. Your boss must have confidence that you are working in his best interest and that you are capable of delivering what he needs (both explicitly and implicitly). Fail to maintain this confidence and your boss will most likely drive you crazy—and will often drive you out.

We've all been there. The boss who last week simply set a goal and gave us the freedom to carry it out suddenly wants to micromanage every phone call we make this week. Sometimes it's because they've lost confidence in us; other times it's because their bosses have lost confidence in them, producing a sort of trickle-down anxiety that may end up with you being hypercritical of the dinosaur diorama your nine-year-old makes for science class. Giving your boss a sense of confidence in you is perhaps the most fundamental of all the implicit needs and the one without which no managerial relationship can succeed.

Understanding the implicit and explicit needs of your boss and his bosses sets a course by which you can align your own efforts. When that alignment is clear and accurate, you're on track to creating an environment in which traction is possible.

Management Value Added

The concept of *Management Value Added (MVA)* is based on a simple question that you should ask whenever you're making a decision about how to invest your time and energy: "What value does management add?" And how can your actions "add value" to any situation in business? That's right—by helping to meet your bosses' needs.

One way to start using the concept of MVA is by sitting down with your boss to discuss his or her explicit needs (the ones written down as part of the company's strategy or the division's official mandate). It shouldn't take long for the two of you to agree on what they are and to prioritize them appropriately. Then ask your boss, "How do you feel I can add the most value?" If your boss responds, "Huh?" you can flesh out the question with additional questions like these:

- "What are the activities I am engaged in when I am contributing the most?"

- "What are the activities that you and the company most need me to do?"

- "What do you consider to be the best and most productive use of my time?"

- "What do you think is the special contribution that I am best positioned to offer to you and the company?"

- "Of all the things that I'm engaged in on behalf of this company, what are the three areas where you believe that I can contribute the most?"

Listen carefully to your boss's answers. Using them as a guide, you can begin to understand exactly how your boss views your contributions. It's quite likely that the way he or she measures your MVA is different from the way you might measure it.

Here's what one of my bosses had to say when I asked him to define my most important areas for MVA:

1. "Hiring, nurturing, and guiding talent; putting the right people in the right jobs with the right goals."

2. "Building capability; teaching my team members and creating an environment conducive to challenging thought and growth."

3. "Staying close to the customers—understanding what's important to them, what their challenges are, and how our company can provide them with solutions."

Of course, this exercise will relate only to your boss's *explicit* needs. (Don't try to engage him in a discussion of his implicit needs. There's a good reason why they're implicit.) Having these priorities clearly defined is an enormous step forward and an advantage that surprisingly few managers enjoy. It provides you with a framework you can share with others on your team and allows you to use the test of MVA in your quest to get past pot banging.

You can use MVA to help you determine how to spend your time, which projects to support, and which meetings to attend. In my case, before committing energy to any new activity, I ask myself: "Will this activity help me achieve my priorities? Will it help me put the right people in the right jobs? Will it help me build capability? Will it help me know and connect with our customers?" If the answer is no, I avoid the activity—even if it sounds otherwise interesting, appealing, or fun.

MVA helps you maintain a focus on the things that matter while earning the support of those you serve. When your boss or someone else in the organization asks you to commit time or energy to an area that falls outside of the MVA priorities you've established, you can talk about how new commitment may affect your main goals and reach a joint decision as to whether a shift in priorities is warranted.

Bridging an Unbridgeable Gap

For some of us the priorities are already clear. The priorities are alive in performance evaluations, and they are written into our planners or are posted on our office walls. All we have to do is keep the dialogue open and use MVA as a criterion for planning our time.

However, for other priorities, just coming to agreement about what's important can be quite difficult.

Consider two managers—Sarah and Rob.

Sarah spent eight years leading a team in the Midwest for a company that she really loved. Recently she'd begun reporting to a new boss on the East Coast—Rob. Early on it became clear that Sarah and Rob were not clicking. Trust was low, and they struggled to communicate. Sarah felt that Rob didn't understand her and didn't appreciate what she had accomplished with her team. Rob felt that Sarah was quick to judge and not open to a new approach.

There they were—unhappy and stuck.

Sarah could have reacted in one of the dysfunctional ways many managers do: by blowing up in frustration and anger, snipping at Rob behind his back until a bitter confrontation was provoked, or quitting precipitously to take a less-than-ideal job. Instead, she took a thoughtful approach, which started by taking a step back to consider her own role in the impasse. Reflecting on the situation, Sarah came to realize that, while Rob wasn't a perfect manager (who is?), she probably had some work of her own to do. She'd worked for a long time without a mentor, a champion, or even a trusted confidante, and she needed someone she could talk to about her job and its challenges, especially during this difficult time.

Sarah decided to hire a personal career coach named Keith Rosen. Keith is a Master Certified Coach and the founder of ProfitBuilders.com, a very successful executive coaching firm based in New York.

Keith helped Sarah work on her communication skills, an area in which Sarah realized she could use improvement. However, as she and Keith walked through a variety of real-life scenarios together, it soon became clear that Sarah *also* needed help with listening skills. She'd been unable to comprehend Rob's explicit needs, and she certainly wasn't accurately interpreting his implicit needs (which as we've noted are always harder to plumb). Keith and Sarah pondered and probed the situation together and came up with a plan.

The following Monday, Sarah went to Rob and said, "I've hired a career coach to help me become a better manager. In working with him, I've realized that one of my main goals is to get in better sync with you. I really want to understand what you need from me and how I can help you be more successful."

The following day, Keith called Rob and introduced himself as Sarah's coach. There was a long silence, and then Rob emitted a long, heartfelt sigh of relief. He began to talk, admitting that, like Sarah, he'd been quite frustrated with their failure to communicate. He felt that Sarah was out of touch with the corporate goals (not to mention his own personal goals). Each time they spoke, he sensed she was reacting to his needs rather than simply listening to them and comprehending them. As a result, she seemed to view every change or new idea as a threat rather than an opportunity.

As they talked, Keith gained a new insight into the dynamic between Rob and Sarah. In Rob's eyes, whenever Sarah challenged or questioned his explicit goals, she was also challenging his implicit goals. Conversely, whenever Rob challenged Sarah's explicit goals, he was also challenging her implicit goals.

The conflict between them really had less to do with corporate strategies or work duties than they'd imagined. It was mainly about a new boss trying to look good and a long-time employee trying to maintain her dignity in the face of disruptive, disconcerting change.

Thankfully, there was no basis for any fundamental conflict between Rob and Sarah. Rob had no need (explicit or implicit) to send a talented veteran manager packing during his first month on the job, and Sarah had no need to end her successful and happy career at the firm. Both really wanted to try to make their new partnership work. So Keith jumped in and spent time with each of them in private, reviewing their explicit needs and helping them interpret their implicit needs. Acting as a bridge, he connected them to one another with a plan that they could each commit to, build on, and maintain.

Sometimes the fit between two managers is so skewed or so damaged by failed attempts at communication that the obstacles to contact seem insurmountable. In such cases, a third party may be able to help you gain needed perspective and work your negative emotions out of the way. He or she can serve as a bridge on the road to greater traction.

If you find yourself in such a dilemma, consider looking for a third-party bridge. Sometimes an independent coach can play this role, as in the case of Rob and Sarah. In other cases, the bridge can be a manager from another department that both parties like and trust, a conflict management counselor or consultant hired by the firm, or a smart and sensitive member of the company's Human Resources department. The key is an open-minded attitude and a willingness to listen on the part of both individuals.

Most communication gaps are bridgeable. Sometimes all it takes is a fresh perspective and a new voice in the room to change the atmosphere from confrontation to cooperation.

Knowing versus Doing—Traction versus Slippage

All too often, when we're most in need of traction at work—at times of high competitive pressure or internal pressure or economic insecurity — we find ourselves experiencing slippage instead. Wheels are spinning, lots of energy is being expended, noise is emitted and sparks fly—but there's no traction and, therefore, no forward momentum.

Sometimes the difference between traction and slippage is obvious. But other times, it can be rather subtle. How can you make the distinction for sure?

If you find yourself removing the same barriers today that you removed last year, last month, or yesterday—you've got slippage. It may not *feel* like slippage to you, because removing that recurring barrier allowed you (at least temporarily) to get something done on behalf of your company. But in a longer perspective, it's slippage—a place where people needlessly spin their wheels time and time again.

Every company is filled with mudholes where slippage is the norm. For example, think about the many varied approval processes you probably face related to budgets, routine spending requests, project go-aheads, hiring or firing decisions, and so on. How many of these processes are empty formalities—hurdles that you (and other managers) must repeatedly jump for no good reason?

Or consider the people problems you've had to "solve" over and over again. There's the gal in marketing who finds fault with every new product launch and never buys into the program until she gets a personal plea to cooperate from someone at the executive level. Or the guy in IT who lets requests for computer upgrades pile up on his desk for months until his boss lays down the law and forces him to act. Or the department that's run like a private fiefdom by a manager who hoards information and devises his own strategic plans that never quite mesh with anyone else's, until a vice president personally intervenes. All of these are classic examples of wasted time, energy, and resources—slippage.

In some cases, we're blind to these corporate mudholes. In other cases, we've accepted them as the way things are. And in still other cases, we're aware of the problems but just can't find the time or motivation to address them.

These kinds of problems aren't confined to the business arena, but crop up constantly in the personal realm as well. How many people do you know who have quit smoking or lost the same ten pounds repeatedly? (Maybe you are one of them.) My own experience with online banking provides another good example. For years I was sitting down twice a month to pay my bills by hand, all the while knowing that online bill paying could save me time, energy, and money (no more stamps to buy). I just didn't commit myself to setting it up. When I finally did, the rewards were immediate, substantial, and permanent. What took me so long?

Behavior like mine reflects what's known as the Knowing *versus* Doing gap—a common problem in business (and life) that the highly respected professors Jeffrey Pfeffer and Robert Sutton have written and lectured about extensively. A handful of companies are aware of these gaps and have created a culture that attacks them. They look for the gaps, create new systems to close the gaps, and periodically evaluate their effectiveness so that necessary follow-up changes can be instituted.

Sadly, such companies are rare. Most of us work in companies where the existence of the Knowing *versus* Doing gap isn't recognized. Consequently, some of our most persistent and debilitating problems are never addressed proactively. Instead, we act only when the pain becomes too great.

What's important is that we open our eyes to see these gaps, then begin to work on the ones where the potential reward for a solution is greatest.

The Good Business Reason—Designing Your Project Portfolio

When we pursue traction, we're looking for ways to drive our companies forward. Sometimes we're stymied by the slippage that we've just discussed. In other cases, the problem is the sheer volume of demands on our time, energy, and resources. If you're a manager with even a modicum of intelligence and ability, you are probably inundated with requests for your help on this or that project, team, or task force. Narrowing these demands to the essential few that ought to become a part of your personal project portfolio is an ongoing challenge.

Regardless of how these projects make it our way, there's a lot of power in a very simple question: *What's the good business reason for doing this?*

Actually I can't take credit for the question. I owe it to my friend Jason Jennings.

An author, consultant, and motivational speaker, Jason has studied thousands of successful firms and in three best-selling books has examined 30 of the best—companies that have grown by more than 20 percent per year for more than 20 consecutive quarters. When profiling Herb and Marion Sandler, the founders and operating owners of World Savings (one of the nation's 15 largest banks and thrifts), he learned that they attributed their success to a corporate culture that never makes a move without first asking that same very simple question: *What's the good business reason for doing this?*

For World Savings, it meant a lot of things that other banks considered essential *didn't* get done. World Savings didn't launch a network of ATMs until years after the competition. The team at World Savings felt they couldn't justify the capital expense because their savings and time-deposit customers (at the time the heart of their customer base) didn't have much of a need for ATMs. It wasn't until World Savings decided to pursue high-balance checking account customers that it made economic sense to install the machines.

Based on that one simple question, the Sandlers created a culture where the justification for every decision needed to be demonstrated and, if possible, quantified. The results have been incredible. World Savings beats their competitors in profitability year after year.

Now I use the same question to help me focus on the projects and activities that make the most sense for me and my company. If something is *really* worth doing, there will be a clear and compelling answer to that powerful question, *What's the good business reason for doing this?*

Here is some additional advice about developing your personal project portfolio—the set of activities and initiatives on which you will choose to focus and with which to become identified.

Perhaps the most important suggestion is to think of your "to-do" list as just that—a *portfolio* of projects. The echo from investment management is no accident. Every project you commit to should be viewed as a personal investment—not of money, but of time and energy, both of which are limited and precious resources. Just as you should think about your financial portfolio is terms of overall risk and reward, so should you plan your portfolio of projects.

Your personality will play a role in the project decisions you make. If you are a high-risk player, you'll take on more high-risk projects, recognizing that the likelihood of failure is significant but that the rewards for success can be enormous. If you are risk-averse, you may take a safer route by sticking to projects you *know* you can bring to successful fruition. Either strategy can lead to success over time. It's just a matter of how you feel comfortable getting there.

Ian Beavis, vice president of marketing for Kia Motors (the Korean-based company that is the world's fastest-growing automaker), told us that he built his career by taking on the projects that nobody wanted—the tough challenges that once solved really defined him as a winner. Quanah Bonrud from Enthusian, the Web-based talent acquisition and management provider, feels the same way, advising, "Do what others are not willing to do, and then do it well."

At the same time, we found that while these managers made their names on their home runs, they also hit a lot of singles and doubles—in fact, they were experts at getting on base consistently and often. Clearly they balance the most difficult assignments with more manageable ones, which enable them to rack up wins quarter after quarter, adding value all the while.

Making Teams Work—Controlling the Cave People

With all of the time we spend working together in teams, we spend very little time learning how to make them work. Sure, we discuss leadership, we talk about buy-in, and we do our best to drive towards clear and meaningful goals. Yet, at the same time, at least half of corporate initiatives never make it from meetings to implementation, and more than 83 percent of corporate failures are driven not by external circumstance, but by simple failure to follow though. Obviously our knowledge of what it takes to make teams effective is lacking.

Without follow-through, we don't have traction. We're back to spinning our wheels. In order to get follow-through when working with a team in a corporate environment, several things are necessary:

- First, we need to create momentum early on by establishing goals that are meaningful and processes that make sense.

- Next, we need to understand the cast of characters we are working with. What motivates them? How do we activate them to invest time in our cause? And how do we prevent the naysayers and the energy-sappers from killing the project?

- Finally, we need to create an environment in which each individual is accountable not to the leader, but to the team—so that the project and everyone involved in it becomes self-driving rather than requiring constant Sisyphean labor (pushing the boulder up the hill through sheer brute force).

Okay, so that's the plan. Now how do we make it happen?

Laurence Haughton has written and lectured extensively about teams, performance, and follow-through. In his book, *It's Not What You Say... It's What You Do—How Following Through at Every Level Can Make or Break Your Company*, he warns us about the dangers posed by the cave people. That is, CAVE people: Citizens Against Virtually Everything. According to Haughton, the cave people are the ones in every organization who go out of their way to kill buy-in, spread negativity, and create failure:

> Just like our bodies have an immune system that assaults everything new and unfamiliar, organizations have their own autoimmune response (a.k.a. the CAVE People) that attacks every new idea and change in direction. So, like doctors preparing a patient for a transplant, leaders must take steps to outmaneuver these antibodies in human form.

According to Haughton, that plan starts by keeping any cave people off your project until *after* you have generated some early critical successes. Having them around is not worth the risk, because killing projects by destroying other people's enthusiasm is what they do.

Oddly enough, in his work as a business consultant, Haughton finds that many companies allow cave people to kill projects even though they recognize the danger they pose. "I get invited into companies after things have gone horribly wrong," he explains, "and management's got a dead initiative on its hands—or one that's mortally wounded. I can't tell you how many times, as I'm re-creating what went wrong, I hear, 'I knew so-and-so would kill our buy-in.' 'Well, if you knew that,' I think in my head, 'why on earth did you let them on the team?'"

At first, it may seem uncomfortable or awkward to work around the cave people, but if you're really going to create change, gain traction, and move forward, it's essential.

The Rest of the Cast of Characters: The Committed and the Compliant

What about the other people who participate in your team? What does it take to understand and motivate them to generate the energy and momentum needed for success?

One way to get started is to sort your team members into two broad categories—the *committed* and the *compliant*.

Suppose you have two team members, each of whom has been asked to deliver your team's business plan to a senior executive. The executive will review the plan and decide whether or not to approve it.

The committed team member walks the plan over to the exec's office and asks the assistant if the executive is available. Learning that he or she is in a meeting that'll end in five minutes, the committed team member decides to wait until the executive is free. When the exec strolls out of the meeting, the committed team member puts the plan into the exec's hands and says, "Thanks for reading this. It means a lot to us and we're really looking forward to your good thinking on this challenge."

By contrast, the compliant team member decides not to wait around. Instead, she simply passes the envelope to the exec's assistant and walks away. She provides no context, no enthusiasm, not even a pitch to the assistant for help.

Committed people are driven by the project at hand. They've caught the passion. They are curious. They want responsibility.

Compliant people are just going through the motions. They may be present physically, but they haven't bought in with their hearts and minds. They'll do the least amount of work necessary to get credit for participating, but they don't contribute new ideas or support the old ones with enthusiasm.

When you know where everyone sits, compliant or committed, you can begin to work on motivating them. Think of it in steps:

1. First, chain up the cave people—don't let them near your project.

2. Next, determine who's committed and who's compliant. Then build early successes with those who are committed and demonstrate this success back to those who aren't. Many people in most organizations will be swayed away from their compliant status toward commitment by evidence of success. You'll find that the momentum created by their shift towards commitment is just tremendous.

With each success, take time to celebrate and demonstrate how everyone can play a role creating even *more* success.

Using Technology to Assure Accountability and Create Traction

As a manager, you're often asked to join a cross-divisional team where your influence is supported not by your power base, title, or role, but rather by the strength of your ideas and your ability to engage people in a common cause. Often these are ad hoc teams created to support projects initiated by senior managers to pursue goals they care about— goals like cost reduction, product and process innovation, or research.

Creating accountability in this kind of situation, where the cast of characters is unfamiliar and it's hard to know what motivates them, is often challenging. Blogs and Wikis, now easier to implement, are beginning to play a powerful role.

As you may know, blogs, which reside online, allow their hosts to share their words, images, and sounds while soliciting a dialogue with their readers. With blogs, the readers are welcome to post responses. With Wikis, anyone can edit the page and improve upon the content.

Originated by software developers putting their minds together to evolve code and later popularized by Wikipedia.com, Wikis facilitate the wisdom of crowds and consistently generate better work. Both blogs and Wikis are being used as business tools by some of today's savviest organizations. 10e20, a Web design shop in New York, decided to launch a blog for each project, requiring employees to post updates on their progress twice a day. Within the first six weeks of the new system, ten projects were completed *early*. (How often does that happen in *your* office?) The blogs played a key role. Being able to read about the other participants' challenges and successes was inspiring for those involved.

Blogs help team members sense the momentum, stay connected to the community between meetings, and really think about, see, and enhance one another's contributions. Blogs also provide visibility into projects for those who have sponsored them, but may not be directly involved. The senior executive who cannot attend every meeting can go online 24/7 for a status report and join the ongoing conversation with personal thoughts and encouragement.

These increasingly simple technologies are facilitating age-old practices in a way that is uniquely convenient for the participants.

Maintaining Traction

There's no doubt that creating traction takes effort, but the rewards are great. We and our companies are at our best when we escape pot banging to do the things that really matter.

When you are exposing your company's Knowing versus Doing gap, reframing your job using MVA, finding ways to build communications bridges between managers, or planning a team effort so that the committed can win over the compliant, you are drilling a layer deeper than those around you. The traction you develop and maintain will enable you to go further and faster than you ever dreamed possible.

2

THE MANAGER'S UNIVERSE

Relationships—The Sum Total of Any Business

As a manager in The Middle, what is the most crucial element you must deal with every day?

Some would reply, "Money." Others might say, "Products." Still others, "Strategies," "Business models," "Organizational plans," or "The corporate vision."

All of these may be important. All are *tools* you need to understand and learn how to wield in pursuit of your goals and the goals of the company. But more important than any of these tools are the *people* you work with and your relationships with them.

After all, to the extent that you've been entrusted with business tools—money, products, services, strategies, and all the rest—it's because of what you've done with and for the other people in the organization. Something in the way you communicate, the way you collaborate to solve problems, the way you listen and learn, the way you direct and coach, the way you disagree constructively, the way you channel your enthusiasm—something in all these *personal* traits has convinced the top brass that you have what it takes to manage. And managing is all about motivating the people around you to work together for the common good.

So "people skills" are not the "soft stuff" of management, something to be given lip service but ultimately less important than the "hard stuff" like financial analysis, marketing strategy, or corporate law. People skills are the *heart* of management, without which everything else is so much sound and fury.

It's deeply ironic that, while we in business carefully count our money, our output, our customers, and just about everything else we touch, we fail to measure what matters most—our relationships. Sure, we amass contacts in our Outlooks or Blackberries or Treos, but do we really evaluate the relationships they represent? Do we analyze where we stand with them? Do we devote resources of time and energy to improving them?

Ignited managers study their relationships the way astronomers study the stars in the sky. At any given moment, some are bright, while some are dimming. Some are moving out of alignment, while others are moving in. Periodically a star may self-destruct in the awesome phenomenon known as a supernova. Other times a new star emerges, one that may ultimately play a central role in your system.

In this chapter, you'll learn how to chart the relationships that make up your business universe. You'll explore how to understand their relative importance, measure your progress with them, and discover ways to improve and strengthen them. This simple system will help you identify where your challenges are and decide where to focus your energies. You'll learn how to visualize the strengths and weaknesses of your relationship network and, as you apply the lessons in this book, you'll be able to *see* the difference as those relationships improve.

Map Your Universe in Five Easy Steps

The following exercise, which we call the Manager's Universe, has many uses. It can be used to map the network of key relationships involved in your routine, day-to-day business life. It can also be used for more specific purposes. For example, suppose you're asked to join an interdepartmental team to help launch an important new product. You might want to create a Manager's Universe map specifically tailored to this project, one that you can use to analyze the relationships that will influence its success or failure.

Here are the five simple steps you can use to create your own Manager's Universe map:

1. At the center of a piece of paper, draw a circle representing you. (Yes, for the purposes of this exercise you are the center of the universe—congrats!)

2. Then draw a ring of six to ten circles on the paper orbiting the first circle. (Think of a planet and its moons.) Each circle represents an important stakeholder in your success—individuals or groups of people on whom you rely and who help to determine your success. (Why six to ten? This is the number of *key* stakeholders to whom most managers relate. If you think you have only two or three, you are probably forgetting about some crucial connections. If you think you have 12 or 15, you are probably getting bogged down with some connections that are much less important; eliminate some of them so as to sharpen your focus.)

3. Fill in the outer circles with the names of your key stakeholders. You'll see in the example shown in Figure 2-1 that one manager (we'll call him Joe) included his immediate boss, his boss's boss

Figure 2–1 The Manager's Universe.

(the chief operating officer), several executives within his company (the director of operations, the director of information services, and the vice president of marketing), two direct reports (his product manager and his service manager), and two important outside groups—his customers and a vital supplier (Owens Company). Why these nine? These are the people who make the greatest difference in Joe's everyday success—the people who control access to key resources, who can provide or withhold the support needed to pursue crucial goals, who can help or hinder Joe's progress toward those goals.

4. Next to each stakeholder, rate the importance of this stakeholder to you in terms of your business success on a scale from 1 (least important) to 10 (most important). This is the first number shown in each stakeholder circle. In Joe's case, his boss and his customers are most important (both rated at 10), while the folks at Owens Company are the least important of those shown in the map (rated at 3). If a particular stakeholder carries a score of 1 or 2, you might want to consider dropping them from the map altogether.

5. Finally, next to the number indicating importance, rate the current quality of your working relationship with this stakeholder on the same 1-10 scale. As you can see, Joe has a great relationship with the service manager (a perfect 10) but a very troubled connection with the COO (rated just 2).

Now that Joe has his universe mapped, he can really begin thinking about where he needs to focus his energies and add more value. Here are some of the specific ways that Joe can use the Manager's Universe map as a self-diagnostic tool:

- Think about each of the relationships included in the Manager's Universe map. Are they built on trust? Do you understand each other? What was your last interaction like? What can you do to deliver value to this stakeholder and help him or her pursue success?

- Focus on the three relationships that are most crucial to you. (In Joe's case, they are his boss, his customers, and the company's director of operations.) How much time are you devoting to each of these connections? Have you been short-changing one or more of these key relationships (perhaps because of a personal aversion or a sense of anxiety)? Have you worked to understand the interests, goals, preferences, and motivations of these key stakeholders?

- Identify the three relationships that are weakest or most troubled. (For Joe, these are the COO, the director of operations, and, in a tie—both rated 6—his boss and his product manager.) What reasons underlie the problems in these relationships? What can you do this week to begin strengthening the ties with each of these stakeholders? What change in behavior (either on their part or on your part) would indicate that the problems are solved and the relationship is on a solid footing?

As you see, you can use the Manager's Universe map to help you develop a plan for managing and improving your network of crucial relationships.

Later in this book, you'll explore the seven Ignition Points that will help you add significant value to your relationships with those around you. Then you can return to your Manager's Universe map and reevaluate your relationships. Over time, the numbers representing the strengths of those relationships should increase.

How and When to Use the Manager's Universe Map

Because your relationships in business are always changing, you'll want to use the Manager's Universe mapping system periodically to monitor the health of your network. You may also want to use it for specific purposes. It's a vital tool when you

- Feel lost, overwhelmed, frustrated, or confused by the conflicting demands of your job

- Are engaged in strategic planning, budget forecasting, or beginning an important new project

- Are impacted by major external change, such as a company reorganization, merger, or acquisition

- Are dealing with one or more new stakeholders, such as a new boss or a new set of direct reports

- Are entering a new role, as when you've been promoted, made a lateral shift, or jumped to a new company

In all of these circumstances, the Manager's Universe map can be a powerful way to organize your thinking about the network of relationships that affects your work. It can help you zero in on the connections that are most important (and avoid wasting energy on those that are less important), identify the most troubled relationships (and help you plan ways to improve them), and keep you from losing sight of relationships that are important but easy to take for granted. An hour spent mapping and analyzing your personal universe can give you a clearer perspective about your job and an increased sense of mastery over its disparate elements.

The same mapping strategy can also be adapted to the broader purpose of career strategy and life planning. For this purpose, you would create a map that includes the main stakeholders with influence over your life as a whole, not simply your success in your current position.

For example, suppose Joe is considering a new job assignment within his company, which will involve moving from California to the East Coast of the U.S. The network of key stakeholders for this decision-making process might include

- Joe's wife (who would have to leave her own California-based job if Joe is to pursue his dream)

- Joe's kids, ages ten and twelve (whose lifestyle and schooling would be affected by Joe's career change)

- Colleagues within the company (with whom Joe may continue to work after the move, and whose help will be crucial to a successful transition)

- Joe's business mentor, Ron (whose advice and wisdom Joe prizes)

Before making any final decision about the proposed career change, Joe will want to think about each of these relationships. Does he know how each stakeholder would react to the move? What degree of support (or resistance) can he expect from each one? Has he invested time to make sure that each stakeholder knows about his dream, understands its pros and cons, and can offer meaningful help, advice, or guidance?

Using the Manager's Universe as a Communications Tool

Useful as the Manager's Universe map can be for individual planning and strategizing, sharing it with colleagues at work can be even more powerful. It's consistent with the transparency that I believe in and will allow you to get a deeper and broader perspective on the world in which you move.

One person with whom you can share the map is your boss. Draw up your universe as how you best understand it and then show it to your boss, explaining its purpose and meaning. Ask him or her to react and comment. You may be surprised by what you hear. For example, your boss may strongly disagree with some of the people or groups you've listed as stakeholders: "Why are you wasting time worrying about Kathy in IT? Her department's not an issue for you. If I were you, I'd be more concerned about Rajid in Finance. He controls the purse strings, and I hear he's looking for ways to cut our budget next year."

In other cases, your boss may have a very different perspective from yours on the strength or weakness of a particular relationship: "Why do you have your connection with Jerry in marketing rated as a 2? I think you two get along great. Sure, he's always grouchy and full of complaints, but that's just the way Jerry is. You should hear what he says about the *other* department heads—he complains about them a hell of a lot more than he complains about you!" Depending on your relationship with your boss, you may choose to show your boss just your list of contacts and how important you feel they are, and not share your strength-or-weakness rankings.

A great question to ask your boss is, "How can I provide the greatest value to the people in my universe?" From his or her unique perspective, your boss can offer insights that will deepen and enrich your understanding of what success in your job really entails—insights such as, "Given the financial pressures we're under right now, the folks in Production aren't that concerned about perfecting product quality. Their main goal is to get goods out the door as quickly as possible. Whatever you can do to keep the plant running 24/7 will make them happy, believe me."

Conversely, the Manager's Universe exercise is also a useful tool to help those who report to you. When a new person joins your team, when one of your direct reports gets promoted or moved to a new assignment, or when a team member is feeling frustrated or stuck, sit down with him or her and have this person create his or her own map. Or bring the exercise into one of your team meetings and invite the entire group to discuss their findings.

This exercise is especially helpful after a reorganization. Most companies will provide employees with memos describing the new reporting relationships, sometimes including org charts complete with ruled and dotted lines that supposedly reveal the crucial connections among individuals and departments. What these charts leave unclear is where the power lies, which *informal* connections will be important, and who will have the greatest impact on your success. Working through a Manager's Universe mapping exercise with your team after a reorganization will enable you to combine input from many sources into a single map of crucial relationships that everyone can work from together, making it easier for your department to hit the ground running once the dust of the reorg has settled.

Understanding Your Boss's Universe

Some managers can't get over their bosses' shortcomings. They count on their bosses to deliver support for their efforts, answers to their questions, and solutions to their problems. When these are not forthcoming (or when they are delivered partially, ineffectively, or too late), the managers in The Middle are disillusioned, upset, and angry.

These expectations and reactions may be understandable. But they're also unrealistic. In the old days of the command-and-control corporation, managers were taught to believe "The boss is always right." Today, smart managers follow a new rule: "The boss isn't always right, *but he has the right to be wrong.*" Once you understand this reality, you can begin to cope with the consequences of your boss's shortcomings and figure out ways to manage productively and happily despite them.

By cutting their bosses some slack, wise managers create an environment where they get some wiggle room in return. They don't fuss about whether their boss's every pronouncement or policy is right or wrong. Instead, they focus on making everyone around them, including their boss, successful.

In the world of business, there's really no substitute for a happy boss. When the boss is happy, there's music playing, the air smells fresher, and food tastes better. So it only makes sense that one of the most important things any manager can do is learn what it takes to make the boss successful.

However, this is easier said than done. For many of the managers we interviewed, a major challenge is determining their bosses' needs. Some of the best advice on this subject comes from Joe Ripp, the former Vice Chairman of AOL and now President and Chief Operating Officer of Dendrite, a provider of corporate sales and marketing solutions. Joe says, "If you can help solve your boss's boss's problems, then your immediate manager will look better and be more successful. Making life easier for the people up the ladder from you will ultimately make your life easier."

Note the key insight in Ripp's observation: Start with your boss, but also consider the perspective of your boss's boss. If you help your boss achieve success with his or her boss (not by going around your boss, but collaboratively), you're really onto something. You're focusing on the issues that matter most at the highest levels of the company—the ones that'll get you the most recognition, the most power within the firm, and permission to pursue all your other dreams and goals.

You can probably see where we're going with this. In order to sharpen your understanding of what your boss needs to succeed, try drawing a Manager's Universe map from the perspective of your boss. Put your boss in the middle and sketch out the network of relationships that are crucial to your boss's success. Rate their importance and the quality of each connection based on your observations of the interactions between them. Analyze the map from your boss's perspective: Which are the most important focal points in the network? Which relationships are the most troubled? And then relate the answers to yourself: What can *I* do to strengthen my boss's connections with the key stakeholders in his universe? How can I make him look smarter, more efficient, more creative, more powerful, more successful?

Everything you do in response to these imperatives will help make your boss happy, and ultimately produce direct benefits for you and your team members.

If you have a boss who truly believes in transparency, you can even share your own version of your boss's universe with him or her and make it the basis for a valuable discussion about your role in that universe. Have your boss correct, expand, and clarify the map as he or she sees it. If this isn't possible, never mind. Use the map you've drawn as your guide. The most important thing is to constantly reinforce your own awareness of the fact that making your boss look and feel good is the smartest (and ultimately most powerfully self-serving) strategy any manager in The Middle can practice.

Igniting Your Network

So far in this chapter, we've talked about the importance of your network of stakeholders without using that much-misunderstood (and often-maligned) word *networking*. In this section, we're going to talk about networking, hopefully providing a new perspective that will help you make this crucial career practice really work for you.

First, a quick story.

These days everyone takes e-mail for granted, and if you're like me, you may be overdue for a cleanup of your inbox. But my friend Brian Tu had his first experience with e-mail a lot earlier than most of us—way back in 1990.

Brian was only about 14 years old at the time, and his father, an early adopter, set up an e-mail account for him. For several years, Brian had only his dad with whom to exchange e-mails. It was fun to do, but so was walking down the hall and talking to good ol' Dad face-to-face. Brian had no real inkling of the burgeoning power of the e-mail medium.

In high school, Brian began meeting other kids via e-mail. With each new e-mail friend, the power of the medium for Brian grew. Friends had friends, and great jokes and rumors and stories began to circulate around cyberspace. In his sophomore year, when Brian got the e-mail address of a cute girl, the Internet took on a whole new level of significance!

Brian was learning a vital truth about networks: Each new addition to any network adds more total value for all those involved. The same happened with fax machines (more offices equipped with fax machines meant more opportunities to use the gadgets) and, a century ago, with telephones.

The same truth applies to your personal business network. The bigger and broader it gets, the more valuable it will be—not just for you, but for every star in the galaxy.

The relative handful of stakeholders you identified when you created your Manager's Universe map are just a start at defining your business network. If your key stakeholders number eight or ten, then secondary nodes in the network may number 30 to 50, tertiary nodes a few hundred, and lesser nodes—some of them no more than points of light with whom you may communicate only once a year or less—may be almost infinite in number.

As the sun at the center of this complex, ever-growing network, you play a critical role. It's up to you to make and maintain the connections that link all these members into a single, living network. By putting a star from one segment of the network in contact with a star from another distant quadrant, you are offering them both an opportunity to generate light and energy together—to produce new value that neither one could create alone.

When people talk about networking, most think about people trading business cards and calling each other for referrals. That's part of it, but networking should really be thought of as *adding nodes*, then *turning them on* in a way that adds value.

My friend John Coulter is a master networker. He lives in Chicago and spent 26 years working with his best buddy from college, Jimmy deCastro, building the largest radio group in the country. Their AM/FM group boasted more than 450 stations when they finally sold it to Clear Channel in 2000. Today, John is a consultant spending much of his time helping early-stage media entrepreneurs. One meeting with John and you know that he is a powerful force, his optimism and energy are inspiring.

As you might imagine from the breadth of his business experience, John's network reaches deep. Call him for a headhunter—he's got 12. Mention you're visiting Cincinnati—he'll rattle off the names of three sales reps, a half-dozen contacts at Procter & Gamble, two top restaurants, and the phone number of a great car service.

John's great memory is an asset. But what really makes John powerful is that he knows what his contacts need and what they are trying to do, and he helps connect them to the people who can do it.

For people like John, networking is about *giving*. When he meets someone new, rather than looking for a referral or an equal handoff, John asks himself one question: "What does this person need, and how can I help?"

If someone has a business idea, John doesn't play the critic. (He accepts the fact that most people have no idea what'll work and what won't, a truth that becomes clearer the longer you work in any business, whether it's movies, publishing, or plumbing fixtures.) Instead, he becomes this individual's champion: "Who can I introduce you to that might be interested in your idea? Here are a few names..." Wherever you're trying to go, people like John help you get there faster. And with each interaction, the laws of karma increase John's own value and success.

Networking as Understanding People's Needs

How do we build relationships with people like John, becoming valued nodes on the network? What it really comes down to is *meeting people's needs*. If we meet others' needs—provide value in ways that matter to them—our needs will be met as well (ultimately if not immediately).

People who believe in this philosophy of networking don't work towards equal, one-for-one exchange. They give for the joy of giving, knowing that the world has a way of sharing rewards.

Of course, knowing *how* and *what* to give to the other people in your network isn't always so easy. With people who are a permanent part of your network (fixed stars in your universe), you have opportunities to communicate, share, observe, and learn what matters to them. With newcomers or slight acquaintances, it may take some insight or intuition.

Generally speaking, business people are usually looking for three types of solutions.

The first type is solutions that'll *make them money*. For example, you can

- Introduce them to potential customers.
- Introduce them to potential team members who can help them earn money.
- Give them ideas for products or services, or brainstorm with them.
- Help educate them about variant business models—show them what can they learn from your business.
- Advocate for them. Maybe drop a favorable reference to them into an op-ed or a letter to the editor in an industry trade journal. Or maybe just send an e-mail to their boss complimenting the great work they did for you.

The second type is solutions that'll *save them money*. You can

- Introduce them to new vendors.
- Give them the benefit of your experience on business systems, procedures, and/or processes.
- Help them find ways to create non-monetary compensation, incentives, and rewards for their employees and suppliers.
- Offer to negotiate favorable deals on their behalf.
- Show them ways to be more productive, efficient, and effective.

Finally, there are solutions that'll *make their lives easier*. For instance, you can

- Teach them how to implement technology better.
- Guide them in their shopping or decision-making.
- Help them plan an event.

- Clip articles or provide them research relevant to their business; in other words, help them learn something.

- Coach them, motivate them, and inspire them.

Once you really get to know your contacts, you'll begin to understand where their needs lie within these categories. If you don't know, ask them: "What's a bigger priority for you right now—finding more customers or trimming expenses? Making more time with your team members or more time with your vendors? What issues are keeping you up at night? Anything I can do to help?"

Once you believe that you understand the problem, clarify your understanding by asking, "Is it correct that finding talented employees is your greatest current concern?" This is an important step, because any solution you provide is meaningless unless it addresses a genuine concern.

Igniting your network is about turning people on. If you deliver real value, they'll feel the pull of reciprocity (it's a human instinct) and ultimately return that value and more back to you or to others in the network.

In Search of Nodes

If you need help in building your personal network, check out one of the popular "social networking" sites now available online. Dan Engel, a successful entrepreneur in Santa Barbara, California, uses LinkedIn (www.linkedin.com) to gather new nodes and light them up. As a member of LinkedIn, you can add your connections and then gain access through them to *their* connections. It's hard to overstate how useful this can be when you need a specific contact. For example, suppose you're a LinkedIn member interested in talking to someone involved in marketing the Pop Secret product at General Mills. You can visit LinkedIn's website, search its listings under General Mills, and chances are if you built your own network, you'll find the friend of a friend of a friend who works at General Mills and knows the relevant manager.

If you're interested, you can even join *my* network on LinkedIn. Just go to www.linkedin.com, search for me, and follow the directions. I'd love to have you as part of my personal universe.

The Need for Speed

A network of powerful nodes is pointless if you don't intend to realize its full potential. However, the more nodes you add, the more significant time constraints become. There simply aren't enough hours in the day to maintain a large network by conventional means. Therefore, you need to add another dimension to your networking program—speed.

Hollywood studio chief Jeffrey Katzenberg has mastered the art of speed networking. Responsible for a large chunk of Disney's success in the 1980s and 90s, he founded DreamWorks SKG with Steven Spielberg and David Geffen and later sold the studio to Paramount. Katzenberg has long been heralded for his close relationships with the Hollywood creative community. You might wonder how such a busy man is able to build and nurture his constellation of relationships (imagine the diagram of *his* Manager's Universe!) while rising to Hollywood's highest ranks.

If you've ever seen him at breakfast, you'll gain some insight. In a year with 260 business days, Jeffrey Katzenberg can find time for 750 breakfast meetings. Yes, we know that doesn't appear possible, but people like Katzenberg live far beyond normal limitations.

Here's how it works. Every morning, Katzenberg sets up shop in the corner of the dining room at one of LA's posh hotels. There he takes three breakfast appointments per hour, 20 minutes apart. Believe it or not, friends of mine who have been his guests tell me they *never* felt rushed.

It happens like this. You arrive at your scheduled time (don't dare be late) and are escorted to Katzenberg's table. The mogul greets you and makes sure you are comfortable. The waiter appears. You order. Katzenberg doesn't. The waiter leaves, and Katzenberg asks, "How can I help you?" As you reply, pitching your screenplay, business plan, or other concept, the waiter returns with your breakfast, plus a small bite for Katzenberg.

After 15 minutes of eating and pitching, you take your last bite, the waiter swoops in to clean the table, Katzenberg replays your needs back to you, offers to do what he can, and stands to wish you a warm good-bye. As you leave, a waiter quickly refreshes the table, and Katzenberg's next guest arrives.

Of course, Katzenberg's time-collapsing strategy produces conversations that are quite different from the usual business interchange. No small talk. No lingering over the choice of omelets. No catching up on the latest gossip. It's all about getting right to the point! By limiting meetings to 20 minutes each, Katzenberg communicates to his guests that *his time is valuable*. The result: Three guests get to run around LA later that day, casually mentioning to anyone interested with whom they just had breakfast. Meanwhile, Katzenberg has maximized his own time and considered three separate business opportunities in the space of time that most people would devote to one!

You probably can't implement Katzenberg's speed networking strategy directly. Most people don't have thousands of players wishing for a 20-minute slice of their time. Some of your business colleagues might even take offense if you sent them packing from the table after 17 minutes of conversation. But the concept of speed networking is critical, and easy to implement with appropriate modifications for your particular circumstances.

Here, in no particular order, is a collection of ideas for speed networking that you may want to try:

- *Never eat alone.* Keith Ferrazi's bestseller of the same name is a brilliant guide to networking, and while the book goes much deeper, the title itself reminds us of an important lesson. Instead of munching a bagel at your desk or scarfing down a sandwich at the deli counter, turn breakfasts and lunches into opportunities to exchange news and ideas with a colleague, client, customer, or source. There's something about "breaking bread" with people that helps to generate an instant bond of fellowship and empathy, which makes mealtimes a perfect opportunity to get to know someone.

- *Get wired.* E-mail, instant messaging, blogging, podcasting—all are powerful tools for adding value to what used to be downtime (commuting, jogging, waiting for your flight, the doctor's waiting room, you name it) and for time-shifting communications into those precious five- and ten-minute segments when motive and opportunity come together.

- *Respond right away.* When you get a message, phone call, e-mail, or letter from someone in your network, respond immediately, while the impulse is strongest, the message clearest, and the relevance highest. Don't stack the "to-dos" in a pile on the corner of your desk, expecting to find an opportunity to devote plenty of time to a "proper" reply. Instead, dash off a quick, top-of-the-head answer *now*, which contains 90 percent of what needs to be said. That's more valuable—and will be more appreciated—than a 100 percent answer two weeks from now.

- *Follow the crowds.* Take advantage of company gatherings, industry conventions, seminars and workshops, and other special events where many of the key people in your network will meet. Attend the parties, speeches, and presentations, and you'll be able to gather information and share news with 15 to 20 important people in less time than it would take to share one dinner with two of them. Always get in the path of the crowd. If they are headed to a seating area, have your conversations near the entry point. Near the end of the party, have your conversations near the door and say a proper goodbye.

- *Create your own groups.* Wish you had an opportunity to mingle with your counterparts in other departments or other companies more often? Invite a dozen key people to join you for lunch every month. Call it "The Second Thursday Club" and hold it at a great, noisy, crowded restaurant where the service is fast and the conversations are always lively. If that works, launch a few other such groups—maybe one for people from a range of related industries, another for alumni of the same college or high school, still another for people who share nothing except a passion for creative business ideas. Gather the right people and you'll soon find that others are begging for an opportunity to join the club.

- *Get your rest.* Paradoxically, taking time out to refresh and recuperate is crucial to keeping your efficiency high. When you're exhausted, your mind starts blinking, ideas fade and vanish, and your response rate slows to a crawl. Learn your own body chemistry and develop a routine that helps you keep it in top form. This may mean a 20-minute nap between afternoon meetings, an hour of yoga twice a week, or a three-day weekend at the shore every two months. Whatever it takes to recharge your batteries, do it religiously lest you fall prey to burnout.

Don't wait until your schedule becomes overwhelming before you consider how you can implement speed networking into your life and your work. Time is precious, and it is limited. Remember that you must collapse time in order to expand your network.

Bosses: Stars, Comets, and the Power of the Network

Having a well-lit network will help you power up a great boss's star (which casts a powerful light on you in the process), or survive the kind of boss who passes through your part of the cosmos like a comet. (You know the kind: full of hot gases and very impressive at first glance, but quickly flaming out into smoke and cinders.)

If you're lucky enough to have a star-like boss, you can connect him or her into your network and share the power of what you have built. If things really go well, your network and that of your boss may combine and increase their values exponentially.

If your boss is more of a comet—someone who doesn't understand you or care about your success—your network may be even more critical. The boss may not like you, but if the other nodes in your network recognize your value as a contributor, your boss will have a hard time letting you go or holding you back without damaging his own place in the network.

When times are tough, the power of your network becomes most apparent.

3

LEADERSHIP IN LIMITED SPACE

The Leadership Dilemma

One day a friend and I were sitting at an outdoor café in foggy Marin County, California, while the sounds of Highway 101 hummed behind us. My friend posed the question, "Can you have a great career in a crappy company?"

It was a simple question, but one I had never seen addressed in any business book.

My friend continued, "We read so much about the great companies— Intel, GE, Southwest, SAS, FedEx, Microsoft—and those with all the heat on them, like JetBlue, Apple, and Google. What about the rest of us? What about those of us who don't work in the best companies? Worse, what about those of us who work in companies that have been through turmoil, companies that have been torn apart? In the midst of the struggle, is it possible to have a great career in a company that is downright crappy?"

It's a poignant question because it focuses so acutely on what I call *The Leadership Dilemma*:

How do you lead in a situation where you are not in control?

During the last ten years, we've had a leadership solution proposed for almost every problem facing us. The books and seminars are endless, each with a different variation on the leadership theme. We've been inundated with leadership myths, leadership fables, leadership secrets, leadership tips, leadership practices, and leadership prayers. There has been so much written and spouted about leadership that some of the core tenets have become clichés, deadly in their boredom. (Have you noticed how eyes glaze over when someone says "win/win" in a meeting?)

Don't misunderstand me—we love leadership. We love the books, we love the people who write them and go on tour to talk about them—ministers, teachers, mayors, football coaches, consultants, academics, even an occasional CEO. They all have something to say, and much of it is actually worthwhile. But why—with all that we've read and with all the training programs we've been to—why is leading people still such a challenge?

One reason is that "leadership," as defined by the books and the consultants, is often better suited for those at The Top than for those in The Middle. So many of the stories of heroic leadership that are told and retold in conferences and around water coolers are about CEOs—the Jack Welches, Andy Groves, Bill Gateses, and Sam Waltons of the world. These are people who have the power to *force* changes on the organizations they head and who don't need anyone's sign-off or permission before launching a new initiative. Can the principles they use to run their companies really work for managers in The Middle like us—managers without the ability to reshape businesses, redirect strategies, or even (in many cases) to hire, fire, and reward employees as we see fit?

The answer is a qualified no. The "leadership secrets" of CEOs work for managers at every level, but only up to a point. And managers in The Middle face unique challenges that CEOs rarely face.

The challenge of *leadership in a limited space* calls for a fresh approach, one that borrows the best applicable insights from the hundreds of leadership books and redefines them for use by ignited managers. That's the purpose of this chapter.

Authenticity and Trust

One of the bedrocks of leadership at *any* level is authenticity. Authentic people are real, refreshing, and comfortable to be around. They don't try to sell you something that they don't believe in. They don't act differently around different people. They are solid. They say what they do and do what they say. You can trust them, and you know where they stand even when you don't agree with them.

In a world where we are constantly trying to understand what's real, what's worth being concerned about and what's not, we never have to worry about them. Authentic people provide the foundations for trust, and for our lives in Quake Country, trust is essential. If we are authentic ourselves, we can be anchors to others and others can rely on us. We can handle the shocks together and rebuild faster in the face of change.

While authenticity serves as the basis of trust, building trust is an active process—one that is of paramount importance in any relationship.

Without trust we have nothing. When we don't trust, we are guarded. We are fearful. We prepare for the worst-case scenario. Without trust, it's impossible to communicate. We're always misinterpreting and being misinterpreted. We're always looking out for the other person's agenda.

By contrast, with trust, we can move fast and get things done. Instead of looking for double meanings, we finish each other's sentences and move forward together to meet new shared challenges.

Trust is emotional. Zig Ziglar (the great teacher, leader, author, and motivator) really says it best: "People don't care how much you know, until they know how much you care."

In my career I've worked with many people who excelled at building trust and others who failed miserably to connect. What's the difference? In most cases, the sense of *caring* is the emotional basis of trust.

Think about the people you work with. Chances are, there is one certain team member that people would do anything for. Let's call her "Kelly." Kelly is the team member who is held in the greatest esteem. If you have trouble with Kelly, most people in the group will automatically assume that the problem must have started with you. Kelly works hard and is uplifted by those around her. She shows people she cares by asking about their families, always considering their needs, knowing their dreams, and actively trying to help them achieve those dreams. (As musician David Byrne once put it, "Sometimes it's a form of love just to talk to somebody that you have nothing in common with and still be fascinated by their presence.") People are important to Kelly, and it shows.

On the other end of the spectrum is a team member we'll call "Ray." Ray works as hard as Kelly, maybe even harder. He cares deeply about the business and he's actually very sharp. But Ray has a problem—in fact, nothing but problems. Ray's days are filled with fights and frustrations. If you have a problem with Ray, everyone assumes it's his fault.

What is Ray's problem? He may have a host of other career-limiting issues, but the foremost problem is that Ray doesn't take the time to show the people around him that he cares. When he tries, his attempts seem empty and phony. He doesn't listen empathetically and demonstrate true caring. As a result, those around Ray believe that deep down he couldn't care less about them—that Ray is only out for himself.

Is this true? Is Ray really a selfish, uncaring egoist? Maybe, or maybe not. Some of the Rays of the world actually don't care about people, and they choose not to fake it. Many Rays subscribe to the old philosophy that "Business is business," and think it means that there's no room for the "soft stuff." They're wrong, of course. Business is done by *people*, and disregarding the human element in business—which means emotion—is a sure way of misjudging, misreading, misunderstanding, miscalculating, and generally messing up any situation, virtually insuring that the project will fail, the taskforce will collapse, and the sales force will fail to meet its goals. You ignore the "soft stuff" of business at your peril.

In other cases, a Ray may simply be deeply shy, often as a result of some psychological wound experienced in childhood or adolescence. Sometimes people who discover that their colleagues and acquaintances consider them "cold," "stand-offish," or "superior" are shocked and hurt, because what comes across as arrogance in them is really an extreme diffidence caused by profound insecurity. If you're in this category, you owe it to yourself to overcome the fear. Get professional help if needed. If the emotions or interests don't come naturally, just do what so many of us do when taking on change—fake it until you make it.

In the end, most people *do* care about others (sociopaths excluded). It's a human instinct fostered by tens of thousands of years of natural selection: As the species evolved, families and tribal groups that cared for one another lived longer, fuller, more prosperous lives and eventually came to dominate over groups guided by the attitude of "Dog eat dog" or, in the words of philosopher Thomas Hobbes, "The war of all against all." Expressing the sense of empathy that is shared by all normal humans isn't a matter of play-acting or gamesmanship. It's about giving yourself permission to unlock the natural reservoirs of emotion that lie hidden inside you and letting them flow on the job, the way they do in your family and social life.

If you're a typical manager, in the next 12 months you'll probably participate in three to five teams with dozens of teammates. Whether or not you're designated as the "leader" of any of these teams is ultimately unimportant. Those who emerge as the *true* leaders will be those who connect with their fellow teammates. It starts with being authentic, which provides the basis for trust. Showing you care will build that trust.

Transparency and Consistency

One of the highest compliments you can give a counterpart in business is to say, "She has no hidden agenda." It's another way of saying that she is transparent.

Transparency and authenticity go hand in hand, and both are essential for managers in the new middle. The people we lead expect, need, and demand transparency from us—today more than ever. In an age when the old rules of the military-style, command-and-control business system have dissolved and no one is sure what the new rules are (or even whether there *are* any hard-and-fast rules), people need to know where they stand with you. They need to know where your power begins and ends, the boundaries of your control and influence, and the explicit and implicit goals you expect them to strive for. None of these parameters are self-evident any longer (if, in truth, they ever were).

Today power is widely distributed, and power levels fluctuate for managers as often as their checking account balances. Organizations are often either matrixed, or decentralized, or organized by cross-functional teams, and all these structures change frequently and unpredictably. So for managers in Quake Country, transparency is more important than ever.

This fundamental shift changes everything about how leaders must lead from the middle. At one time, a style of "playing your cards close to the vest," hoarding information to be doled out as it suited you, was an arguably unfair, but often effective, means for gaining control. Today this approach doesn't work, and the manager who tries to use it often loses control as well as the trust and respect of his teammates.

The transparent manager is less a "boss" than a coach or mentor. This shift requires greater expertise from us, as well as increased closeness to the work and to the needs of our people. And when our people need more from us than we can give, we need to help them in pursuit of their needs. We need to help them navigate our organizations, sell their ideas, and build their careers.

Managing this way means dropping the façade of the all-powerful, all-knowing leader to be admired, feared, and unquestioningly followed. It means operating as the first among equals, captain of the team, wielding, for everyone's benefit, the power you've gained by virtue of your knowledge, skill, and willingness to serve. And it means revealing the real you behind the discarded mask of "the boss"—in other words, being transparent.

To be transparent, you must also be consistent.

It's simply not possible to have varying standards (of work quality, ethical behavior, or social values) and remain transparent. Transparency allows people to know your authentic viewpoint—what you really stand for—so that they can anticipate your attitudes, make decisions consistent with your shared values, and operate autonomously with greater confidence and with less fear and uncertainty. If you're inconsistent, no one can tell what you really believe. (It doesn't matter what you *say*—your inconsistent actions will betray you every time.) This makes you impossible to "read" and prevents you from being transparent.

Thus, transparency means applying the same principles in the workplace as in your personal life. Unethical behavior often goes along with compartmentalization. Think of Enron, WorldCom, Adelphia, and a dozen other recent corporate scandals. Undoubtedly, most of the executives and middle-level managers who cooked the books, defrauded customers and investors, and violated well-known norms of corporate behavior thought of themselves as upstanding citizens, good family members, and thoughtful friends and neighbors. They were able to participate in on-the-job corruption only because they compartmentalized their values, separating "business" or "work" from the rest of life. It's a common phenomenon—hence the popularity of sayings like, "Business is business," which are all about the notion that somehow the ethical standards of the marketplace have no connection with those of ordinary human beings.

In some circumstances, compartmentalization is necessary for mental health. A soldier must draw a bright dividing line between the brutal acts of killing he must perform on the battlefield and the way he manages anger in a family, work, or neighborhood setting once he returns home. But maintained for too long, compartmentalization leads to the condition known as *cognitive dissonance*, a form of anxiety (often unconscious) resulting from inconsistency between one's beliefs and one's actions.

At its most extreme, cognitive dissonance can even be a fatal condition, as when the "pillar of the community" is exposed as a corporate fraud and ends up a suicide—crushed by the pain that results when the wall between two selves is breached and the contradiction can no longer be maintained.

No one is ethically pure. We all fall short of our own moral standards from time to time. This gap between the ideal and the real is natural and perhaps even a healthy condition, because it challenges us to grow closer to the ideals we cherish. What's dangerous is trying to deny the existence of this gap by pretending that different spheres of activity can support greatly different moral codes. Each of us is a single human being and must behave that way to be completely sane. This is the crucial link between consistency and transparency.

Defining Honesty

"All too often we hire people for what they know and fire them for who they are"—insightful words that explain a lot about what goes wrong in corporate America.

In Quake Country, where trust is fundamental, businesses consistently make the mistake of hiring people based exclusively on their knowledge, skills, and experience rather than on their character. When scrutinizing potential new hires, we analyze their resumes, evaluate their achievements, and note their educational credentials—but we rarely seek a clear understanding of their values. Conversations about values and honesty with people we barely know feel awkward, and today's concerns around employment law and the potential for litigation on the basis of discrimination makes managers even more hesitant to probe such personal matters.

Yet if we are to trust each other on the job, we must arrive at a shared definition of honesty. If we don't, we'll be on a collision course toward mutual misunderstanding, betrayal, and recriminations.

You may wonder: Is it really necessary to *define* honesty? Don't we all know what it means to be honest? Not so fast.

Fifty years ago, in the more homogeneous (and more socially restrictive) world of mid-century America, colleagues at work generally lived in the same neighborhood and often were of the same race and religion, and shared similar values. If not, then it was likely that they would get plenty of time to know one another—after all, in an era of virtually guaranteed lifetime employment, teams often worked together for decades.

Today coworkers are not so similar. In a more mobile and more diverse America, we work with people from different religions, ethnic groups, and educational backgrounds. We may work together for just a few months or years, not decades. And, as a society, we don't necessarily share a common definition of honesty any more than we agree on other basic values. As a result, there's ample room for misunderstanding, confusion, and mistrust.

Have you ever known someone who believed that responsibility for the truth goes no further than their lips? It's happened to me.

Several years ago, the business I worked at was booming and our operation was expanding quickly, which meant that new teams were being thrown together at a breakneck pace. I was assigned a new sales rep I'll call Tom. One morning, Tom asked me to sign off on a large advertising program he was putting together with a client. It looked lucrative and I was pretty excited about the opportunity. But before giving my approval, I asked the questions I always ask before accepting any deal: "Why is the client doing this? What does the client expect?"

Tom paused for a minute, then said, "The client is doing this to grow their business. They're in a real hurry to sign." He pushed the form toward me, as if silently urging me to initial it without asking any more questions.

But I persisted. "Why are they in such a hurry?"

"Well," Tom answered reluctantly, "I didn't tell them this. But they're under the impression that if they sign this deal with us, we won't sell any advertising to their competitors. So they want to move fast and block them out."

"That doesn't make any sense!" I responded. "You know we don't offer exclusivities."

Tom tried to reassure me. "Oh, sure, I agree, this isn't an exclusivity. They just think it is. We won't put it in the contract."

Now I was really concerned, and I challenged him. "So, in other words, you're lying to them."

Tom was taken back. "Absolutely not! I never lied. I don't know how they came to that belief. I didn't say it, but somehow they believe it. I just didn't correct them. So come on, let's get this deal closed." Tom sincerely had no idea why I was making this so hard.

Of course, this deal was dead on arrival. When I buy something, I expect the person selling to me to think about my best interests and point out anything in the deal that may not be consistent with those interests. If I find out later that certain things were not disclosed, I consider the sales rep accountable. That's part of my definition of honesty, and I try to apply it no matter on which side of the bargaining table I'm sitting.

I explained this to Tom without shaming him but rather asking him to see this negotiation from all sides. I also let him know that, while he may believe that others in the business world play the angles, we should aspire to higher standards. In that way, we can build long-term success we'll feel good about.

Tom never brought me a sideways deal again.

As this story illustrates, there are many definitions of honesty. Small distortions considered lies in some cultures don't classify as lies in others. Among some Japanese business people, saying no is considered rude. To avoid it, they will use circumlocutions and demurrals: "What you ask will be very difficult for us to do... I am not certain whether this is possible... Perhaps this matter is something we need to consider more carefully later on..." and so on. Another Japanese person would recognize this as a polite no, but many a Western businessperson has misinterpreted such a statement as a mere bargaining ploy or even as a yes with a caveat attached. In the subsequent dispute, accusations of dishonesty often fly despite the fact that the real problem is not dishonesty, but a deep cultural collide.

Even within our culture there are double standards that often lead to confusion. When a man's wife or girlfriend asks, "Do I look fat in this dress?" he'd better "lie"—if that's the right word to describe an answer such as, "You always look great to me!" And many of us have worked for bosses who send subtle signals about the kinds of bad news they are and are not willing to hear from a subordinate. There are even entire companies where the word "problem" is tacitly prohibited; what other people call problems are referred to as "issues" or "concerns" or even "opportunities." Some would describe this as "spin" or "tact" or "being political," but others would call it "lying." It's not obvious which evaluation is correct.

What's important is not that we all adhere to one definition of honesty, but rather that we talk about these matters and come to an understanding with the people we work with.

So how *do* we talk about these things? We're not suggesting that every interview with a potential new hire include an hour in Starbucks discussing the 50 scenarios in which they could take advantage of you. But it's important to find ways to probe value issues at the start of any new business relationship.

When I'm hiring new sales reps now, I tell them the story about Tom to give them a sense of what I feel is fair disclosure. I also tell them a story that comes from the gut (literally). I'm usually on some type of diet, and my sweet wife is always trying to help by cooking foods that are low-fat, or low-carb, or whatever the latest diet rage is. This sometimes poses honesty challenges for me. For example, suppose that while my wife is driving across town to get low-carb dressing for my salad, I stop off on my way home from work to have a burger at Johnny Rocket's. Do I owe it to her to say something about my detour? My answer is yes. As a participant in the weight-loss program, I owe it to her to tell her everything (and take my well-deserved lumps for deviating from the plan). I tell new hires this story and let them know that I expect no less from those I work with.

There are other approaches that smart managers have developed. D. Scott Karnedy of XM Satellite Radio has a contract he shares with potential team members during the interview process. The contract states what his expectations are and what people should expect of him, including the ethical standards they will share. For years now, he has been having his people sign off on this contract their first day on the job, and they appreciate the sense of transparency and mutual respect it fosters.

For a team that's already in place, we recommend devoting time during your next meeting or offsite conference to consider an ethical situation with which you or a team member have been confronted and then really discussing it. Let everyone suggest the best ways to handle the situation. Then look at your company's guiding principles and arrive at a standard of behavior that everyone can understand and commit to.

This kind of ethical consistency keeps people on track and continually reminds them about what is important. In today's business world, we cannot talk about these issues too often.

Playing It Straight

One common sin against transparency is using the office grapevine to send back-channel messages rather than delivering the word directly in a private conversation.

Imagine that you have a team member named Martha who has been taking two-hour lunches. People are beginning to notice and complain about the big hole in the middle of Martha's workday, and you know you have to do something. But what?

One option would be to announce in your next team meeting that lunches should last no longer than an hour. Another would be to talk with Martha about the problem one-on-one. Either solution would be acceptable. But what *doesn't* work is the indirect approach that all too many managers use: You keep asking where Martha is around two o'clock in the afternoon. You wonder aloud why she hasn't finished her project. Your hope is that Martha will get the message. Maybe someone on the team will pull Martha aside and warn her that her long lunches are making her look bad in front of the boss.

It's easy to slip into the indirect approach. In the short run, it avoids confrontation and reduces the stress of conflict. But in the long run, it tends to *create* more conflict through confusion, uncertainty, and misunderstanding. Team members start gossiping about Martha. They wonder why you haven't spoken with her directly, and perhaps attribute to her some sort of special status or power that makes you "afraid" to confront her. Some other team members also begin taking two-hour lunches, consciously or unconsciously testing your ability to set limits or to establish fair rules that apply to everyone. Next thing you know, half of your team members are spending their days arguing about the length of lunch hours rather than getting their work done.

In companies where indirect forms of communication are habitually used, the potential for misunderstanding and resentment is enormous. Consider what Shari McGuire, a manager with a Fortune 500 financial institution in Minneapolis, had to endure as the result of a manager sending a message through indirect, symbolic means.

Here's Shari's story:

> "One year, our manager threw a big party to celebrate the first anniversary of several employees in the department. We had cake and gifts and even took photos which were displayed on the bulletin board. It was nice and everybody felt good about it. Until several weeks later, when a coworker and I were celebrating long-term anniversaries with the company. She'd been with the company 20 years, and I'd been around for 10 years. Did we get a party? A cake? A gift? No—we came to work to find a memo and a token gift on our chairs. That was it!"

> "Needless to say, I learned a lot about how *not* to treat your employees from that manager."

Shari's manager had probably given little thought to the message she was sending through her different kinds of celebrations. But it doesn't take long to conclude that he placed a high value on "new blood" while holding long-term employees in disdain. This certainly isn't the policy at the bank, and the indirect message being sent here was really destructive to morale.

As a manager, you need to think continually about the messages your words and deeds are sending. Make certain that you *know* the messages you want to convey and that you convey them openly and clearly—not in veiled fashion through symbols, hints, or gestures.

The New Golden Rule

So much of what we learn when we study the principles of leadership centers around the so-called Golden Rule: "Do unto others as you would have them do unto you."

The Golden Rule is practically universal and can be found in the ethical and religious teachings of many nations. It has worked well in many settings (including the workplace) for thousands of years, and will continue to work when applied to people of the same culture.

However, in today's increasingly diverse world where a typical workplace may include people from half-dozen ethnic and racial backgrounds, disparate social classes, both genders, and a variety of sexual and religious orientations, the underlying assumption of the Golden Rule is becoming dubious. As diverse people, we have diverse needs, interests, goals, and desires. Therefore, to assume that what we want for ourselves is what others want is often no longer valid.

This challenge to the Golden Rule applies to simple social questions. For example, I have great respect and admiration for items handcrafted from wood. A fine teak desk set, box, or bowl would be a wonderful gift for me, something I would deeply appreciate. On the other hand, cultural experts say that most people from the Middle East don't have any deep-rooted fondness for wood. Perhaps it's because of the lack of trees in their native lands, or because of the fact that wood does not hold up well in their dry climate. So maybe a classic wooden sculpture is not the best gift idea for a colleague from Dubai.

Thus the need for a New Golden Rule: "Do unto others as *they* would have you do unto them." In other words, strive to serve, reward, and respect others—not in the way that *you* prefer but in the way that *they* prefer. And how can you know what they prefer? It's as simple as asking.

This principle applies to much more than gift-giving. It applies to every human connection between you and the people you work with. If you strive to know and understand the interests, values, and goals of the people you manage, your colleagues, and other business associates, you'll be better able to incentivize, reward, help, and bond with them.

Some of the concrete ways to apply the New Golden Rule include the following:

- Make a discussion of career goals part of every job appraisal or coaching session with your team members. Rather than *assuming* that Deb and Jerry want a raise and promotion next year (because that's what *you* are working for), ask them about their dreams and desires. Maybe Deb is more interested in exploring a lateral shift to a similar job in a department elsewhere in the company (a move that you could help facilitate by making a few phone calls to your friends in that department). Maybe Jerry would most appreciate being able to work from home two days a week so that he can spend more time with his newborn baby son (a change you'll have to negotiate on his behalf with the rule-makers in Human Resources).

- At the start of every new business partnership, explicitly discuss the underlying goals of all the parties so that the policies and procedures you establish can help everyone get closer to their real objectives. For example, suppose you are establishing a joint venture with another company for the development of a new product or service that both companies will market. How would each company rank the importance of such disparate goals as speed to market, initial product quality, cutting-edge design, breadth of market appeal, and ease of use? You may discover that the goal you rank first is low on your partner's priority list, in which case the way you each manage the project may need to be seriously adjusted in order to avoid mutual disappointment.

- Make a habit of exploring with your boss what you can do to make his job easier, more productive, and more successful. Don't assume that what he or she *says* is always a completely accurate description of what he or she really *needs*. (Like anyone else, bosses often feel constrained by cultural and social norms that make openness and transparency a challenge.) Instead, proactively ask about the biggest challenges and problems your boss faces, and then discuss how you and your team can help solve them.

The New Golden Rule also relates to one perennial management challenge: How do you deal with the eccentric, egotistical superstar employee, the worker who contributes a lot to the company by his or her sheer brilliance but who refuses to follow the rules that others readily obey for the good of the team?

The New Golden Rule suggests that everyone deserves to be treated as an individual rather than according to cookie-cutter standards of right and wrong. This is true—but at the same time, when one person habitually abuses this approach by violating group norms and making life hard for the rest of the team, where do you as manager draw the line?

As a manager who has had to deal with more than one arrogant superstar in my day, I've found that people *will* accept the notion that the rules can be bent for a particular person, provided they understand the circumstances and accept the idea that the rule-bending serves some greater good—and provided that there are limits to what the superstar can get away with.

For example, I would rule that an extremely high-producing member of a team may be permitted to skip some meetings that others must attend and perhaps turn in paperwork that is less than thorough—so long as the higher-than-average productivity continues to pour in. But the superstar will *not* be allowed to be verbally abusive to other employees (or of course to customers and clients), and the minute his or her productivity slips, it's back to living within the norms.

And I will be totally transparent about these arrangements with everyone on the team. They need to understand that we are all paying a price in flexibility for the sake of money generated by the superstar. In my experience, the other team members will accept the situation if they understand it and if I'm consistent about it—and if I'm prepared to be equally flexible when other people need it (for example, when a female team member is pregnant and needs to make job-sharing arrangements).

Ultimately, the New Golden Rule is about learning to look at the world through fresh eyes—to see things as others see them. It's an essential skill for any effective manager to learn.

Making the Little Things Count

Elias Plishner, at age 30, is finally starting to look a little older than 17, which is a good thing for Elias: No more wearing fake glasses to meetings or struggling to find a hairstyle that will add years to his age. As the Vice President of Online Media at the Universal McCann Advertising Agency in Los Angeles, Elias is finally starting to feel as if folks are listening, and while he'll take a little credit himself, he also credits the winds of the Internet revolution at his back.

As the "online media guy" in a big advertising agency historically focused on the print and television categories, Elias was charged with trying to convince clients to commit a greater proportion of their media dollars to online advertising. This wasn't an easy assignment. There were some dark days after the initial vogue for Internet advertising faded. Audiences hated intrusive pop-up ads, and advertisers thought the little banners that appeared next to people's e-mail messages were lame.

But eventually consumers began spending so much time online that Internet advertising became increasingly attractive. The ads themselves got better and bigger. Soon marketers were playing TV spots online and harnessing the power of click-here shopping to sell products and services directly to consumers. Now online advertising is a recognized industry force, and Elias's phone calls are getting returned more often than not.

During the tough times, Elias learned some important lessons that he sticks to today. Like many managers, he had to lead his team through a period of challenging (and ever-rising) goals, limited resources, and a lack of clear career paths. Lacking final authority over his team members' compensation, Elias's ability to motivate people was limited. Why follow someone who at the end of the day may or may or may not be able to reward you?

To Elias's credit, he was forthright with his people about what he could and could not do for them. He recalls a time when one of his team members clearly deserved a pay raise—several months prior to the date when company rules would permit it. Elias went to bat for the employee, used all his best negotiating skills with Human Resources, and came back with a reasonable compromise. Elias met with the team member and explained in detail how and why he'd been able to win some, but not all, of the negotiating points he'd asked for—an early raise, but smaller than Elias had wanted, along with some additional give-and-take on other issues. "I want people to know I'm fighting for them, even though I can't get them everything they may deserve."

Still, Elias wanted to figure out how he could add more value to the life of his team. His initial answer came from his identity as a certified Internet nerd. Elias had a true passion for online media, and he began to see his role as that of coach and counselor. He taught his reports everything he knew about the Internet, coached them on working with clients, helped them develop sales and marketing plans that would boost their clients' business, and showed them how to convey the importance and excitement of the Internet.

Elias urged his team members to view learning as their highest priority. "Your job is to be a sponge," he would tell them, "soaking up everything there is to know about online media." Then he would give them an opportunity to put their knowledge into action, bringing them along on client presentations and meetings (including those that would normally be considered "inappropriate" for lower-level workers elsewhere at the agency). He explains, "Putting people on the firing line, learning what keeps clients awake at night and what makes them happy, makes them feel as though they're part of the process. It's motivating, and that's why I do it."

Elias's coaching enhanced the success of his people, and they respected him for it.

Over time, however, Elias began to find the work less than fulfilling. The job was complex: His team would create ads, buy media, review reports, and then get bogged down in reconciling the resulting spreadsheets and software programs that tracked results. More and more, Elias's role seemed limited to hours of number-crunching and enforcing deadlines. It was fun to help grow a new industry and help marketers build their businesses, but there were times when the sheer volume of paperwork left Elias feeling bored and depressed. And inevitably this attitude was conveyed to Elias's team members. Morale fell, and with it productivity.

Then Elias got an idea.

Like millions of other people, Elias read the best-selling book by journalist Malcolm Gladwell, *The Tipping Point: How Little Things Can Make a Big Difference*. The book's central theme is that small actions can have effects that are many magnitudes greater if they happen in just the right time and place. Gladwell recounts how nationwide fashion trends often originate with the choices made by just a few of the right people ("connectors," who anchor a network of people ready to be influenced), and how a series of seemingly insignificant actions (such as crackdowns on subway graffiti, turnstile-jumping, and harassment of motorists by squeegee-wielding windshield washers) launched a chain of events that led to a dramatic reduction of crime in New York City.

Inspired by Gladwell's insight into the power of small actions, Elias sensed this might be the kind of idea that could reenergize and motivate his team. He then scheduled an offsite meeting. As preparation, Elias gave copies of *The Tipping Point* to his team members and asked each one to write a one-page paper about something small they'd done in their lives that had a serious impact.

At the offsite meeting, the team members shared their stories. Some were touching, some were amazing, and some were funny. The way in which sharing these stories solidified the team was remarkable. But that wasn't Elias's main goal. His real purpose was to institute the Tipping Point Awards.

Each month, a member of Elias's team would be celebrated for something small he or she had done that had a big impact. Maybe it was coming in on a Saturday to look at competitors' advertising and sharing the findings, which in turn caused clients to increase their investment. Maybe it was helpfully transferring an inbound call from a stranger who happened to be the CEO of the company's global parent. These were actions that started as fairly ordinary examples of good work but ended up having more meaningful results, deserving to be celebrated.

Through all of these strategies—coaching team members to share their specialized bodies of knowledge and thereby enhance their own careers, fighting on their behalf even when he lacks the power to win every battle, and helping people to see the bigger value in the small daily actions that make up their jobs—Elias helps to connect his team members to their work and gives them a greater sense of the value they are creating. He is authentic, and he leads with transparency—two traits that are increasingly important for ignited managers.

Resilience, Optimism, and the Leadership Quest

As managers in Quake Country, we ride the same emotional and psychological shock waves as our people. While we may absorb the tectonic shifts a little earlier, the thrill, the fear, the impact are equally powerful. And the ways in which we as managers react almost always affect our team members' response.

This imposes a serious responsibility on the manager. As leaders, we must have more resilience. We must bounce back faster. We must have a viewpoint that is appropriately positive and leads people to a better place faster. But how?

It's not easy to maintain your equilibrium when the people around you are reacting (or overreacting) to the latest wave of bad news, unsettling change, or competitive attack hitting your company. But resilience is more than just an inborn personality trait. It's a skill that can be learned and improved over time. Highly resilient people do three things very, very well when faced with change:

1. First, they accept the new reality. They've developed an attitude that says, "The past is the past. It cannot change. Here is what is real today. Let's examine it together, figure out what it means (and doesn't mean), and discover some ways to make it work for us."

2. Second, they are great at improvisation. They pick up the pieces available to them right now and make the most of them. Unlike less-resilient people, who may go to pieces in situations where the familiar rules no longer apply, resilient leaders say, "Business as usual doesn't seem to be working any more. Let's forget our old ways. What new approaches can we try? What lessons can we apply from other companies, other businesses, or other situations outside of the business world?" And when one attempt fails, they are ready to move on to a second, and a third, and a fourth... until they find a new system that works in the changed landscape.

3. Finally, in insane times, resilient people draw deep personal strength from their own sane values and beliefs. Regardless of where things are headed, they know what they believe is right and they work toward it.

People get those deep-rooted values from many sources. For some, it's religion—perhaps in the form of a church, synagogue, mosque, or other community of faith, or perhaps in the form of a book or a set of teachings they find nourishing and enlightening. For others, it's family, friends, or another group of people who help to remind them of what's truly important and restore their spirits through fellowship and good times. For still others, it's a place or an activity that provides emotional and psychological comfort—body-surfing at your favorite beach, painting water colors in your neighborhood park, cooking chili for the gang in your backyard. Discover what helps you stay anchored in your personal values and return to that source frequently, especially during times when the ground beneath you and the walls around you are trembling.

The people you work with who don't have a clear and consistent set of values may find life in Quake Country a source of fear and confusion. But you can help by letting them borrow yours. If you are forthcoming and free with the principles that you rely on, it's easier for other people to pick them up and try them out. Maybe someday they'll internalize them as their own.

Whatever the case, use your optimism and inner strength to guide and support them. We're all attracted to optimism and those who can instill it in us.

So much of leadership is about setting people on a course that they feel good about, and so much about feeling good is based on attitude. But how can you feel good when you are in the deep valleys, struggling without resources, uncertain whether there's a payoff ahead?

Many of the greatest leaders share the notion articulated by the great teacher of philosophy and mythology, Joseph Campbell, that each of us is the hero of a personal quest. Each of us is the central character in a search for greater meaning in which a series of challenges must be encountered, understood, and overcome. No two people have exactly the same quest; no two people will discover the same deeper meaning in life. But people can share a part of their quests, helping one another along the way while their paths intersect.

This perspective on our lives gives optimism a new meaning. Recognizing that life is a quest, we begin to see the daily stresses, setbacks, and calamities as wonderful twists in the plot—logs to jump, rivers to cross, and mountains to scale. Each obstacle we surmount makes us wiser, stronger, and more enduring. And knowing that each of our team members is on a quest of his or her own deepens our appreciation of their individual talents, needs, and uncertainties. Whatever the circumstance, we can work together in the knowledge that our people are progressing towards their own fulfillment.

We are reaching the potential within ourselves to lead.

So what is the answer to the question my friend asked that foggy day in Marin County? Is it possible to have a great career in a crappy company?

After a chuckle and a bit of thought the answer came to us. It comes down to how you wish to measure your value. Do you measure your value based solely on what you create for yourself? Or does your definition include the value that you are able to help others create?

We all want to be winners in the leadership quest, but for true leaders the big payoff is also in the growth that occurs on the journey.

4

MANAGING YOUR EMOTIONS

Road Rage in the Marketing Department

For many of us, our time in the car is the only time we get for ourselves. It's where we start and finish our workdays, getting a chance to reflect on where we've been and where we hope we're going.

The highway is also an amazing place to study human behavior. Comedian George Carlin was on to something when he remarked, "Have you ever noticed that anybody driving slower than you is an idiot, and anyone going faster than you is a maniac?" Of course, Carlin's observation is really more of a comment about how we perceive other people than about how other people drive: We all tend to assume that our preferred driving speed is the "correct" one, and therefore react with intolerance or even anger when someone else chooses a different speed.

Think about the last time you were cut off while driving. Could anything feel more unfair? Some idiot managed to cross five lanes of traffic without signaling, then squeezed right in front of you, missing your bumper by inches. You were forced to floor the brakes, trying desperately to hold your lane. Remember how you reacted?—Your heart raced, your skin got flushed, and adrenaline pumped through your system, generating the ancient "fight-or-flight" syndrome that saved the lives of our cave-dwelling ancestors when confronted by a hungry sabre–tooth tiger.

You were angry—really angry. But mingled with the anger was a powerful emotion that triggered it. The emotion was fear. For a split second, you could almost hear the crunch of metal and glass, feel the searing pain as your car slammed into the embankment at the side of the road and rolled over, crushing you... But it never happened. The chemical reaction to the fear flooded your body, producing the road rage that followed.

Every day, people get cut off at the office. They suffer surprises, shocks, and assaults, all challenging them at a primal level. Underlying the anger they feel is fear: fear of loss, fear of embarrassment, fear of failure. No wonder that, on any given day, more than a million American workers are out on "stress leave," putting themselves on ice because they are simply too raw-nerved to face their fears in a productive fashion. Others, unsuspecting and tired, choose the wrong responses. They lash out in anger, putting others on the defensive and turning the workplace into a battle zone. A handful "go postal," committing acts of physical violence that shatter relationships and destroy lives.

In this chapter, you'll learn about tackling intense feelings like fear, anger, shame, and despair head on, and about how to keep these powerful emotions from contaminating your decision-making. You'll discover several dangerous paths down the slippery slope to emotional and psychological imbalance, and learn about techniques for avoiding that quicksand.

Emotional Intelligence

Emotions are rarely something that we can control. We can't prevent a sudden unexpected event from stimulating a primordial emotional urge. But though we can't eliminate the onset of fear, we can control the way we respond to fear. In the battle against fear, we have two strong tools. For the fear that catches us off guard, we have our *emotional intelligence*—the ability to take a step back and choose the appropriate response before leaping ahead and adding to our pain. For the fear that comes from confrontation, hard conversations, or forced choices, we need to be supported by a *Bigger Yes*—something that is greater than our fear, something big enough to power our courage.

Emotional intelligence, often abbreviated as "E.Q.," stormed the world of management thinking in the early 1990s, when journalist Daniel Goleman published his best-selling book *Emotional Intelligence: Why It Can Matter More Than IQ*. It spawned a series of spin-offs and copycat books, but the original work is still well worth reading (Goleman's a clear and persuasive writer), so by all means pick up a copy and glean from it what you can.

Without trying to summarize all of Goleman's insights, let me share with you one aspect of emotional intelligence that I find most compelling and useful. It's the simple idea that *you and your emotions are two different things*. The feelings, thoughts, reactions, impulses, desires, repulsions, urges, fantasies, and longings that flow through your brain and body at any given moment are interesting and often reveal truths about you and what is happening to you that are important. But they are *not* "you." There is a separate entity—a deeper self—that is fundamentally unaffected by these changing states and remains consistent from minute to minute, day to day, even year to year. This is the real "you," the locus of your existence and the connecting link among all the experiences and memories that make up your life.

It's important to distinguish this real you from the momentary flow of emotions. Why? Because when we confuse the two—which we're prone to do in moments of intense feeling—we lose the capacity for objective thinking. Instead, we become so caught up in the instantaneous emotion, whatever it may be, that we identify with it and surrender our sense of self to it. As a result, the emotion takes over, seizing control over our behaviors, summoning up ideas and images that support it and fueling *further* emotional reactions. Our whole self becomes a slave to the emotion and devotes itself to satisfying whatever craving it generates. If the emotion is fear, we become devoted to fleeing. If the emotion is anger, we become devoted to expressing rage through violent words or deeds. If the emotion is grief, we become devoted to wallowing in misery.

Of course you've experienced this. When we're very young and immature, it's our dominant mode of existence. A baby experiencing hunger *becomes* hunger, and his or her wails of hunger are inconsolable and unceasing until the longed-for mother appears. A little child frustrated by a parental "No!" *becomes* his anger, and the result is a tantrum—kicking, screaming, blubbering, biting, howling—that may go on for hours until exhaustion sets in and the child's system simply shuts down.

Part of growing up is learning how to separate ourselves from our passing emotions. And most of the time, we're all capable of doing this. When your stomach growls during a late-morning meeting, you don't throw a fit and demand lunch as you might have done when you were a toddler; instead, you wait for a decent break in the conversation and then politely ask, "Anybody else feeling ready for a sandwich?" That's what being a grown-up is all about.

The problem arises during moments of *intense* emotion. That's when your primitive, animal-like instincts, which don't know how to distinguish your *self* from the emotions you *experience*, try to take over. Chemicals flood your nervous system, overwhelming you with powerful impulses. The next thing you know, you are saying or doing something you'll later regret—expressing emotion unrestrained by civilized mores, thoughtful reflection, or even enlightened self-interest.

I don't mean, of course, that you're likely to fling yourself onto the floor and start howling like a two-year-old. (Though there are CEOs whose behavior isn't all that different.) Under strong emotional pressure, you may find yourself snapping angrily at colleagues, unleashing sarcasm, whining about how hurt or upset you are, or even breaking down in tears. It may feel good for a moment or two—it's such a relief to give the emotion a chance to express itself. The reactions of those nearby will quickly remind you that uncontrolled behavior is considered "childish," even "infantile," and is unlikely to get you what you need or want in the long run.

Instead, remember to *separate* yourself from the emotion. The next time you're feeling some powerful emotion at work, take it as a cue to *slow down*. Rather than *expressing* the emotion, take a moment to *observe* it. Shut down the self-talk that *embodies* the momentary feeling—inner dialogue like, "That S.O.B.! How dare he talk to me that way!? I'm going to teach him a lesson once and for all!" Instead, open up a dialogue that *reflects* on what is happening inside you: "Wow, I'm really angry! It gets my goat when Harry criticizes my work in front of my staff. It makes me feel embarrassed and upset. And this time it feels worse than ever before. Maybe it's because it's the second time he did it this month."

There's a world of difference between these two reactions. The first strengthens and reinforces the emotion, increasing the inner pressure you feel to express it forcefully. The second examines and analyzes the emotion, helping you to understand its causes. In the process, it tends to cool the emotion, gradually letting you achieve mastery over it.

Having experienced whatever emotion you are feeling, and then having separated yourself from it, you will be in a position to *choose* your response to the situation rather than being controlled by intense feeling. One of Daniel Goleman's recent articles describes new research by the consulting firm of Hay/McBer based on a random sample of almost 4,000 executives from around the world. This research uncovers six different leadership styles, described in Goleman's shorthand as Coercive ("Do what I tell you"), Authoritative ("Come with me"), Affiliative ("People come first"), Democratic ("What do you think?"), Pacesetting ("Do as I do, now"), and Coaching ("Try this").[1]

In a particular setting, any of these leadership styles may be effective (although some—especially the Coercive style—can be dangerous and must be used with caution). But the most notable finding cited in Goleman's article is that effective leaders are able to use more than one style, depending on the circumstances and the nature of the problem they are currently facing. In fact, the great leader chooses the best management style for an occasion the way a great golfer chooses the perfect club for a particular shot.

One hallmark of the exceptional leader is the ability to move flexibly and smoothly among styles—using the Authoritative style, for example, when a clear direction from the top is required, shifting to the Affiliative style when it's more important to heal emotional rifts among the members of a team, and then moving to the Pacesetting style when it's crucial to get quick results from a motivated, competent team. Of course, it's only possible to achieve this level of flexibility when you've mastered your emotions sufficiently to be in command of yourself, and therefore able to freely choose the most appropriate way to interact with your colleagues.

Your Bigger Yes

It's all well and good to talk about "counting to ten" or "taking a deep breath" when emotions start to overwhelm you. There are situations in

---

[1] Daniel Goleman, "Leadership That Gets Results." *Harvard Business Review*, March-April, 2000.

life, and at work, when powerful stressors simply *can't* be controlled by an act of will. There are times when you need a more powerful source of inner strength. For me, the best of such resources is something called "The Bigger Yes," a phrase familiar to many from its use by author Stephen Covey of *Seven Habits* fame.

Ambrose Redmond put it this way: "Courage is not the absence of fear, but rather the judgment that something else is more important than fear."[2] Having The Bigger Yes is having something more important driving you—something that gives you the courage to stand up in the face of fear, anxiety, anger, or any other overwhelming emotion and do what you *know* is the right thing. Your Bigger Yes may be your principles, values, or sense of justice. It may be your knowledge of a better opportunity. Whatever it is, your Bigger Yes is stronger than the emotions that are trying to control you, and it gives you something to cling to rather than allowing the emotions to sweep you away.

Consider the case of Michael Drake.

Mike left his private practice as an executive talent recruiter to join Freddie Mac, which as you may know is the independent financial corporation chartered by Congress to improve liquidity in the mortgage marketplace and therefore help more Americans own their own homes. Although Freddie Mac undoubtedly does a lot of good work that benefits millions of people, it's an organization with a very conservative, risk-averse, even repressive internal culture—a culture Mike characterizes as "based on fear." This atmosphere has been intensified since 2003 as a result of public battles over Freddie Mac's accounting practices, especially in regard to their use of so-called derivative hedges, complex financial instruments designed to mitigate interest-rate risk. It's a potential scandal-in-the-making that has made folks within Freddie Mac understandably nervous about virtually *any* decision they made.

Like many Freddie Mac employees, Mike wanted the company to have a fresher perspective. Unlike most of the others, however, Mike was given a powerful opportunity to create positive change. In his new role as the person in charge of hiring for the organization, Mike was given

---

2 Understanding Panic Disorder, "Understanding Panic Disorder." Available online at http://www.geocities.com/Heartland/Valley/2669/panic.html

the goal of hiring 1,000 new employees within a year—a huge influx necessitated by the derivatives controversy and the drive for greater oversight it produced. These new people would ultimately constitute 20 percent of the 5,000-person Freddie Mac workforce.

Mike saw the assignment as an exciting opportunity to do something much bigger than just recruit a few employees. This was a chance to help change the overly bureaucratic, fear-based culture of Freddie Mac.

However, many others at the company wanted to maintain the comfortable status quo. A struggle between the two sides was already in high gear when Mike arrived. There were so many policies holding people back, and all these policies were being challenged and defended by warring factions.

Unsurprisingly, Mike soon found himself embroiled in these battles. Some of the wars he had to fight were purely administrative—which didn't mean they were simple. For example, in the hiring system that Freddie Mac had used for the past 32 years, a new recruit would not be assigned an employee number until his or her first day on the job. Unfortunately, routine procedures like buying a computer or a phone and assigning office space couldn't *begin* until that number was in place. The result: New employees would have to sit around in borrowed cubicles for two weeks with nothing to do, a ridiculous and morale-draining way to start their tenure at Freddie Mac. It sent each new employee the deadly message, "Hey, around here it doesn't matter whether you're working or not."

You might think that solving this problem would be an easy matter once it was identified. You don't know Freddie Mac. "It was unbearable," Mike recalls. "For three months, I was banging my head against a stone wall. All I heard was comments like, 'It doesn't matter,' 'Why do we need to change?' It was incredibly frustrating."

Nothing happened until one day the corporate chief of information technology called Mike to vent his personal frustration. With his department in the midst of its own rapid expansion, the CIO had discovered that his halls were filled with new-hire refugees—homeless, computer-less, phone-less, and unable to get anything done. "Why do we have this ridiculous system?" he wanted to know.

Here was the opening Mike had been after. "It's because, up till now, nobody's wanted to make fixing the system a priority."

"Well, it needs to be a priority."

"I agree," Mike said. "So pick up the phone and call your tech people and tell them that."

The CIO made the call, and within three days the problem was solved. Now new employees are assigned a number one week before they join the company, so they can have their personal infrastructure in place from day one.

Other obstacles Mike faced were more substantive. The hiring process at Freddie Mac required that each candidate not only receive the endorsement of the hiring manager, but also an endorsement from each of the other team leaders. This "veto power" made the work of getting candidates with fresh perspectives and new ideas into the organization very difficult. If even a single interviewer felt threatened by a candidate with game-changing perspectives or ideas, he or she could simply shut the candidate down—no questions asked.

After a few candidates (whom Mike had really believed in) failed to make it through the process, he decided to take a more aggressive stance. He began questioning the managers, forcing them to defend their positions on job candidates. Challenging the prevailing culture at Freddie Mac in this way wasn't an easy thing to do. "I was scared at first, but I believed that what I was doing was right for this company. That's what got me through the fear."

The initial response from the other managers was shock and resentment. Who was this new guy who dared to rock the boat by criticizing their dicta? But in time, the managers began to see that Mike's motivations were sincere. The candidates he was pushing had smarts, energy, and commitment, and they were in fact the kinds of new workers that Freddie Mac needed to carry out its program of reform. The other team leaders gradually accepted the fact that Mike knew what he was doing, and little by little, they stopped pushing back against his hiring recommendations.

Changing a corporate culture is never an easy task. It takes years of blood, sweat, and tears, and even then is often only partially successful. Throughout his time at Freddie Mac (he has since moved on), Mike found working within that bureaucratic world frustrating at times. It would have been easy for him to allow emotional reactions like anger, despair, cynicism, and hostility to overwhelm him. How did he control these feelings? It went back to Mike's commitment to something more important than his day-to-day struggles on the job—his Bigger Yes.

Here's how Mike explains it:

> "Each day I wake up, look at myself in the mirror, and say, 'Today, I am going to do what I know is right for this organization. It doesn't matter what anybody else says. It doesn't matter whether I make friends or enemies. It doesn't even matter if my efforts succeed or fail. If somebody else sabotages what I'm trying to accomplish, so be it. What matters is that I do the right thing. If I do that, I'll feel good about myself when I go to bed tonight."

Mike's fearless commitment to his personal values in the midst of corporate intrigue is greatly strengthened by his career and financial situation. Before joining Freddie Mac, Mike had enjoyed some success in his personal consulting role. Before *that*, he had had a successful career at a large and growing for-profit corporation in the technology world. He'd managed his money well, accumulated a nest egg, and had gotten to the point where he knew he could weather any storm. These experiences had left Mike with a feeling of inner confidence and independence that on-the-job conflict couldn't shake. "It helps a lot to know that, even if I were to lose my job at Freddie Mac, I would be all right. I'm good at my job, and I know others who will pay me well to do it. I've got some money saved, and I'll be fine no matter what happens. *I'm just not going to be afraid.*"

There's a great irony here: Mike Drake can do what's right for *others*—he can put his company and his team of employees first—because he's already taken care of *himself*. Unlike some "company men" who are helplessly dependent on the good will of their corporate employers and live in terror of the pink slip, Mike can stand on his own. And this enables him to be a *better* employee—more honest, more independent, more truly loyal. Mike can see what's right for the company and stand up for it because of the strength provided by his Bigger Yes.

In the end, a company filled with frightened "company men" is far *weaker* than a company made up of strong individuals like Mike Drake—men and women who have options for life *outside* the company.

When a manager's not fearful about losing his job, he sits in a much healthier place. He can help his team because he has a solid foundation on which to base his actions.

Your Own Bigger Yes

Building your own Bigger Yes can be done in several ways. When it comes to moral, legal, and ethical issues, your own values must serve as your guide. When it comes to your career, having options like Mike's helps support your Bigger Yes. This means building and constantly refreshing your strong network of personal connections, as we discussed in Chapter 2, "The Manager's Universe." It may mean having a list of ten executive recruiters with whom you've built and maintained relationships over the years. It may mean nurturing your reputation as an industry leader by writing articles for trade magazines, making speeches at conventions, or volunteering to serve on the boards of industry organizations.

Management guru Tom Peters recommends freshening up your resume every quarter, even if you have no intention of looking for a job and regardless of whether you are employed by a company or by yourself. Sitting down every quarter to measure your accomplishments and plan how you can become more valuable in the quarter ahead is a valuable exercise for helping you keep your career on track and making sure that your Bigger Yes is continually growing.

Finally, like Mike Drake, make a point of managing your personal finances so as to bolster your real and psychological independence. Too many people get into the habit of spending every dollar from their periodic bonuses and salary increases on "the good life." "Hey," they think, "What's the point of working hard and making good money if I'm not going to enjoy it?" Sometimes they use their spouses or kids as an excuse: "Oh, we've *got* to buy that $2 million house in El Ritzo Canyon—it's in the best school district in the state." They end up with scanty retirement savings, no financial cushion for tough times, and a growing mountain of credit-card and home-equity debt, all of which makes them hostages to their jobs, unable to consider walking away when the personal, professional, or ethical stresses become unbearable.

Hollywood types—directors, actors, and such—like to talk about having "Screw You Money" in the bank. It's a specific amount of savings that they feel would enable them to say to any mismanaged studio or overbearing producer, "I'm not going to take your abuse any longer—I quit." Having Screw You Money in your investment account is a great idea no matter what industry you're in.

How much would it take? That's up to you—your lifestyle, your family needs, your financial obligations (like parents who need help or children's educations), your spouse's career status, and the nature of job-shifting in your industry. Some people feel they need a full year's income to have the ability to say "screw you" and walk away from a job; for others, six months is sufficient.

Yes, it's challenging to save six months' worth of income. Most people never do it. Setting this as a goal will require quite a bit of self-discipline—scaling back the vacations, eating out less often, buying less extravagant gifts for holidays and birthdays, and so on. But believe me, once you have your Screw You Money in the bank and experience the sense of freedom and integrity that only your Bigger Yes can provide, you'll find that your level of on-the-job fear is ratcheted way, way down.

Fending Off the Fear-Mongers: Amplification and Compression

As much as you work to guard against it, there may still be times when fear finds a way to push you down a slippery slope, potentially damaging your relationships with your team. This is especially likely to happen when you work with the kind of person I call a *Fear-Monger*.

Have you ever had a manager who seems to enjoy taking a piece of bad news and running around the office with it?—Sharing it, fanning the flames, theorizing on all the negative implications? This is the m.o. of the Fear-Monger. (In truth, it's a way of behaving we all get caught up in sometimes.)

It's easy to see how it occurs. The Fear-Monger gets his buttons pushed somehow—perhaps by a bad set of quarterly numbers, a rumor about corporate cutbacks or impending firings, a triumph by some arch-competitor inside or outside the organization. The Fear-Monger becomes angry, anxious, and confused. He wants to talk it over, not just once or twice, but eight or ten or twenty times, hoping to make sense of it all, to somehow *conquer* the adversity by finding words with which to define and delimit it. Meanwhile, everyone else is just getting brought down—feeling worse with every rehashing of the bad news.

Here's a hideous example of fear-mongering from my own career. I was working at a small television station in Monterey, California, when a new general manager (I'll call him Josh) took over. In classic style, he began bashing the prior management team, thereby insulting everyone who'd been a part of the old team. Then he laid off about one-fifth of the staff, handling the firings in a cold-hearted manner. Everything he said and did reinforced the same depressing storyline: Things were bad, very bad—and only Josh could save us.

As time passed, Josh's profound negativity only seemed to get deeper and darker. He ordered the receptionist to keep the glass entry doors to the building locked. If anyone wanted in, she'd have to run out with a key to let them in. Imagine being one of our customers in this quiet, idyllic community, having to jump and wave outside on the sidewalk in a desperate attempt to get the receptionist's attention so you could be let in.

One day, Josh even became convinced that a moving truck parked near the station contained a bomb. He telephoned the police, leading to incredible embarrassment for the station when they showed up and, of course, found nothing inside the van except moving pads and a furniture dolly.

Fortunately for us, Josh's worries about the station were just a manifestation of his own dark view of life, not a reflection of the actual status of our business. Unfortunately, he managed to drive away more than half the staff, ultimately forcing us to combine our operations with those of a competitor, so that our station no longer functioned as a stand-alone entity. Josh's fear-mongering actually destroyed the business.

Okay, so fear-mongering is clearly a destructive force. But what's the appropriate way to deal with bad news? The answer is not to go to the opposite extreme, as all too many managers do. They prefer to ignore bad news, as if pretending it never happened will make it go away. Troubles are papered over with happy talk, and team members become afraid to speak the truth, sensing that the psychology of management is too fragile to cope with it.

Clearly some position between the extremes is the right one. Workers want their managers to be authentic and transparent, but at the same time they want their managers to lift them up rather than to wallow in the mire of negativity. How can you be transparent and honest about your company's problems while at the same time leaving people feeling good about themselves, their company, and their future?

The best managers use the simple two-part technique of *amplifying* the best news and *compressing* the worst. They don't alter the facts. Instead, they choose to expand upon the hopeful possibilities in any situation and avoid dwelling on the negative ones.

In Hollywood, where drama is the order of the day, Marc Sternberg is Vice President and Group Advertising Director for the *Hollywood Reporter*. Marc tries to take a realistic view of the ups and downs of business. "It is what it is," Marc says when his team suffers a setback. "Now, what can we do to make it better? It's not that we don't try to control the outcomes of our business dealings. We do that all day, and oftentimes we're quite successful. It's just that when things don't go our way, we refuse to allow these occurrences to become trend lines. Instead, we go straight to work on elevating our situation."

Another manager, Christine Wagner, says it this way: "Around here, we have long weddings and short funerals." Once again: Expand on the positive, even turn it into a cause for celebration; acknowledge the negative, then move quickly on toward a more hopeful future.

The philosophy here is simple yet easy to forget in the heat of the moment. The next time significant news comes your way and your people are standing by waiting for the report, ask yourself these questions:

- Is the information true and verifiable? (If not, don't even *think* about broadcasting it around the company. The last thing companies need is to have their managers in The Middle contributing to the rumor mills that tend to work overtime even without such help.)

- Who will be helped by this news, and who will be hurt? (Think about ways to couch the information so that the benefits will be enhanced and the damage will be minimized. For example, is it possible that someone's job may be in jeopardy? Reduce the embarrassment by giving them an advance heads-up if you can, and by offering them whatever contacts, advice, help, and support are in your power.)

- What are the positive scenarios that might arise from this news? (Be prepared to spell these out explicitly for your team members. Don't assume that they understand the implications of any development—what's obvious to you may not be to someone else who is less plugged in to the corporate grapevine and less cognizant of the big picture than you are.)

- What are the negative consequences that come to mind? Are they real? If so, what are some ways to overcome them? (Be prepared to address these as well. If you know that people will react with exaggerated fears, debunk their paranoia with hard facts. If the negative scenarios are real but avoidable, acknowledge them and be ready to offer a plan: "First thing tomorrow we're forming an emergency task force to address the following three concerns...")

People want information and will never ask you to stop telling them, regardless of how much it hurts them. They'll love you if you not only give them an honest weather forecast, but also offer a poncho for the rainy days and a beach chair for the sunny ones.

Keeping Your Balance between Your Company and Your Team

As managers in The Middle, the fulcrum point we all live on is skinny and sharp, and if we fall off we're likely to get jabbed in the backside as we tumble to the ground. Balancing on the fulcrum is not just a function of our place in the org chart, it's also what our teams and our leaders expect of us. To lead, we can never live tilted too far to one side or the other. Where we are needed is The Middle—the vital balancing point.

Life in The Middle involves a natural tension. When conflicts arise, it takes courage to keep your balance. The Middle is where the peacemakers, the negotiators, and the connectors live—the ones responsible for making things work despite the emotions that rage around them.

The balance that managers in The Middle must maintain has many facets, but here is one of the most important rules to remember: *When managers fall off point, they usually tilt either too far towards the company or too far towards their team.*

The company-tilted manager toes the corporate line at the cost of his own integrity and that of his team. Ever see the cult movie *Office Space*? It's a new management classic. The company-tilted manager is personified by Lumbergh, the funny and tragic antagonist of that picture. Lumbergh spends all of his energy managing up. His boss is his client, and everyone else is just that—everyone else. When policies are handed down by senior management, Lumbergh communicates them as inalterable facts like commandments chiseled into stone tablets, with no translation, no context, no enthusiasm, and no advocacy on behalf of his team. Lumbergh is a mere mouthpiece, the proverbial "empty suit" who has stopped thinking for himself and simply echoes the management line. As a result, he has earned no respect from his team members, and he gets exactly the amount he has earned.

Do you suspect that you may have become a company-tilted manager? Don't worry, it's not necessarily a fatal condition. You can recover, but it's hard work. It starts with listening to your people and making a real effort to understand their view of their jobs, their place in the organization, and their expectations of you. You must probe the members on your team who are most honest with you in order to understand your team's perceptions.

Then you must go out of the way to engage your team members in conversations, all of which are likely to be eye-opening and some of which will probably be painful. If you've screwed up in the past by failing to represent the concerns and interests of your team, you'll have to spend some time addressing those failures. You'll need to share with your people what your intentions were and how you reached the decisions you did. If you're not proud of the outcomes or have regrets about your actions, apologize. It won't kill you. In fact, being transparent about your mistakes can be incredibly powerful. Failure to do this will just allow the existing gap to widen and accelerate the inevitable, painful end of your tenure as leader of the team.

On the other side of the spectrum is the *team-tilted manager*. This kind of manager believes that leadership is about serving the team—and they're right about that. What they miss, however, is that leadership is *not* about serving the team *to the extent of sacrificing all else*. They tilt too far towards their teams by ignoring other crucial elements of leading in The Middle. Though well-meaning, they end up damaging their teams rather than helping them.

Team-tilted managers fall into two categories: the *fighters* and the *lovers*.

The *fighters* believe the business world is a tough place, and therefore they must act as warriors on behalf of their teams. They challenge outsiders, they resist high authority, and they bully in defense of those they lead. For their teammates, this is sometimes exciting. "At last!" they say, "We've finally got somebody who's on *our* side!" And for a time, the productivity and morale of the team may skyrocket.

In the long run, however, the effects are usually damaging for all involved. The fighter loses his effectiveness over time. Turned off by the fighter's hostility, allies gradually distance themselves. Those offended by the fighter stop offering their support. Eventually, the organization's negative view of the fighter casts the whole team into a shadow.

After one fighter was removed from his leadership role, I had occasion to talk to some of his former team members. I quickly discovered that they had a very negative view of their firm. "Those people at headquarters don't care about us and will blame us for anything and everything that goes wrong," was their attitude. "We need somebody to go to war for us, or else we'll get no respect." I was reminded of the bizarre worldview that grows up in a cult: The leader convinces his followers to share his paranoid attitude about the outside world, depicting himself as their savior and the only person who *truly* cares about their well-being.

By contrast, the *lovers* are managers who are willing to sacrifice their personal interests for the benefit of their team members. They work extra hours covering for team members who go home early, silently fix mistakes made by their people, and give everyone who works for them consistently high ratings (even when the quality of their work is borderline).

Unlike the fighter, who offends everyone, the lover offends no one by refusing to stand up for what's right. The fighter has become so strongly affiliated with the team that he's abdicated his roles as coach, mentor, guide, and field general. He can lead cheers—*but he can't call a play.* The lover ultimately becomes a weak link that threatens to bring everyone down unless he's removed from the leadership position to which he is so ill-suited.

When you allow yourself to fall off center in either direction, you hurt your team and create an environment that fosters poor results both for the company and for every individual involved. Remember the horrific disaster that struck the space shuttle Columbia in February 2003? It led to the deaths of the entire crew and practically destroyed the space shuttle program. The committee charged with investigating its causes found that management at NASA had created an environment in which key engineers were afraid to speak up about unsafe practices—and when a few did, they were ignored and ultimately silenced.

It's obvious that company-tilted managers at NASA had abandoned their role as advocates for the engineering teams. Maybe they hadn't considered the dire consequences of failing to support their teams; maybe they were afraid to act because they didn't have a Bigger Yes in place. Whatever the reasons, the inability of the managers in The Middle at NASA to maintain their balance may have been what cost seven astronauts their lives.

On the Road Again

So we begin our chapter where we started. Another maniac flies across highway lanes. Tires squeal, horns blare, and suddenly the out-of-control vehicle is looming in front of you, dangerously close. But this time your reaction is different. Calmly you apply the brakes, open a space in the road ahead, and change lanes to pass the cut-off artist. There's no road rage. In fact, you're laughing.

What happened? You changed your point of view, and so set the stage for a different emotional response. With the tools you now have to deploy, you can make these changes and set a new course, managing fear and anger back into the dark, quiet recesses, where they belong.

5

THE DEADLY LACK OF
EMPOWERMENT TRAP

The Self-Empowered Manager

Jeanne Bogre is marketing manager for Danly IEM, a Cleveland-based company that is the leading manufacturer of die sets, die-making supplies, and machine components for industries in North America. (Think about the people who make machines for factories. Danly IEM sells products to *them*.) Jeanne is in a challenging place. Not only is it a male-dominated industry (and, yes, Jeanne has had to deal with her share of sexist attitudes, usually veiled but no less powerful for that), but it's also an industry in which quite a bit of outsourcing is going on, generating a lot of fear among rank-and-file employees about their jobs moving to Asia or Latin America.

Under the circumstances, many managers in The Middle would be paralyzed by uncertainty. What's going to happen to our company? Will we pack up and move to Mexico or Singapore or Korea? If we don't, will we end up losing our market to cheaper competitors from those lower-wage lands? If the answers to these questions are unclear, how do I motivate my people without lying to them? It's one of those times when life in The Middle can be excruciating.

But Jeanne Bogre has found ways to turn the anxiety into opportunity. Rather than reacting to the outsourcing trend with denial ("I'm going to pretend this isn't happening until they cart up my office supplies and ship them overseas") or resistance ("I'm going to fight to keep every job in the USA no matter *how* much money we lose in the process"), Jeanne is saying, "Let's recognize what's happening and figure out how to make it work for us." That includes finding the potential benefits of outsourcing both for her company and for herself, personally.

Jeanne's ability to seize the outsourcing opportunity begins with an attitude of flexibility—a quality that distinguishes Jeanne from some others in her industry. "The guys in upper management obviously tend to be older than middle management," she explains. "Most of them have families and strong domestic ties. So they don't want to travel to the overseas venues where a lot of our business is starting to migrate." Jeanne has no problem with traveling, and so she has volunteered for foreign assignments more senior managers shied away from. In the process, she has walked through doors that otherwise would have been closed to her.

"Let's say I'm working on a project in Asia," Jeanne says, "where a lot of factories that need our products are now being built. This is a brand-new market for us. That means I have a lot more flexibility to set standards and to create business practices than I would in our current market. If I wanted to change some system here in the States, everybody would want to know why. There'd be a lot of push-back. Not in a new market. I've found you've got much more room to grow as a manager if you're willing to tackle a new project for your company. I was able to set up my own pricing structures and my own distribution networks in places like China and India because I was the expert on those markets—just because I was willing to *go* there and learn what made them tick."

Now Jeanne is using her knowledge base to expand the parameters of Danly's business. "More and more companies are looking to buy products like stampings, car fenders, hoods, whatever, in Asia. But they don't know a lot about how the business works over there. That creates an opening for Danly. We've built up a lot of experience in Asia, and we have a guy running our joint venture in China who gives us more knowledge about manufacturing and distribution in China than the majority of people in our industry have. Why don't we sell that knowledge as a service?"

Jeanne is leading Danly's new effort to do just that. "We can help our customers with anything from locating products to finding companies that can manufacture stampings or toolings. We can help U.S. business people organize their trips to China, give them the key contacts they need, and coach them on how to negotiate successfully over there. And for each service we can charge a fee."

Jeanne and her team are developing the profit model for this new service-based business right now. Its potential is enormous. The concept wouldn't even exist if Jeanne Bogre—manager in The Middle—hadn't grabbed the bull of outsourcing by the horns and asked, "How can I make this work *for me?*"

Jeanne's story illustrates the special capability of managers in The Middle to recognize business opportunities that top-level executives, more distant from the needs and problems of customers, may overlook. As management guru Rosabeth Moss Kanter has said, "Because middle managers have their fingers on the pulse of operations, they can also conceive, suggest, and set in motion new ideas that top managers may not have thought of."[1] It's the power of the fulcrum at its best.

Everybody's Favorite Excuse

Jeanne Bogre's story also illustrates the (frequent) hollowness of one of the favorite excuses cited by managers in The Middle for failing to solve problems, seize opportunities, or follow through on initiatives—the *lack of empowerment.*

This alibi takes many forms. Sometimes managers complain about the lack of support for their ideas from above: "I've proposed solutions for our divisional problems dozens of times. They either get shot down by my boss or else disappear into some kind of black hole and are never heard from again."

Other times they blame bureaucracy or red tape: "Around here, you can't get permission to try something new until three budget directors, two strategic planners, and five departmental heads sign off. By the time you get the paperwork done, nobody even remembers what the project is about."

---

[1] Rosabeth Moss Kanter, "The Middle Manager as Innovator." *Harvard Business Review,* July-August, 1982, page 95.

Other managers say they are hampered by structural problems: "It's obvious what we need to do to fix our marketing problems. But it's not in my job description. And if I tried to get involved, I'd have the folks in marketing screaming bloody murder about my trespassing on their turf. Who needs the aggravation?"

Still other times, they blame a lack of time, energy, or resources for their failure to act: "Sure, I have an idea or two about how to expand our business. But I'm already working 60-hour weeks just putting out fires and making the business we've *got* work halfway smoothly. When am I supposed to launch something new, between 1 and 3 a.m.?"

These excuses may *sound* valid. And in a minority of cases, they may hold a little water. There are companies where bureaucratic rules genuinely hamper initiatives from The Middle. It's certainly true that many managers are coping with badly-stretched resources, making it very challenging to find time or money to launch new programs. If you've tried every strategy we'll outline in this chapter to seize and wield power from The Middle and still failed to make a dent in your company's traditional ways of doing business, it may be time to think about moving on.

In reality, when managers blame lack of empowerment, they are often simply copping out, covering up the *real* reasons for their failure to achieve what they say (and probably believe) they want to achieve.

Opening up Asian markets and creating the model for a new form of service-based business was *not* part of Jeanne Bogre's job description at Danly IEM. However, she simply volunteered for assignments no one else wanted, discovered the business opportunities lurking there, and started making them happen. Jeanne understands how to navigate the *real* power structure of her company rather than waiting around for someone to bestow empowerment upon her.

In most organizations, unspoken realities counter the oft-spoken excuses about lack of empowerment:

- Yes, bosses may shoot down or ignore good ideas from their underlings. But there's wisdom in the old saying, "It's always easier to get forgiveness than permission." Many managers try to pursue new ideas through "official channels" when such bureaucratic routine isn't strictly necessary. Much of what people seek approval for does not need approval. We do it, in part, because getting approval makes us feel good. If you can free up a modicum of time and money to try something new, why not simply *try it*—and present it to your boss later on, once you have some successes, however modest, to point to?

- Yes, red tape can be frustrating. When you run into a short-term No, you are being called to supply a Bigger Yes. If an idea you want to develop is truly meaningful and important to you—and provided there is a good business reason for doing it and it really adds value—then be persistent. Rework your proposal and present it again; seek the resources you need through other channels; scale back the idea and launch it as a "pilot project;" or simply put the idea into "turnaround," as the folks in Hollywood say, and wait for the right time and place to try again.

- Yes, business structures (from inter-departmental rivalries to information-hoarding silos) can make it hard to try new things. Bring your networking skills to bear. Identify the three people from neighboring business units whose help you *must* have to make your new project work and figure out how to make them your best friends. (Remember to think about divining their explicit and implicit needs and finding ways to help them achieve them.) Maybe your new project will end up being a "joint venture," with revenues, profits, and kudos shared among the participants. The important thing is to get it off the ground using whatever wall-busting techniques you find necessary.

- Yes, resources can be scarce—especially the most precious resource of all, your own time. If the new idea you want to pursue really matters, you can create the time to do it—as Keith Rosen explains.

Seizing the Tools of Empowerment

As you saw earlier in this book, Keith Rosen is a Certified Master Coach with a world of experience in helping managers in The Middle become more effective and empowered. Lack of time is one of the most common complaints he hears from his clients. "So many times," Keith says, "managers will come to me and say they're inundated with work. They have so much work on their plate they don't know how to get it done—let alone find time to expand their creativity into new areas. We start having a conversation about what they have to do and about the time it all takes."

"This leads," Keith says, "to the big question: Do you have any opportunity to delegate some of that work to other people? They usually admit, 'Well, I *do* have some other people I could delegate this stuff to.' The question then becomes, 'Well, why aren't you delegating more? What do you think is holding you back?' And then they say, 'Well, of course, Keith, if I want something done right I have to do it myself.'"

Suddenly the *real* problem is looming in sight. It's not that the manager's job has been poorly defined by the corporation, giving him or her too much to do in the allotted time. It's that the people who make up the work team don't have the manager's confidence, either because of a lack of skills or the manager's own failure to train, coach, and communicate with them.

For most managers in The Middle, then, being swamped with work is not "the problem." It's a symptom of the problem—which, once you drill a little deeper, is revealed to be a failure to create and lead an effective team that can take work off the manager's desk and get it done.

"Ultimately," Keith says, "the true role of a manager is to make your people more valuable. If you choose the right people and then work to make them continually more skilled, more autonomous, more independent, and more self-driven, they're going to do what they need to do in the first place. Therefore, you no longer have to manage as much as you used to, and you don't have to handle so much of the work yourself. If you create a team of highly-competent, internally-driven people who work together towards a shared goal, you'll find yourself spending less time putting out fires and more time being creative and truly productive."

If lack of time is one of your big complaints—and for most managers in The Middle, it is—don't wait around for the top brass to double the size of your staff. It's up to you to seize the tools that can help you empower *yourself*. These include

- Using the power of *hiring* to build a team that's made up exclusively of high-skill, high-energy, positive-thinking achievers. Can't find the right candidate after 20 interviews? Try rewriting the job description, rethinking the credentials you seek, and reeducating the Human Resources department about what you're *really* looking for. Then interview 20 more people... and 20 more if necessary, rather than settling for someone who will act as a dead weight on the rest of the team.

- Using the power of *firing* to eliminate people who just don't fit. The moment you *know* the fit isn't right, take action. You are *not* doing anyone a favor when you make excuses to put off the inevitable. Every month in which a not-quite-competent or not-quite-appropriate person remains on your payroll, you are wasting money, diverting your own energy and attention, and sapping everyone else's morale. Of course, you hate firing people—that's a sign that you'll probably do it humanely rather than cruelly. Get it over with sooner rather than later so that everyone can move on to better things. Chances are the person leaving the party will ultimately appreciate it as well. There's nothing worse than living with the pain of a poor fit.

- Using the power of *organizing* to solve persistent problems once and for all. (We talked about this in Chapter 1, "Action with Traction.") Sit down today and identify the five kinds of fires you find yourself putting out week after week. Each one represents a systemic breakdown. Draw on the knowledge of your team or other colleagues to figure out how the systems should be changed to keep the same fires from breaking out again. Then implement the new systems. The amount of time you spend on repetitive problems should shrink from 50 or 60 percent to 10 or 20 percent, freeing up energy for the ideas that lead to growth.

- Using the power of *choice* to focus on high value-added activities rather than wheel-spinning exercises or tasks that you *like* but that don't generate benefits for you, your team, your boss, or your company. We all fall into routines. If you've been in the same job more than six months, the chances are good that you have five to ten weekly activities that you do simply out of habit. Identify them and either delegate them to someone less expensive or more appropriate (if they really *ought* to be done) or simply eliminate them. (You may well discover that the report you've been spending two hours on every Friday morning simply ended up in someone else's circular file—they'll be relieved not to have to deal with it for 15 seconds every Friday afternoon.) Repeat the same exercise six months from now. It's like making your computer run faster by uninstalling the software you never use.

Feeling unempowered? Like Jeanne Bogre, don't wait for someone to give you power. Use the techniques we've highlighted to free up some of the power you *already* have, most likely without even knowing it.

The Wagon Train Effect

This is not to imply that organizational barriers won't affect your use of power. Of course they will. One of the most significant barriers, which few people consciously recognize, is what we call the *Wagon Train Effect*—the tendency for every process in an organization to move at the same pace.

If you were a pioneer traveling West with a wagon train, it wouldn't matter if the horse you had hitched to your wagon could run like a Kentucky Derby winner; you would move no faster than the *slowest* horse in the chain. Similarly, no matter how agile, creative, and productive one department or one manager in a company may be, the organization's overall speed of response is usually determined by the *slowest* business unit. It doesn't matter how great a software company's marketing or sales or service teams may be; if the research team can't produce great new products fast enough, the company's sales are going to go into the tank.

The Wagon Train Effect tends to retard change and enforce a needless uniformity. It also tends to disempower managers whose skills exceed organizational norms. In other words, if you have the talent to manage an organization the way Secretariat could run, you're apt to be pretty frustrated as a team player in most companies. It's equally frustrating to be part of a company where a single department is the equivalent of a broken-down mule, slowing down the parade for everybody else.

How can you combat the Wagon Train Effect? It's not always possible for an individual manager to solve this problem. Here are some strategies that work:

- *Feed vitamins to the slowest horse.* Obviously, you can minimize the Wagon Train Effect by jump-starting the performance of the department that is most seriously dragging down the team. Sometimes all that's required is an infusion of resources: more employees, more money, and better equipment. Sometimes new leadership and a new sense of direction are needed. As an individual manager, it may not be in your power to do a lot to help the weakest horse on your team. However, you can at least highlight the nature of the problem and encourage the organization to concentrate remedial efforts where they're most needed rather than instituting across-the-board remedies (most of which will be wasted).

- *Decouple from the wagon train.* If you run a department that's noticeably faster, more effective, and more productive than the others in your business, you may be able to find productive ways to use the excess capacity that don't rely on those other departments. For example, suppose you run a design department with creative capabilities that exceed those required by the rest of the business. Why not offer design services on a consulting basis to non-competitive outside companies, thereby creating a new source of revenues and profits and keeping your people busy, productive, and happy? Or suppose you manage a super-hot marketing team, but your company can't produce great products fast enough to keep your people pumping. Consider serving small outside companies that can't support their own marketing organizations and that produce goods or services that are compatible rather than competitive with those your company offers.

- *Link your horse to another caravan.* In some cases, you may be able to look for opportunities to shift your departmental linkages to another part of the organization more in tune with your capacities and needs. For instance, if the sales group that services your division is having trouble keeping up with the flow of product offerings you are creating, maybe there's another, more dynamic sales team elsewhere in the company that would welcome a new set of challenges.

The Wagon Train Effect is one of the most difficult organizational problems to master, and one that often produces an effect of disempowering capable managers. If you find yourself stuck in a slow caravan, try one of the strategies described here—it may work for you.

Sources of Power

Ah, you may say, it's all well and good to speak about taking power rather than waiting for it to be handed over—but isn't it true that power is a limited commodity that some people in the corporation have more of than others? I can't achieve the power of the CEO just by *acting* like a CEO, can I?

Of course, that's true. The amount of power you can claim simply by *taking* it is not unlimited. (Thank heaven—otherwise, every business would be like a lawless tribal nation, in which power belonged to whichever warlord was most aggressive about seizing it.) That's why it's important for every manager in The Middle to understand something about the true sources of corporate power—which are a bit different from what you probably have been raised to believe.

In a classic article written almost 50 years ago but still stunningly applicable today, social theorists John French and Bertram Raven identified six sources of social or organizational power. Each has a unique source, and each must be used in particular ways to be effective[2]:

- *Reward power* is based on the perceived ability to provide positive consequences or remove negative ones. As a manager, you have reward power to the extent that you control the raises, bonuses, work assignments, and other desirable (or not so desirable) consequences meted out to the members of your team.

---

[2] John French and Bertram Raven, "The Bases of Social Power." In *Studies in Social Power*, edited by D. Cartwright. Ann Arbor, MI: Institute for Social Research, 1959, pages 150-167.

- *Coercive power* is based on the perceived ability to punish those who do not conform with your ideas or demands. You wield coercive power whenever you fire someone or exile them to your personal "doghouse"—for example, by sending them to bleak and snowy Schenectady, New York for a conference in the middle of the winter.

- *Legitimate power* (also called *organizational authority*) is based on the perception that someone has the right to prescribe behavior due to election or appointment to a position of responsibility. Your legitimate power comes from the title on your business card and your place on the org chart. It's greater if the perception exists that you "deserve" the job because of your talents or other personal qualities.

- *Referent power* is based on association with others who possess power. This is an interesting one. Two managers with precisely the same job title may have very different levels of referent power if one is more closely associated with the CEO. A junior-level staffer at News Corporation may have significant referent power because her last name happens to be Murdoch. You may also enjoy referent power through association with someone powerful *outside* the organization; that's why (for example) a chief of staff for the President of the United States can get a prestigious job at virtually any law firm or consulting group after leaving his White House job.

- *Expert power* is based on having distinctive knowledge, expertise, ability, or skills. Most managers in The Middle rose from staff or line positions in which they developed and exercised special knowledge and skills, and these abilities give them expert power they can use as managers. Thus, the manager of a group of engineers or editors or scientists or salespeople gets respect and deference, in part, because they know that she was once a great engineer, editor, scientist, or salesperson in her own right.

- *Information power* is based on controlling the information needed by others in order to reach an important goal. Information power is derived primarily from *using* the information you obtain to empower and support those on your team, rather than from hoarding it in secrecy. In most organizations, managers in The Middle serve as conduits for information, data, strategies, goals, and philosophies from top management to individual contributors, as well as conduits for news from the front lines to top management. Thus, Middleshift managers can wield a great deal of information power, and it flows in at least two directions—from the top down and from the bottom up.

This list of power sources is fascinating in itself. But French and Raven went further. They also examined how power derived from the various bases affects both *attraction* (that is, a positive feeling on the part of the recipient towards the agent who uses power) and *resistance* (that is, a negative feeling on the part of the recipient toward the agent who uses power).

They concluded that the use of power from the various bases has significantly different consequences. For example, reward power increases attraction while creating minimal levels of resistance. (This explains why most people tend to suck up to their bosses during the weeks before bonuses are due.) By contrast, coercive power typically decreases attraction and causes high resistance. (Think about the complaints, bitterness, and anger that erupt in an organization after an upheaval results in firings.) However, French and Raven also noted that "the more legitimate the coercion [is perceived to be], the less it will produce resistance." Thus, coercive power *combined with* legitimate power tends to be more effective than coercive power alone.

The French and Raven system offers an interesting way to analyze power in *your* organization. Think about your boss. What sources of power does he or she draw upon? What percentage of his or her power is derived from each source? Does this change from time to time? (When the team is working together to "crash" a major new-product development project, the boss may derive most power from expertise—the ability to contribute breakthrough ideas to solve problems. Later, when the new product is being launched, his or her power may derive mainly from the ability to win support from the CEO and the EVP of marketing—referent power, in other words.) How do people respond to the boss's uses of power based on the various sources? How and when is attraction greatest? What uses of power provoke resistance? Could the boss do something different to minimize resistance—for example, by taking steps to increase his or her reliance on some other power source?

You can perform the same kind of analysis on others in the organization—on yourself, of course, as well as on other key players, including the CEO. You can also consider the company-wide patterns that characterize power flows in your organization. In some family-run businesses, referent power based on closeness to the founders is the dominant form of power. In some technical or creative companies (think Intel, Pfizer, or Disney), power is derived mainly from expertise—scientific brilliance or movie-making genius. In some organizations, power is based primarily on control of information. For example, during the second term of the Clinton White House, those with the greatest perceived power tended to be those who knew the "inside dirt" about the Monica Lewinsky scandal, the associated investigations, and the impeachment proceedings. When an organization is abuzz with gossip, you can bet that some serious information-based power-mongering is going on.

If you feel unempowered, clues to the reasons may be uncovered through an analysis of the French and Raven power categories at work. You may be trying to wield a kind of power that is severely undervalued in your organization. If the people in your company tend to recognize *only* legitimate power, they may be unmoved by your truly awesome displays of expertise. Conversely, if you find yourself in a setting (such as a research institute) where expertise is *the* currency of power, you'll probably get nowhere trying to impress people with your fancy title (legitimate power) or your friendship with the dean (referent power): "Never mind that—how many patents do you own?"

Igniting the Power of Change

Too many managers get frustrated with the perceived obstacles to their empowerment and simply tune out and give up. They begin treading water, collecting paychecks, and maybe getting a modest promotion from time to time, but never make any *real* difference in the organizations they call home. Over time, they stop playing the game; they lose their skills, their connections, and their self-confidence. They usually end up being relegated to the bench or to mop-up duties.

It's so sad. And so unnecessary.

Joe Ripp, a long-time veteran of the corporate wars, knows a thing or two about how to build careers inside organizations. Asked recently what he'd say to a manager in The Middle who feels disempowered, Joe said:

> "You're probably right to feel that way. Most mid-level managers feel that sense of restriction. You're stuck in a box and you're told to manage your box. Yet you're looking around and saying, 'There are a lot of things that we should do better.' And it's frustrating to be able to do so little to make things change.
>
> "If you're the kind of person who gets his whole team focused on that question—What can we do better?—then that becomes part of the normal routine. You can work with your people on that. Because remember, they're struggling with the same question. Just like you, they want to get more out of life than a nine-to-five routine. Like you, they want meaning. Like you, they want to make a difference.
>
> "Don't just say, 'I'm not empowered,' and give up. Instead, keep asking the question. Organizations won't change overnight. Your reporting structures won't change overnight. Your day job isn't going to go away. You still need to do your day job—that's what you were hired for. Asking that question puts your job in a bigger context and pushes you forward on that search for meaning.
>
> "Let me give you an example. While I was the chief financial officer of Time, Inc., I was asked once to give a speech to the Accounts Payable department. And here, in essence, is what I said: 'You're sitting in our offices, processing lots of things—papers, columns of numbers, spreadsheets. I'm sure it gets boring at times. But think about this. You see more information about what we spend and therefore what we *do* than anybody else in the corporation. Maybe you should think about this question: What should we be doing with all this information? Is there anything we can do with it that could add value to this company?'

"I ended my speech. They applauded politely. And I went away.

"Four months later, I had a surprise visit from the woman who headed the Accounts Payable department. 'Remember the question you asked in your speech? I've got your answer.'

"She showed me a brochure she'd received in the mail from Dun & Bradstreet. They were selling a service that would consolidate all of your accounts payable, giving you the credit file number for each vendor so that you could figure out what percentage of your spending they were.

"Maybe this doesn't sound like a big deal. But at the time, Time, Inc. was a decentralized organization with about 15 different accounts payable centers. And the parent company, Time Warner, was a much *bigger* organization that was also totally decentralized. There was no one place where you could add up the spending information and say to a vendor like IBM, 'Do you know that we spend X hundred millions of dollars a year with you? We should be getting a better discount.' Logical and sensible as this was, it was simply impossible.

"Here was this woman, a supposedly lower-level manager, offering the solution. So we followed her suggestion and bought the Dun & Bradstreet service for about $175,000. Overnight we were suddenly able to make sense of the 20-odd billion dollars of spending for the entire corporation. And within a year we had task forces organized to go after specific levels of spending on paper, printing services, trucking—you name it.

"We ended up saving about 5 percent on our purchases, which amounted to at least $1 *billion*. Yeah, with a B. All from this one idea floated by a middle manager. All because she was focused on that simple question: 'What can we do that will make a difference?'"

As Joe Ripp's story illustrates, empowerment isn't mainly about org charts or job descriptions or reporting relationships. Sometimes it's as simple as *asking the right question*... and not stopping until you come up with an answer.

The Power of Righteousness

In most organizations, power is usually taken, not bestowed. If you don't know how to wield power, you probably won't get much done, even if you are the CEO. If you *do* know how to wield power, you can accomplish a lot more than your job title alone might suggest. But there's an important corollary that too many managers forget: *You must take power for a righteous reason.* Otherwise, whatever power you *do* obtain is likely to be short-lived and ultimately ineffectual.

"Righteous"—did we really say that? Perhaps our language is sounding a little like what you'd hear in a superhero movie: "Always remember," intones the wise old mentor to his young acolyte, "You must use your powers for good, not evil!" So be it. As we've said, one of the keys to finding meaning in your life is to start thinking of it as a quest in the heroic Joseph Campbell mode. So, yes—you are a superhero of sorts, endowed with unique abilities, and your job is to use those abilities to the fullest in the service of a worthy cause of your own choosing.

Many people have only a vague idea as to why they get up and go to work in the morning. Of course, they need to pay the rent and buy non-fat lattes at Starbucks, but there are millions of ways to make money. Why work at *this* job, the one job of all jobs that you hold today and to which you will devote the greatest part of your time, energy, heart, and soul this week, this month, and perhaps for some years to come? What mission does it embody? Why do you want power? What do you plan to do with it? And above all, why do you *deserve* it?

You earlier considered *legitimacy* as a source of power. In our democratic times, legitimacy isn't so much conferred from above as granted from below. In politics, it's called "the consent of the governed," and it's considered the basis for any meaningful social structure. In business, it goes by different names, including "credibility," "leadership," and "charisma." In any sphere, you can't get it unless you deserve it; and you don't deserve it unless you intend to use it for the good of all rather than for selfish ends.

This is the weakness of the Machiavellian approach to management. It focuses on using manipulation, intimidation, and deceit to seize and maintain power, which is viewed as an end in itself. Machiavellian tactics often work for a time. In the long run, most people are willing to lend their support to a leader only when they respect his objectives and see some potential benefit to themselves in his purposes. Why should they work hard and zealously contribute their creativity to an organization if the end result is simply to allow one leader, or a handful of leaders, to buy their third houses and their sixth cars? *You* wouldn't do it—why would anyone else?

Before you attempt to take and use any power within your organization, you'd better consider seriously the question of purposes. Do you want power to satisfy your ego, increase your income, and annoy your enemies? If so, you're not likely to enjoy it for very long. Or do you want power so that you can build something of lasting value for the company, its customers, its employees, and all the others whom it touches? If so, you may find that a large and steadily growing number of people will be willing to entrust you with their time and energy, empowering you to make your righteous dreams come true.

Imagine that this morning a brand-new boss, a person reputedly of great power and wisdom but previously unknown to you, has taken over your company. Promptly at nine o'clock he walks into your office, shakes your hand, gazes deep into your eyes, and asks this one-word question: "Why?"

What is your answer?

PART II

GET MORE PURPOSE

6

IGNITION POINT 1:
THE PROCESS

More Purpose: The Ignition Points for Managers in The Middle

The first section of this book was about more power. We get more power by performing the basic parts of our jobs well. We get power through performance and through the growth of our own confidence. Part I was about what managers need to do to recapture that confidence in themselves.

Now, in the second, core section of this book, we'll talk about more purpose. The seven Ignition Points we'll describe in the chapters that follow represent things that managers in The Middle can do better than anyone else in the company. For it is the ignited manager, uniquely positioned and righteously empowered, who can combine the element and create the light. It is here, at these ignition points, where managers can achieve their highest purpose.

Many managers—not just women—run up against a glass ceiling at some point in their careers, an invisible barrier that stalls their upward progress. It's frustrating, but inevitable, a result of the fact that business hierarchies are shaped like pyramids, getting progressively smaller the higher you rise. There are just too many hard-working, smart, and talented managers in The Middle competing for a few C-level positions to satisfy them all.

Here is where leverage is needed and real purpose must be divided and demonstrated. The skills and techniques represented by the Ignition Points will help deliver that sense of purpose. Don't just take our word for it; consider what research into managerial careers has shown. "Unlike middle managers who stalled in middle management," concluded one expert, "successful middle managers focused on improving essential skills and establishing performance records during the frustrating wait for advancement."[1]

Don't assume that the value of the skills represented by the Ignition Points will always be obvious. Learning often generates value in powerful ways that we cannot always see and usually can't predict. For example, think about how Steve Jobs, the brilliant and creative CEO of Apple, applied unorthodox skills in a thoroughly unexpected way. The story begins with reminiscences from Jobs's college years:

> Reed College, at that time, offered perhaps the best calligraphy instruction in the country. Throughout the campus, every poster, every label on every drawer, was beautifully hand-calligraphed. Because I had dropped out and didn't have to take the normal classes, I decided to take a calligraphy class to learn how to do this. I learned about serif and sans serif typefaces, about varying the amount of space between different letter combinations, about what makes great typography great. It was beautiful, historical, artistically subtle in a way that science can't capture, and I found it fascinating.
>
> None of this had even a hope of any practical application in my life. But ten years later, when we were designing the first Macintosh computer, it all came back to me. And we designed it all into the Mac. It was the first computer with beautiful typography. If I had never dropped in on that single course in college, the Mac would have never had multiple typefaces or proportionally spaced fonts. And because Windows just copied the Mac, it's likely that no personal computer would have them. If I had never dropped out, I would have never dropped in on this

---

[1] Leon E. Wynter, Leon E., *Wall Street Journal*, August 5, 1999. Online at http://www.careerjournal.com/myc/diversity/19990805-wynter.html.

calligraphy class, and personal computers might not have the wonderful typography that they do. Of course it was impossible to connect the dots looking forward when I was in college. But it was very, very clear looking backwards ten years later.[2]

In Part II of this book, we'll teach you—or perhaps remind you—about some of the familiar and unfamiliar skills that managers can apply to bring unique value to their companies. Connecting the dots is up to you.

The Power of the Process Master

If your company is like most businesses, it engages in myriad processes. Each contributes to the greater mission in ways large or small.

For instance, the conception, design, manufacturing, packaging, shipping, marketing, selling, and servicing of any single product involves dozens of processes. Some are simple and self-contained—for example, the process in which Sally in the warehouse reads an SKU off an order printout, picks the right box off a shelf, and places it on a conveyor belt to be carried to the mailroom for shipment to a customer.

Others are complicated and complexly interrelated—for example, the web of processes that kicks into gear when a customer visits the Dell Computer site, chooses and customizes a laptop design, and orders the Dell factory to assemble one for him, pulling together parts from many suppliers and combining them into an intricate technological object that *must* work correctly the first time.

Many of these processes are customer-facing; others are purely internal, but no less important. (If the process that generates your payroll check stops functioning, how many more weeks will you keep showing up in the office?)

In some sense, these processes *are* the company. Without them, there are no goods, no services, no sales, no customers, no revenues, and no profits. People come and go, but processes—once developed, codified, and set in motion—tend to perpetuate themselves until someone

---

2 "'You've got to find what you love,' Jobs says." Stanford Report, June 14, 2005.

deliberately changes them (which is often easier said than done). The sum of the processes defines what the company does and determines whether or not it is successful.

So it's not surprising that one of the most powerful ways for a manager in The Middle to add value is by knowing the processes his company engages in... and knowing them cold. That means knowing each step (what happens and what doesn't), who does it (and how and why), the steps that can be skipped or abbreviated, and the steps that can't. It means knowing the connections among steps and how a mistake or omission at any point in the network is likely to reverberate elsewhere. It also means knowing the individuals who handle the processes, along with their quirks, strengths, shortcomings, needs, and vulnerabilities.

The Process Master knows all these things and can deliver the backstage tour that exposes elements of the business that no one else sees or even knows exist. She understands better than anyone else how to get things done, what's waste, what's not, and where the disconnects are. She understands where unique value is created and where the cracks exist through which value leaks away. (These things usually happen in places that senior management is scarcely aware of.) When a company is in trouble, the Process Master can help to save it by identifying where money can be saved, products improved, and services enhanced through streamlining, simplifying, and rejiggering.

Legend has it that on the pirate ships of yore, the most powerful man was not the man with the most doubloons or the hardest fists or even the biggest pistol. The most powerful man was the one who held the map and (more important) knew how to read it. With his help, captain and crew had a chance of returning home safely—without it, no chance at all. The Process Master of today is like the man with the map.

It would be nice if all the Knowpower that makes a Process Master could be easily captured and written down somewhere. Unfortunately, it's impossible. In most companies, the fraction of process knowledge that is explicit and stated in a manual, workbook, form, or Web site is between 15 and 25 percent. The rest is implicit and secreted in the brains of company veterans, usually managers in The Middle who have learned the ropes through years of daily experience. It's made up of thousands of fragmentary data points such as

- Who's the first guy you call when the assembly line shuts down? And who do you call when the first guy is on vacation in Tuscany for two weeks?

- What's the latest possible date for changing prices in next season's catalog before it goes to the printer? And in a drop-dead emergency, what's the *real* latest possible date we can get away with, without having Lou at the printer's shop come after us with a machete?

- How much money did the company spend on limousine services for the top brass last year? *How* much?! And if we tried to cut that by 30 percent, would we end up *losing* money because of the time the big shots would waste dictating memos of complaint about the inconvenience of having to drive their own rental cars instead?

- Why do we package our 3-inch long products in plastic bubble cartons that are 12 inches long? And would reducing the packaging by 50 percent be a smart environmental-and-money-saving ploy or a boneheaded move that would make our products invisible on the store shelves alongside the competition?

Who knows this kind of stuff? Ninety percent of the time it's a cadre of smart and plugged-in managers in The Middle, without whom the company would soon grind to a halt. The rest of the time it's a handful of rare, brilliant senior managers who never forgot the crucial importance of grass-roots knowledge.

By the early 1870s, John D. Rockefeller, then in his thirties, was already one of the most successful and richest business men in the world. One day while touring one of his Standard Oil plants, he watched a machine soldering caps onto five-gallon tins of kerosene for export. After a few minutes, he asked the manager in charge, "How many drops of solder do you use on each can?"

The manager replied, "40." Rockefeller asked whether they'd ever tried 38. The answer was No, so Rockefeller told them to try it. Unfortunately, the cans leaked when sealed with 38 drops of solder. But not with 39 drops. So Rockefeller ordered that 39 drops of solder be the new standard for sealing kerosene cans.

In the first year, the change saved $2,500. Over time as the business grew, the savings multiplied. Decades later, in retirement, Rockefeller beamed as he told the story and bragged about the hundreds of thousands of dollars he'd saved the company with that one little change.[3]

Now *there* was a Process Master.

Being a Process Master is an incredible way to multiply the value you produce for your company and everybody connected with it. It also multiplies the importance and value of the role you personally play, which produces, in the long run, enormous rewards for you.

Harnessing Knowpower

A core part of the Knowpower of the Process Master is to recognize the difference between how the company's systems work in theory (according to the employee manual, the org chart, or the assumptions of the CEO) and how they *really* work. The difference is often huge. And when it's ignored, disastrous wastes of time, energy, and money may occur.

Will McDonald (not his real name) is an IT manager for a major financial services firm whose customers include both corporations and individual clients. ABC Bank is a well-run organization, frequently honored as a "most-respected" company in industry polls and magazine surveys. But that doesn't make them immune to the missteps that can occur when the Knowpower of their managers in The Middle gets overlooked.

According to Will, ABC has always had an entrepreneurial corporate culture, with top managers who like to delegate as much authority as they can and an understanding of the need to involve managers in The Middle in most key decisions. But over time, this non-hierarchical spirit has gradually subsided. It's probably inevitable. Over the past decade, ABC has grown from 3,500 employees to 40,000, making it much harder to push decision-making down to the lower levels of the

---

[3] Ron Chernow, *Titan: The Life of John D. Rockefeller, Sr.* New York: Random House, 1999, pages 180-181.

organization. Furthermore, ABC's growing diversification in the financial services businesses, coupled with the complex demands for public reporting of financial data imposed by the new Sarbanes-Oxley regulations, have made the organization more cautious and conservative. Decision-making is becoming more centralized.

As we say, these changes may be inevitable. But the dangers inherent in the trend toward centralization surfaced when the company took the enormous step of implementing a new system of customer relationship management (CRM) software across the organization.

Will explains, "Most of ABC's CRM applications had previously been developed in-house. This made it relatively quick and easy to develop and implement upgrades and changes requested by the operating divisions. But of course, our home-grown software didn't fit any industry-wide standard. So the specialists in our IT organization were very supportive when salespeople from a nationally-known supplier came calling with their proprietary CRM system."

The leaders of the relevant IT department were enthusiastic about the CRM software and sold the project to senior management. But when the change was announced, Will and many of his colleagues were concerned. "The outside supplier offers a fine product," Will says, "but when we analyzed what it would take to integrate it with our existing systems, we realized it was going to be a major effort that would take more than 18 months. That's a major disruption to our business."

Other problems became apparent when Will discussed the new software with his internal clients, the ABC business units. As they analyzed the new program's capabilities, it became clear they would lose some of the functionalities that the existing system provided them, as well as the flexibility in implementing upgrades and changes that they'd always enjoyed.

Unfortunately, ABC's senior management had failed to include IT middle management in its feasibility analysis before signing on with the outside supplier. The impracticality of the new plan only became apparent later, when IT middle managers like Will met with the business units to discuss its implementation. As a result, the project slowly died, but not before costing ABC several million dollars.

What's the lesson? That any company considering a major change to one of its processes needs to involve managers with Knowpower—the Process Masters who can help identify the real-world obstacles to making the change successful. And managers in The Middle, like Will, need to step up to volunteer their expertise when significant decisions are being contemplated (provided, of course, that they get wind of the decisions in time).

There's a silver lining to this story. ABC's internal procedures have been changed to avoid similar situations in the future, including a new system for sampling middle managers' views and opinions whenever major decisions are being made. And perhaps the CRM fiasco was necessary to make the need for this change obvious. "If this had been a smaller project, it probably wouldn't have generated the awareness necessary to drive change within the organization," Will says.

By contrast, a similar change process at a European telecom company—a Deutsche Telekom subsidiary with $3 billion in revenues in 2003 and approximately 10,000 employees—went much more smoothly precisely because a key middle manager helped to design the program.

Pressured by declining revenue growth, the company's senior management had concluded that operating costs had to be reduced to meet their parent corporation's profit expectations. So the CFO enlisted the help of a big multinational consulting firm to develop a company-wide cost-reduction effort. Fortunately, the company delegated a group of top-performing managers in The Middle to work on the project alongside the consultants.

One of these managers (we'll call him Henrik) was asked to identify cost reduction opportunities in the company's network operations department—by far the largest unit in the organization. Henrik had started with the company as a technician back in the 1960s, worked in a series of leadership positions, and had reached a fairly senior position (two levels down from the chief technology officer) by the time of this project.

Just like at most companies, payroll costs at this telecom firm represented the single biggest item addressable by cost-reduction efforts. Jittery about possible layoffs, most people in the organization were understandably hostile towards the project team. But Henrik found a way to significantly reduce costs *without* layoffs. Thanks to his deep knowledge of the company's internal processes, including the daily routine of technicians in the networking operations department, he realized that a minor reorganization could enable the techs to handle a significantly higher workload. So instead of laying off people, he proposed that the technicians' newly freed-up capacity be used to in-source most of the equipment installation and line-activation work that had previously been handled by independent contractors.

It didn't take long for the top brass to recognize the merit in Henrik's ideas. The installation processes were brought in-house, saving the company as much money as if they'd laid off 200 employees. They also avoided exorbitant severance payments (which would have consumed all the cost savings in the first year), to say nothing of the incalculable damage to employee morale and productivity that layoffs would have produced.

Is Henrik some kind of management genius? Not at all—just a middle management Process Master applying his detailed, ground-level Knowpower about how company processes *really* work to the challenge of adding value. In this case, with spectacular results.

How Do You Fix the Processes? Try Asking

Practically every large company has its share of dysfunctional processes. It's not due to management laziness, ignorance, or stupidity (at least not usually), but simply a natural outcome of the way organizations grow. In the heat of the daily battle to serve customers and keep the revenue flowing, no one wants to shut down everything for retooling. It's quicker and easier to patch a process here, throw a few people at a problem there, shuffle some lines on an org chart there, and hope that the whole Rube Goldberg contraption just keeps chugging until the next quarter. As a result, systems tend to get jerry-rigged rather than planned with thoughtfulness and insight based on an all-inclusive overview and analysis.

That's the bad news—and it's the reason you probably find your daily job pock-marked with frustrating encounters with bureaucracy that no longer works (if it ever did). But it's also the good news. It means that, in most organizations, there are significant opportunities for cost savings and improved efficiencies waiting to be seized by managers in The Middle who take the time to apply their process Knowpower to fixing the accumulated problems.

We could tell many stories to illustrate this powerful truth. Here's a great one that features an inspiring manager you've already met in these pages—Joe Ripp. It's about a program Joe helped created at AOL that yielded nearly $600 million in savings, money desperately needed to help the online service company remain profitable during a time when its base of dial-up customers was shrinking.

Joe explains, "AOL was about an $8 billion enterprise, generating profit margins of between $1.5 and $2 billion. So we were spending about $6 billion every year, and every dollar either generated or didn't generate value. My job was to ask, 'Are we sure we're maximizing the value of every nickel we spend?' That meant looking at every process and asking *why* are we doing this? Is this process adding value by attracting customers, improving efficiency, enhancing service, or generating revenue? And if not, why shouldn't we just shut it down?"

When Joe began asking these questions, he encountered initial resistance. In part, it was due to the natural tendency of people to push back against change. "The immediate answer to the *why* question is usually, 'That's the way we do things here,'" says Joe. "It takes time for people to realize that it's not a good enough answer."

AOL's past history of business success strengthened the pushback. "Our success actually blinded us," Joe explains. "Because we were so profitable, we didn't recognize that some of the decisions we'd made had actually *not* been very effective. We needed to find a way to separate our real success factors from the phony ones."

For support and guidance, Joe called in a team from McKinsey & Company, maybe the most prestigious consultant firm in the world. They helped design what came to be called the Operational Effectiveness Program (OEP) for AOL. The idea was to find and save value for the organization through cost containment, revenue improvement, system enhancements—any and every process improvement they could identify. But even more important was the cultural change Joe wanted to introduce to AOL. Joe wanted his pushy questioning about the value of specific processes to become the norm throughout AOL.

As OEP began to take hold, Joe made a discovery. "Once we got underneath the covers," he recalls, "we discovered that our managers were managing averages. In talking about processes, they'd say things like, 'My average salesman is selling X dollars' worth of services.' 'Our average disconnect rate is Y.' 'The average retention rate is Z.'"

Joe began to suspect that something was being missed in all the focus on averages. For example, suppose the average satisfaction rate for a particular segment of customers was 85 percent. What did that really mean? Joe realized it meant there were a lot of customers—tens of thousands, perhaps more—who were actually very unhappy with their service. They represented a real threat to AOL's future, like a hole in the bottom of a bucket through which water was inexorably leaking away. The question was *why* they were unhappy. What was going on? What were the issues that troubled customers? How were their needs and expectations changing? "We had to do a lot of digging to get deeper than the average," says Joe. "That's the only way to move the average up."

"The average customer doesn't care about your average," Joe continues. She only cares about her own experience with you. So we spent a lot of time 'de-averaging' AOL. We got under the covers and asked, 'If on average we're doing X, Y, or Z, what does the distribution around the average look like, and how do we drive value by improving service for the people with the biggest problems?' In the end, you can't fix an average. You can only fix things for specific customers—individual people."

Digging beneath the surface measurements that AOL had previously focused on enabled Joe and his people to identify dramatic opportunities to improve the company's investment planning, shifting funds from processes that added little or no value to others that paid off in terms of customer satisfaction and sales growth. "In certain areas we cut our costs pretty dramatically. In the end, the OEP program yielded more than $800 million of incremental value—$500 million in reduced costs and $300 million in enhanced revenues. All because we started asking questions about what we were doing and why—and not being satisfied with halfway answers."

Cost-cutting isn't the only benefit of rethinking and streamlining your company's processes. Every needless step you can eliminate makes your team's work easier, less stultifying, and more rewarding.

Collaboration in The Middle

Fixing processes as Joe Ripp did is a powerful way that managers in The Middle can add value to their companies. Another is finding ways to bridge the process gaps that often prevent company departments and divisions from working together. This isn't easy to do. There's a lot of talk about "borderless organizations" and "seamless integration." But most companies are still organized into silos where work, ideas, and communications flow up and down, but never crossways. You'll be in a better position to overcome these barriers if you took to heart our advice from Chapter 2, "The Manager's Universe," specifically about the importance of networking. If you know your counterparts in other departments well enough to call them when questions or problems arise, you're ahead of the game—and better off than a lot of managers who allow org charts and official reporting relationships to limit the people they talk to.

One company that desperately needed to improve collaboration between departments was Overstock.com, the discount e-tailer who reported 2005 revenues of $804 million. They'd developed a strategy to improve customer retention and increase sales by rethinking the role of the contact center—in reality, four centers staffed by more than 400 agents whose job is to handle customer requests and problems using phone, email, and instant chat systems. As some other direct merchants have done, Overstock wanted to transform customer service from a *cost* center charged simply with making customer complaints go away as efficiently and cheaply as possible, into a *revenue* center through which products and services could be cross-sold and upsold, customer relationships strengthened, and satisfaction rates improved.

It's a powerful strategy when it works. But there are dangerous pitfalls. Customers hate getting the hard sell when they're already steamed about a problem with a past order—which is the chief reason why they reach out to the contact center in the first place. A company needs unusually fast and responsive IT systems and interface designs to make customer contacts more enjoyable than frustrating. (Ever dutifully punched in your 10-digit phone number and 12-digit order number when ordered to do so by a recording—only to be asked by a human being to repeat the same information two minutes later?)

Even the measurement systems for managing the contact center need to be thoughtfully redesigned if the center is to be repurposed. Traditionally, contact center personnel are judged on average length of call—the shorter the better. That makes sense if the objective is simply to solve customer problems as quickly as possible. But cross-selling and upselling take time. How do you balance the new objectives versus the old definition of efficiency? The right solutions aren't obvious.

So Overstock.com was taking on a challenge that called for unique understanding of company processes and how they connect—not only the processes for managing the contact center itself, but processes for sales, marketing, shipping, financial controls, information technology, and more. Like most companies, Overstock.com didn't have any one person with the comprehensive, detailed, ground-level knowledge needed to link all these systems effectively.

Two managers in The Middle came up with a counter-intuitive yet brilliantly effective approach. Tad Martin, vice president of merchandising and operations, and Kamille Twomey, vice president of online marketing, actually moved out of their separate offices and set up shop in a new, shared space—two desks, two computers, and two phones, along with file cabinets, family snapshots, and all the other paraphernalia of an office home.

What about the privacy that most managers consider a perk of their jobs? That was gone. And that was precisely the point:

> "We hear each other's phone conversations—and we *should* hear each other's phone conversations," says Martin of their shared quarters. "So much of what we do and the decisions we both make affect the customer's experience. So much knowledge is

passed between merchandising and marketing. It just made sense to do it in real-time rather than waiting for another meeting."[4]

Martin and Twomey realized that reshaping some of their company's most complex and important processes meant delving deeply into those processes and sharing their knowledge of those processes as intimately as possible. The best way to make that happen was for them to live together (at least during work hours) so as to create a profound, gut-level sense of what was happening in all the relevant departments every day—the kinds of problems that arose and the nature of the solutions needed.

Not every manager will need (or want) to move in with a colleague. But ignited managers are uniquely positioned to break down the silos that all too often make departments and processes in the same company mutually incomprehensible and prevent meaningful collaboration. It's one of the most powerful levers you can use to add value in your mid-level role.

Change Happens at the Intersections

Revamping a contact center isn't the only kind of challenge that calls for cross-departmental fertilization. Precisely because true collaboration across functions and departments is so rare, the creative results that are generated when people who don't always work together join forces are often unique. And the more your company's organizational structure *discourages* collaboration, the more important it is for managers to push hard to make it happen.

Sunil Mehrotra, most recently president of consumer media services at Homestore.com, spent eight years as a manager at GE, one of the world's most profitable and best-managed corporations. It's also huge, complex, and inherently difficult to navigate. Linking people and processes together to let creative sparks fly is very hard to do at GE. But the surrounding company is so powerful that, when the juices start the flow, the resulting energies can be awesome.

---

[4] Lauren Gibbons Paul, "Hub of Activity." *CMO* magazine, April 1, 2005, page 34.

"GE was a matrix organization when I was a middle manager there in the 1970s," Sunil explains. "That meant most of the work happened in teams, where you had to try to influence people who may not report to you, such as peers from other departments. It was also a process-driven, data-driven, and highly analytical company. And when you have a matrix organization driven by very detailed processes, the processes can take over and the organization can lose sight of the marketplace, the customers, the products and services—all the things that the processes exist to serve.

"The challenge for managers in The Middle is especially great and middle managers, who don't have the authority or the responsibility to change the processes on their own, can feel handcuffed."

In this kind of environment, being a change agent is hard. But Sunil has been studying how GE's processes work to learn how to make change happen.

One of the great GE success stories that Sunil likes to recount is the Spacemaker line of products. "GE was late getting into the microwave oven business," she recalls. "The Japanese were there, the Koreans were coming on strong, and microwave ovens was a category that was rapidly growing when GE finally entered the market."

GE had some catching up to do. They needed a breakthrough concept. How did they come up with one? Sunil explains: "A multifunctional team was formed. It included industrial designers, product managers, and market research people who joined forces to explore new ideas for microwave ovens. Among oth er things, they spent hours together sitting behind one-way mirrors and listening to focus groups of consumers talking about working in the kitchen. And as they listened, they realized that countertop space was a scarce resource, already crowded with toasters, blenders, food processors, and other gadgets. Where would people stick their new microwaves? It was a problem."

The designers and the product managers and the marketers looked at each other, and light bulbs switched on. Why should the microwave have to sit on top of the counter? Why not raise it *above* the counter by attaching it underneath the hanging cabinets? "Would that solve the problem?" the designers asked. "Will the oven still work?" the product managers asked. "Can you *do* that?" the marketers asked. Yes, yes, and yes. The Spacemaker brand was born, and with it the vehicle GE would ride to dominance in the microwave oven market.

"There was no revolutionary technology involved," Sunil observes. "All it took was a cross-functional approach. The traditional product development process where the product managers define the requirements for market research could not have created this breakthrough product. The guys in market research conduct the research and feed a report to the product managers. And the product managers, in turn, outline product specs for the designers to try to match."

What's wrong with this traditional approach? On paper, nothing. In reality, a lot. Each disconnect in the process represents a hole where an idea can easily vanish. For example, when product managers aren't directly involved in market research, they get no direct exposure to customer needs. It's *possible* that the the lack of countertop space might have come through in a packaged report. But then again, it might not. The Spacemaker might never have been conceived—or, more likely, it might have emerged at some other company.

Sunil spells out the lesson. "The magic happens when middle managers get together. They're the ones who are closest to the problems, whether the problems belong to the customer, the end-user, the distribution channel, or the factory. That's where middle managers live. And when they're thrown together to solve a business problem, leaving aside ego involvement and fear of failure, they can tap the knowledge that resides in different areas and bring it all together in new and creative ways. Change happens at the crossroads, the intersections where different processes and disciplines meet."

It almost sounds simple. But there's no formula for making it happen on command. Sunil acknowledges that processes are important, especially in a large, complex organization like GE, but processes can sometimes stifle creativity.

Here's how Sunil sums up the Spacemaker experience: "To be able to increase the odds that your organization is creatively connected to customers, you have to transcend your processes. And middle managers are uniquely suited for that challenge."

Making Mergers Work through the Insights of the Process Masters

Maybe the greatest process challenges arise when companies merge. Even two firms that are fundamentally similar in terms of their spheres of operation, markets, management styles, and cultures often find it daunting to make the necessary connections among people and systems. And no one knows these difficulties like the managers in The Middle who are charged with overcoming them.

I have a buddy in the book publishing business who likes to recount this story (the names have been changed to protect the guilty):

> "A company I used to work for has lately been on an M&A binge, buying one small publisher after another to boost their revenues and expand into new markets. Last year, I was strolling the floor at an industry convention when I ran into a woman I know who's a middle manager at this company. She's in charge of book production processes—everything from having raw manuscripts copy-edited through the shipping of finished books into the company warehouse.

> "After greeting Betsy, I asked her how she was coping with the latest round of acquisitions. She rolled her eyes. 'I'm at my wit's end!' she said. 'I walked into the office one Monday and was given 500 new books to publish next year. They're all in various stages of production at Jones and Company—some being edited, others being designed, others being typeset, still others at the printer. The Jones people have been using a completely different set of software tools to manage the processes, and it's taking us weeks just to figure out how to translate their terminology and protocols into ours. Their policies are different, their editorial standards are different, even the sizes of the books they produce are different—which matters because the cartons and pallets at our warehouse were designed to fit the books we make. The fact that their entire staff is 2,000 miles away doesn't help matters. I've got people working 14-hour days trying to meet impossible publication schedules that we

have to meet if we're going to hit our revenue targets. Frankly, it's a nightmare."

"I gave Betsy my condolences and resumed my stroll around the convention floor. Who should I meet half an hour later but Betsy's boss, the executive vice president who ran her division and had masterminded the merger.

"I greeted Gary and said, 'Congratulations on the Jones acquisition. I guess you guys have your hands full integrating the two companies.'

"Gary just stared at me. 'What are you talking about?' he said, spreading his hands wide. 'It's all done!'

"I stared back. For a minute, I thought one of us was losing his mind. Then I realized what was going on. Gary fancies himself a grand strategist—not the type to get his hands dirty with the messy details. He leaves those to people like Betsy. He sincerely believed that, once the acquisition papers were drawn up and signed and a few dotted lines were penciled in on the org charts, the merger of the two companies was complete! He had no idea about the problems Betsy and her team were wrestling with—which was the *real* work of integrating two companies."

Fortunately, not every top executive is as clueless as Gary. Some have realized that fitting two companies together is a complex task that requires extensive consultation with both organizations' Process Masters—the managers in The Middle who understand how things really work and can figure out how to mesh the systems and people into a new, effective whole.

Steve Wall of Right Management Consultants (RMC) has built a specialty out of focusing on the crucial role of middle managers in mergers and acquisitions. Steve and his team at RMC have developed a unique process they call *organizational due diligence*. It's a vital supplement to the traditional intensive financial analysis that's normally associated with the term "due diligence." RMC merger experts will examine the company to be acquired from the point of view of strategy, culture, leadership, competencies, organizational structure, and processes. The idea is to determine how well the two organizations to be merged will fit together; to identify cultural, stylistic, and process differences that may create barriers to the successful execution of strategies; and to develop a detailed plan for overcoming those differences—one that goes far beyond Gary's method of waving a pencil at the two companies and declaring "It's all done!"

Steve and the RMC consultants involve managers in The Middle in their organizational due diligence process. It begins with extensive interviews, group discussions, and surveys designed to elicit managers' feelings about the cultures and the informal, unspoken processes at each company. For example, when RMC worked with a global hospitality firm (Company A) on a merger with another, smaller hotel chain (Company B), it discovered dramatic differences between the cultures of the two companies. Company A was cautious, conservative, professional, and highly organized; Company B was people-oriented, social, more relaxed, and slower-paced.

It's easy to imagine the conflicts that would probably ensue if the two organizations simply combined their financial, purchasing, hiring, and other processes into a single unplanned lump. Employees accustomed to life at Company A would probably accuse their new colleagues from Company B of being lazy, disorganized, careless, and undisciplined. The folks from Company B would consider their counterparts from Company A uptight, anxious, authoritarian, and stuffy. Workers from Company B might (consciously or unconsciously) sabotage the carefully-designed processes from Company A, sending back paperwork half-completed or three weeks late; workers from Company A might respond with threats, complaints, and punishments. In short, the merger could quickly turn into a disaster.

To prevent this nightmare scenario, RMC arranged for middle-level managers from both companies to meet and spend time together learning one another's strengths and weaknesses, coming to understand their varying cultures, and developing ideas for a *new* culture that could be shared effectively by both parts of the newly merged organization. They talked through the processes used by both companies for various tasks, explained the rationales behind their varying systems, and drew up plans for combining what was best in each company's approach. By the time RMC's culture-merging program was completed, managers from Company A were talking appreciatively about what they could learn from their counterparts at Company B—and vice versa.

You don't need a consulting company to spearhead a similar effort at your company. If a merger or acquisition is in the works, don't react as many managers in The Middle do. They go into defensive mode, spending their days tracking down the latest rumors about What It All Means—who's up, who's down, who's in, who's out, and which executives will emerge from the consolidation as the *real* winners.

Instead, realize that a time of upheaval is an opportunity for you to shine. Talk to your boss (and perhaps your boss's boss) about how your Knowpower can help make the transition a smooth one. Offer to inventory the processes your department runs, map the connections to other parts of the firm, and be part of a team to plan and implement the changeover.

Making this offer will benefit you in several ways:

- It establishes you as supportive of the new regime rather than as a malcontent and potential rebel.

- It gives you a role in establishing the new order—which may mean an opportunity to shape it to your liking.

- It makes you all the more essential to any "new guys" who end up running your operation—after all, who better to interpret and manage the new system than the one who created it?

- It provides you with a positive outlet for the nervous energies inevitably stimulated by a corporate shakeup.

- And it adds value to the company—which is what they pay you for, remember?

It's yet another advantage to being a true Process Master—the fact that, no matter what kinds of storms may rock your company, there will always be a need for the person who holds the map and knows how to read it.

Be that person.

7

IGNITION POINT 2: THE PEOPLE

The Power of the Linkmaker

Picture a mass of some 100 billion living cells, each operating like a kind of on/off switch, always either resting (off) or shooting an electrical impulse down a wire-like structure (on). Each of these structures generates a tiny electrical charge, and from their ends they spit out chemicals that trigger impulses in other nearby cells. The cells are called neurons, the wires are axons, and the trigger chemicals are transmitters with names like epinephrine, norepinephrine, and dopamine.

Welcome to the neural network known as the human brain. The continual flow of energy from one cell of the network to another is how the brain creates intelligence—by generating new neurological connections, constantly creating new connections among cells; in effect, rewiring itself to send information to new portions of the brain where language, memory, motor skills, unconscious behavior, emotions, and hundreds of other functions are controlled.

The ignited manager does the same thing for the company—transmitting information through new pathways. But, of course, the rewiring that the manager does isn't biochemical, because the nodes being linked aren't neurons in the great mass of gray matter that makes up the human brain, but rather individual people inside (and sometimes outside) the company who must work together to make things happen. And instead of being based on the flow of electrical impulses through fluids, the corporate rewiring by which information gets transmitted uses many forms of communication among people, from face-to-face conversations to e-mails, letters, memos, formal reports, and notes scrawled on sticky yellow notes.

We call effective managers who do this kind of rewiring *Linkmakers*. They know people throughout the company, know what they know, and know how to link one person to another so as to make new things happen.

The Linkmaker may or may not be exceptionally knowledgeable, skilled, or creative. He or she may be a Process Master, for example—but maybe not. The Linkmaker's special talent doesn't grow out of any individual capability. Instead, it grows out of the ability to tap knowledge that resides in the organization and in the connections among the many people who make up the organization, rather than in any single individual.

At first blush, this kind of knowledge may sound vague. If it doesn't exist within the head of a particular person, where is it really? And how can it be accessed for the good of the company? In fact, research suggests that *organizational* competencies are actually more powerful and more crucial to success than individual competencies.

One reason is that organizational competencies are less vulnerable than individual competencies to being stolen by competitors. A rival company may lure away this or that employee, thinking it is siphoning away your firm's unique strength, only to discover that what made the employee so effective was actually a team ability that mysteriously vanishes when the individual is separated from the group.

Even more important, organizational competencies not only tap individual talents, but also *combine* those talents in ways that have unique psychological, intellectual, and emotional resonance. Here's how one group of experts on organizational dynamics puts it:

> "Understanding middle managers' perceptions... can reveal valuable group-level competencies that are facilitated by the organization's culture. For example, in a corporate video, Herbert D. Kelleher, CEO of Southwest Airlines, describes

the firm's competency in turning planes around quickly as having a 'balletic quality,' as all the different workers perform their tasks."[1]

Think about that notion—a "balletic quality" to the work of airline employees as they clean the cabin, refill the gas tank, perform safety checks, replenish supplies, and perform all the other jobs that go into turning around a Boeing 737 jet between flights. Where does that quality reside? Not in the mind of any one employee, or even in the plans and protocols spelled out in the Southwest manual. Rather, it describes a quality that all of the perceptions and actions of the various workers share as they race through their tasks. Each employee is acutely aware of what each of the others is doing and of how their jobs intersect. They know which tasks must be performed first and which must be done later. They know how the paths of the various employees will cross and intersect as they rush around the plane, and where they may collide if they're not careful. They know what must happen in the event of some unexpected glitch—the discovery of a camera left on board by a passenger, for example, or a disabled smoke detector in one of the lavatories—and they have in mind the sequence of steps they will take to deal with it *without* delaying the other processes.

All of these perceptions and actions are interwoven in a complex fashion that—when it works right—resembles a carefully choreographed dance. This dance has been created not by any one managerial genius, but rather by hundreds of Southwest employees throughout many years of working together, experimenting, and figuring out the best techniques for getting things done with the utmost efficiency and clarity and even a bit of aesthetic pleasure (hence Kelleher's appreciative word, "balletic"). And it doesn't reside in any single mind but rather in the shared culture of many minds.

So what is the role of the Linkmaker? He or she has a special sensitivity to and awareness of this kind of organizational competency. The Linkmaker knows where it exists, what kinds of challenges tend to trigger it, and how to tap it. He or she also understands how it can be disrupted, what it takes

---

[1] Adelaide Wilcox King, Sally W. Fowler, and Carl P. Zeithaml, "Managing Organizational Competencies for Competitive Advantage: The Middle-Management Edge." *The Academy of Management Executive*, May 2001, page 95.

to protect and nurture it, and how to transmit it to new hires and to future generations of employees. And the Linkmaker uses knowledge of people—both in the abstract sense of understanding human psychology and in the concrete sense of knowing and caring about the co-workers he or she interacts with daily—to serve all these goals.

The Linkmaker uses the touchstone of People Power to accomplish things that can't be done by any one individual. Making this happen requires knowing people and how to appeal to their higher purpose. The Linkmaker can lead people across the company to do what's right, tapping disparate skills, knowledge bases, and personal qualities to create a dance of achievement that can be beautiful to behold.

The talents of the Linkmaker are crucial to organizational success. No wonder Quy Nguyen Huy, after conducting extensive research on the subject, had the following to say: "A new executive's fresh ideas don't have a prayer of succeeding unless they are married with the operating skills, vast networks, and credibility of veteran middle managers."[2]

What the Linkmaker Knows

Making links is a skill that takes thought, practice, and commitment. Linkmakers thoroughly understand who the right people are for which task, and they build personal connections within their network to match management needs to their proper connection points. They continually work to identify new ways to apply resources and direct teams. In the process, they assume leadership roles, identify best practices, and collapse time to gain productivity. Being a Linkmaker means combining your knowledge of how things really work with your network in a way that really drives success.

Here are some other specific skills that Linkmakers develop over time:

- *The Linkmaker can solve in minutes problems that otherwise might take days.* The Linkmaker understands intra-company relationships at a level deeper than what's reflected on any org chart. So when a process breaks down, a new project gets

---

[2] Quy Nguyen Huy, "In Praise of Middle Managers." *Harvard Business Review*, September 2002, page 72.

stalled, or a change initiative refuses to take off, the Linkmaker can identify which people are likely to be the source of the trouble and which people can provide the remedy. He or she can provide simple yet powerful people insights like, "Ed in accounting is the bottleneck—he hates making decisions and tends to sit on paperwork rather than sign off on it. So any time you have to run something by Ed, be sure to give him a definite deadline and call him with a reminder the day before."

- *The Linkmaker understands and can articulate the company's core competencies.* Every organization has some unique strengths that make it special and potentially offer it a competitive edge. Yet surprisingly, many companies don't recognize those core competencies. Instead, they like to claim, "We pursue excellence in everything we do," or even point to areas of weakness as if *those* were the keys to their success. By contrast, Linkmakers know the company, its people, and how their talents combine in unique ways. They recognize and appreciate those "balletic" abilities that make a company special, whether they involve turning around a jet, designing a fabulous new product and getting it into stores in record time, squeezing every drop of waste out of a manufacturing process, or energizing the sales force to reach a seemingly impossible quota as the year-end deadline approaches.

- *The Linkmaker knows what's possible and how to prioritize in a business world where we are overwhelmed by choice.* Because the Linkmaker understands the company, its people, and its competencies, he or she can help top management make smarter decisions about where to focus and what goals to set. When a company needs a quick fix to improve the numbers for the upcoming quarter, the Linkmaker can help identify places in the organization where low-hanging fruit can be harvested: "The folks in customer service work at full capacity during January, but things slack off in February and March. We can move a third of them to temporary slots in sales support to clear up the backlog of orders and get that revenue booked." And when a company is making plans for long-term growth, the Linkmaker can suggest which capacities need to be upgraded in support of the broader agenda.

- *The Linkmaker can quickly identify disconnects and knows how to remedy them.* Most corporate initiatives—whether you're talking about new product launches, market expansions, company acquisitions, or new business ventures—tend to flounder. In comparison to the rosy scenarios created by strategic planners, they almost always take longer, generate lower revenues, amass higher costs, and produce more errors than anticipated. Linkmakers can help anticipate such problems before the fact and can help solve them after the fact. They know, for example, when a particular group of employees lacks time, energy, motivation, knowledge, skill, or interest to tackle a new set of responsibilities, and they can help craft a realistic plan for fixing the deficiencies so that the new project will have a prayer of succeeding.

- *The Linkmaker knows the truth of the old adage, "In union there is strength."* Linkmakers are attuned to the interpersonal, interdepartmental, interdivisional, and cross-functional relationships that make life in any organization complicated. They know which people can't stand one another and which ones have a mutual admiration society; they know which groups have a reputation for being stuck-up and stand-offish, which are considered lazy and sloppy, which are crackerjack problem-solvers but low on people skills, and which are supposed to be the "party crowd" that's fun but not very reliable. And most important, they know how to find the right motivational buttons to push to help these disparate groups work effectively together.

- *The Linkmaker knows how to operate just below the radar.* Most of the knowledge and skills that give the Linkmaker his special power are unofficial, even subliminal. You'd never write these things down in a company manual or publish them on your Web site (for one thing, you might get sued). And many people are uncomfortable even discussing them explicitly. The Linkmaker understands and respects these sensitivities. He or she knows how to be discrete in making judgments, tactful when sharing them, and subtle when using them to oh-so-gently manipulate people toward producing the results she desires.

Igniting the Network

As we've discussed earlier, communicating with your network is a crucial part of your everyday work. It's also a vitally important part of what makes the Linkmaker so powerful. Linkmakers cultivate their networks assiduously and energize them frequently, igniting them with fresh information, calls for action, requests for help, and invitations to participate. If you want to be a powerful Linkmaker (and you should), expect to spend the bulk of your time at work massaging your people connections. In fact, according to one estimate, most managers spend 50 to 80 percent of their workdays in "communication activities of some type," ranging from face-to-face conversations and coaching sessions to group meetings, e-mails, letter-writing, phone conversations—you name it.[3]

It's crucial, however, to invest your time and energy in communications that *matter*. One pitfall that many managers fall into is wasting time on forms of communication that are content-free and therefore don't contribute either to anyone's individual knowledge base or to the competencies of the organization as a whole.

Perhaps you know (or are) someone afflicted with info-mania. It's an easy trap to fall into. The new technologies of communication—e-mail, instant messaging, BlackBerrying—are so fast and easy to use. But, looked at objectively, the symptoms are clear. Staying in touch with your network isn't about tracking multiple forms of technology every minute of the day and night. It's not about sending or receiving hundreds of e-mails every day. It's especially not about sending one-word missives like "Thanks" or "Okay."

It's about connecting with people only when you have something significant to share. If you do this, people who see your return address on an e-mail message will open it first.

Furthermore, the benefits from communication that is *proactive, focused,* and *purposeful* are far greater than those you get from communication that is *reactive, scattershot,* and *purposeless*. Note the description used by the psychiatrist cited in the study: "workers are literally addicted to

---

[3] Charles Kerns, *Value-Centered Ethics*. Amherst, MA: HRD Press, 2004.

checking e-mail and text messages during meetings, in the evening and at weekends." (No wonder people sometimes call the popular communications device a "CrackBerry.") The word *addiction* describes behavior that is out of control—an activity that drives *you* rather than vice versa, and that grows in intensity and compulsiveness even as its original motivation fades. (Once a drunk is really hooked on booze, the stuff doesn't even taste good any more—he just drinks it to be drinking it.)

Note, too, the reference to "checking e-mail and text messages during meetings, in the evening and at weekends." You've experienced it—being out to lunch or at a party or a ballgame with a friend who keeps breaking off the conversation to respond to a beep or a buzz. It's rude, yes. But as a communications strategy, it's also hopelessly ineffective. When you e-mail during a meeting, you miss the content of the meeting even as you send and receive information electronically with half or less of your brain. When you interrupt a conversation with a colleague to check out an instant message, you disrupt your relationship with that colleague and undoubtedly lose at least 50 percent of the information he or she is trying to communicate—especially the portion that is transmitted non-verbally through gesture, facial expression, vocal inflection, and body language. As you multiply communications channels, you subtract value.

Are you interested in making *real* connections with people—the kind that the true Linkmaker values and deploys? Here's how it's done:

- *Make the first move.* Having an "open-door policy" is only a start. Don't sit in your office and wait for people to come to you. Visit them where they live and work. Ask them to explain what they do, how they make decisions, what they value, how they think. Every such encounter adds a node to your network and increases the People Power available for you to call on.

- *Focus on one person at a time.* This is a skill that the world's best leaders cultivate. While in conversation with someone, work on shutting out distractions so that you *really hear* what they have to say—and not just its surface meaning but also its subtle undertones and emotional resonances. Few things are as flattering as being listened to with care and attention. Lavish this on the people that matter to you, and you'll be amazed at their readiness to follow you.

- *Have a purpose.* When you communicate, have a goal in mind. It could be open-ended ("To get a better understanding of what Andrea in Finance does all day and how she affects my department") or very concrete and specific ("To tell Andrea about the new incentive plan I'm considering and find out what questions she may have about implementing it"). Once you've achieved the goal, move on. Communication isn't about mindless chit-chat—it's about meaningful contact.

- *Turn your channels on and off with deliberate intention.* Rather than continually interrupting yourself, make conscious decisions about how and when you will communicate. During an interview, don't answer the phone or glance at the computer screen. During a conference call, don't flip through your inbox or scan your e-mails. And when you *know* you will be too distracted to concentrate, tell people so: "This is a bad time. Let me finish this report and I'll stop by your office to talk in 45 minutes, okay?"

How Linkmakers Build and Use Their Networks

Steve Mummolo managed an in-house design team for US Search, a firm that is a leader in using technology to track down information about people for purposes as varied as employment background checks, screening of nannies or building contractors, or searches for someone's long-lost classmate or sweetheart. He exemplifies how the Linkmaker builds an ad hoc network to get things done when the explicit structure of the company isn't working.

Steve had a problem. In June 2003, US Search merged with the Enterprise Screening division of First American to form First Advantage, a Florida-based firm. The merger expanded the company and added many new resources, but it also threw the firm's internal systems into a temporary state of confusion. Departments like Finance and Human Resources had to devote time to examining their own processes and figuring out how to unify the two organizations. At this inopportune time, an urgent design challenge meant that Steve had a desperate need for more talent on his staff—and he needed them yesterday.

"In the wake of the merger," Steve recalls, "the HR people were really unclear as to what the hiring process would be. I tried the logical channels. Our new in-house HR rep said he didn't handle recruiting. So then I called Florida where our parent company is based. They said, 'Well, we can sort of handle it, but we don't know exactly what you need.' And when I explained that I badly needed some design help, I was handed a huge ball of red tape to unravel. To start the hiring process, you needed two weeks' notice, and you needed to fill out a collection of forms and get approval from executives all the way up to the CEO.

"This doesn't work with a design team. When you need help for a hot project, you need it right away. You don't have two weeks' notice."

So Steve took it upon himself to handle the recruiting process. How? By using his skills as a Linkmaker. "I spoke with people at several different staffing agencies. I preferred one particular creative group because they pre-screened and did all the background checks on everybody. I wound up orchestrating the recruiting process, hiring the people I needed, and then plugging the information into our HR systems."

The process took a little time and patience. "I just went and tracked down all the people I needed to get approval from," Steve explains. "For example, I went to Legal and said, 'This is what I'm doing and here are the contracts from the headhunters. I need you to review them.' My friend in the Legal department turned it around for me in a day. In the end, we got it all done quickly. I'd been dancing around with HR for months. Once I started acting on my own, I had a candidate that I was making an offer to in less than 30 days."

Here is where many managers in The Middle would raise the empowerment issue.

How do you get permission to do something like this that is worthwhile but outside of the company's ordinary procedures? Steve did it by using his knowledge of how to push his boss's buttons.

"I'm a designer, basically. Numbers are not my thing. But I knew that Bob, my boss, would want a financial justification for this. So I ran the numbers. I figured out how much time I and my people were spending on trying to get the hiring done, and I calculated how much money all that time was worth. Then I could show Bob how much money we would save if I could push it through on my own. What could he say? 'That makes a lot of sense,' he told me, and I was off and running."

Creating and using an ad hoc network of outside recruiting firms and in-house advisors wouldn't have been Steve's first choice. His out-of-the-box solution was driven by sheer necessity. "At the end of the day," he says, "if my team's work doesn't get finished and we don't get to market our product and we start losing revenue, I can't blame my problems on HR. It's up to me to make it happen. So I did what I had to do."

What are some of the lessons to be learned from Steve's adventure in Linkmaking?

- When you're trying to get something done, use the proper channels first.

- Then, if the official procedures don't work and you find you must make an end run, do it in a politically sound way: Explain your reasons, get your boss's support, and keep people informed.

- Above all, show results. If you can make your network pay off in tangible ways that benefit the company, you'll be a hero. If not, you won't.

Steve recalls, "I didn't try to hide what I was doing. I would call HR almost daily and explain what I was doing, who I was talking to, and how the process was unfolding. They could see that I wasn't trying to steal anyone's thunder—I was just trying to get some results. I didn't want to start too many fires along the way, because I knew that at some point I would have to deal with these people again."

Today, the hiring process at US Search is far more efficient, and Steve may never have to resort to Linkmaking tactics in that area again. He views what he did as a stopgap measure to bridge a difficult time in the company's evolution. Most important, it worked—because of the Linkmaking prowess Steve employed.

Leadership, Management, and the Secret of People Power

One key to management is understanding the differences among people and making those differences work for, rather than against, the organization. To use our terminology, great managing is largely about Linkmaking—knowing the people around you, understanding what makes them tick, and connecting their knowledge and skills in ways that will make powerful things happen for the organization.

Brad Edmondson illustrates this lesson. Currently a freelance journalist and consultant, Brad was formerly a manager and editor-in-chief at *American Demographics*, a magazine that is now part of the *Advertising Age* publishing operation but that was owned by Dow Jones during Brad's tenure there.

During his years as a manager, Brad discovered that understanding what makes people tick and being able to empathize with them is crucial to having a network that can produce results. In his case, the people he was supervising were writers like himself—which gave him a leg up in terms of understanding how to motivate and encourage them:

> The only way to really manage writers is to have a personal, first-hand understanding of writing. It's a complex process that includes fact finding, research, rumination, analysis... then coming up with the outline, coming up with the lead, figuring out how to draw readers into the story you have to tell. Reporters need to develop very, very quickly, the ability to zero in on what is the most important fact. What makes the story unusual? And what will maintain an average person's interest? The best writers become very skilled at detecting bullshit. Reporters have the best BS meters because they have to—and because they see so much BS.

> Only an experienced journalist can really understand how it all works. If you don't know what a great lead paragraph is from having written one, it's very, very hard to explain to someone else.

> So managing reporters is a unique challenge. Sometimes being a good writer and being a complete egomaniac go together well. And you need to know your team members well enough as people to understand when they're working out some sort of

personal issue in an office context and need to be given a long leash. Basically, if you can just keep them close to meeting their deadlines and isolate their tantrums and outbursts—which is possible—then you can keep getting production out of them. Which makes it all worthwhile in the end.

Brad also discovered that disciplining these creative egomaniacs, while sometimes necessary, involves an unusual degree of sensitivity and tact:

When somebody blows a deadline—which is the worst failing in journalism—rather than just firing that person or sticking them on the obituary desk, you need to understand why it happened. Because sometimes there are very good reasons. Or when you give somebody an assignment and have high hopes for the story only to be disappointed by what gets turned in, what's really crucial is to follow up with the writer and have a frank talk about why they let you down. Because when you're doing creative work, there are frequently reasons that make failure unavoidable. And so, as a manager, you need to understand that sometimes the quality of a creative worker's output is beyond their control.

So if you just fire someone who disappoints you once or even a few times, you may end up discarding somebody who could be a great source of good work for years to come. That's why you have to take the time to really know and understand people before making judgments.

One of the best pieces of management advice I ever heard came from a publisher I used to work for. He said, "I'll put up with attitude if I get performance." And sometimes the best reporters have a whole lot of attitude. It's because they tend to have a complete hatred of bullshit. Unless, of course, it's their own!

So, for Brad Edmondson, effective managing is a lot more like chess than checkers. It's not a game with interchangeable pieces to be pushed around the board wherever the boss happens to want them. It's about pawns and knights and bishops and rooks and queens—each with unique talents, vulnerabilities, flaws, skills, and problems, and each ready to contribute when they are placed in exactly the right place at the right time. (Remember what Herb Kelleher said about "the balletic quality" of turning around a plane at Southwest Airlines? He might just as well have called it a chess game. Both are about the intricate, cunningly-designed flow of objects and forces in space so as to achieve specifically desired results.)

Like Brad, the ignited manager has a history of experience and success with the work he is supervising. He remembers what the challenges are (what it means to write a great lead paragraph) and can empathize with the problems his team members face.

He also develops his Linkmaker skills to a high degree and uses them constantly. He learns to sniff out people who have the instincts and the talents he needs to make the operation go. Then he works with them to maintain their productivity. When necessary, he works around their personal foibles so long as they meet the most essential goals. When problems arise, he doesn't simply punish or humiliate the team member—instead, he delves into why. And when problems are genuinely beyond people's control, he recognizes that and responds appropriately rather than blowing off people with the potential to contribute.

The Essential Ingredient: Trust

In this chapter, we've talked a lot about the importance of communication and its crucial role in the work of the Linkmaker. Unless people are ready and able to share ideas, insights, data, experiences, objectives, and plans with one another, the network that connects them is useless and will never generate the energy that makes things happen.

That readiness can never exist without the essential ingredient of trust. People who don't trust one another won't talk openly about what they know and what they want to do. When trust is absent, information gets hoarded, processes become opaque, teams break apart into self-serving units, and, as the flow of data through the networks slows to a trickle, the organization as a whole gets stupider.

Dan Puckett is Director of Finance and Sales Operations for Affymetrix, a biotechnology company with more than $300 million in shares, a market value of $1.3 billion, and about 900 employees, of whom Dan manages 14.

Dan's chief value of Affymetrix is as a Linkmaker. On practically a daily basis he finds himself in situations where he has to broker or build bridges between two groups. In part, his linkage role is indicated by his title, because Dan helps to draw intellectual and information connections between the two (sometimes conflicting) roles of financial management and sales management. But the role also grows out of Dan's personal qualities and the history of his position in the company.

When I spoke with Dan, he'd been in his job for just seven months. But he'd devoted that time to building positive relationships with those in the department, especially the sales people. It's important because one of Dan's roles is to work through the details of sales agreements before they are officially approved by the company, making sure they make economic sense and don't violate any company policies or standards. Sometimes this can be a touchy process, especially when a particular sales person is pushing to meet a target and is eager to get Dan's buy-in on an agreement that might be borderline.

"Most of the reps will call me straight up and talk through deals," Dan explains. "We have a good enough relationship now so that they're willing to be very open with me about what they're trying to accomplish. They know I'll support them if they do the right thing. There are still one or two people in the group I don't know that well, so they may not be comfortable coming to me with tough questions just yet. But that'll come with time and just a matter of working with the people longer."

One of Dan's toughest jobs is dealing with so-called rep letters every three months. A rep letter is a disclosure statement that confirms that all aspects of every sales arrangement are known and have been disclosed. It's Affymetrix's way of ensuring that their sales people don't make any side arrangements in order to clinch a deal—an aspect of squeaky-clean management that Dan takes very seriously.

"Just this morning," he told us, "we had an issue that came up related to a commitment we made to a customer. I had to talk with one of the VPs of Sales about why we have the rep letters and what's so important about them, making sure he understands why corporate finance monitors these things and why we've got to be sure these letters are complete and timely."

Why is Dan the best-placed person to make sure these commitments are met? "I'm the person that they've got some trust in. I work with them every day and make sure the lines of communication are strong. And the trust extends up the line through our organization, which is very helpful. The VP of Finance is the person to whom I report, and was in my role previously. From her history, she's got relationships with a lot of the sales reps. That means they have a lot of trust in me and my boss and are pretty quick to open up about any problems they're having.

"Without that trust," Dan concludes, "I couldn't do my job. And it would also impact the sales team. If they didn't trust me or my department, they wouldn't reach out for support with analysis and modeling and other functions that only Finance can do. Our relationship would become an adversarial one instead of a partnership. We'd be forced to play games to try to find out the information sales would be hiding from us, and everybody would waste a lot of time and energy. In the end, sales would suffer and we'd all lose out. So trust is the key to making things work."

Dan's lessons for other would-be Linkmakers are as follows:

- *Take time to develop trust.* Make it a conscious goal, especially during your first year in a job.

- *Be open to questions and communications of any kind.* Reward openness through a positive and supportive attitude. This helps build your network and ensures that lines of contact will be open in times of crisis, when the flow of information is absolutely vital.

- *Build off past relationships.* When someone else on your team has earned the group's trust (as is the case with Dan's boss), piggyback on that connection to build your own alliances.

In time, your network will be humming with the sound of ideas moving, intelligence being generated—and things getting accomplished.

8

IGNITION POINT 3: THE MESSAGE

The Power of the Translator

Ever look around your office and find yourself saying (or at least thinking), "It's like the International Departures lounge at Kennedy Airport around here"? In today's diverse and globalized world, where a workplace is likely to find WASPs and Latinos and South Asians sitting next to people of Russian and Italian and Chinese and African-American descent, that's not an uncommon reflection. And most of the time we consider this a great thing. Our growing diversity means we can draw strengths from people of many personality types, life experiences, and philosophical and mental makeups. But diversity (as you may also have noticed) sometimes creates challenges. Getting everyone on the same page in terms of company goals, methods, work habits, and communications styles can be a little harder when no two team members come from exactly the same background.

Just as at the United Nations, the talents of a Translator may be helpful.

But in reality, the diversity challenges of our workplaces go even deeper than the obvious level of ethnic and cultural diversity.

What about diversity of skill sets? Think about the people you work with every day. Do the bean counters in Finance think and talk and plan and judge in exactly the same way as the creative types in Product Design? Do the folks in Marketing always see eye to eye with the people in Legal? Do the staffers in Human Resources, the computer whizzes in Information Technology, and the MBAs in Corporate Planning—not to mention the guys and gals in the mailroom—all share the same world view?

You know they don't. In fact, as we mentioned each of these categories of workers from a typical office, didn't a visual image flash across your mind? Isn't it fairly clear to you which group of people is more likely to wear gray pinstripes and which to wear jeans? Which group carries MP3 players and which group carries today's *Wall Street Journal*? Which group goes clubbing and which group goes to bed early?

Stereotypes? Sure. We all store stereotypes in our brains. They're over-simplifications, and unfair and very dangerous to use when working with individual people who have a way of defying expectations. But in many cases they also encapsulate a grain of truth.

That's why we need Translators in our workplaces; not primarily to help connect people of different ethnic backgrounds, but to help people of wildly different viewpoints and values to understand one another and unite behind common corporate goals.

This third Ignition Point is about the power of the Message. One of the key roles of today's manager in The Middle is to understand top management's vision for the future of the company and then somehow find ways to translate that vision into actionable ideas that our diverse workforces can all relate to, buy into, and support.

In a way, it's a two-part challenge. The first part is knowing management's needs, goals, and intentions. This in itself is not easy, especially considering how poor a job many executives do of formulating their corporate vision and presenting it in a coherent, understandable fashion to the managers in The Middle (let alone those at deeper layers of the organization). It's not enough to hear what the executives are saying; you also need to know the implicit messages, the unspoken motivations, and where you stand today in the long-term history of the company. Understanding what the top brass *really* wants sometimes requires all the analytical skills and personal sensitivity we can muster.

(In some cases, of course, there *is* no true vision from the top. Many companies state their goals as "growing revenues, reducing costs, and delivering quality"—which isn't much of a vision. When that's the case, the job of the manager in The Middle is even more complicated: He or she must also *create* the Message as well as translate it.)

And that's just the first part of the challenge. The second part is conveying the Message to your team members, using all the many languages and dialects they speak to make the corporate objectives both understandable and acceptable. Yes, it's about "What's in this for me?" But that's not all. It's also about, "Why should I care?" "Why does this appeal to my deepest personal values?" and "How does this fit into the narrative I'm constructing of my personal life quest?"

This Ignition Point is quintessentially about being the manager in The Middle. With the corporate Message on one side and our teams on the other, we need to find ways to make that Message actionable. The Translator's role is to get groups working together to find a common language and put the company's goals into a context that will motivate and even excite people.

How the Ignited Manager Can Create and Sell a Saving Message

We've already alluded to the special challenges that arise when one company acquires another. In today's business world where mergers and takeovers are occurring more frequently than ever, the talents of the Translator who can help people from wildly different corporate cultures find a common language and coalesce around a shared message are incredibly important. Here's the story of one such manager—Sunil Mehrotra at General Electric, whom you met earlier in connection with the Spacemaker story.

In 1985, GE acquired RCA's consumer electronics business, the great old company famous for its radios, TVs, stereos, and other consumer electronics gear. GE's goal in making the acquisition was to strengthen its position in consumer electronics, not just by obtaining RCA's customers, but also by piggybacking on the knowledge and skill that RCA had developed over decades of creating products for that marketplace. (GE's CEO, the already-legendary Jack Welch, had made it clear that he wanted the firm to be number one or number two in every market it operated in—nothing less would suffice.)

So logically enough, GE merged its consumer electronics division with RCA's. RCA, at the time, had the number one market share in consumer electronics in the US, while GE was fourth or fifth. Yet GE had acquired RCA and GE was a dominant, highly profitable corporation, while RCA was struggling—despite the fact that, in the consumer electronics business, the acquired company was stronger than the acquiring company.

This made for a curious and challenging managerial situation. As the merger and reorganization shook out, all the senior managers at RCA ended up being people who'd been brought in from GE to run the organization, while the managers in The Middle were from RCA— almost like the yeoman farmers who suddenly find that the manor house on the hilltop is now occupied by a set of new and unfamiliar nobles. What's more, GE and RCA had corporate cultures that were very different. So this was not a marriage made in heaven.

We'll let Sunil pick up the story from here:

> I'd been with GE before and was hired back from Chase Manhattan to head up RCA's market research and competitive analysis department. I was soon promoted to be the general manager of the RCA brand, responsible for televisions, VCRs and camcorders. As the brand manager for these businesses, I had to make changes and improvements in the merged organization by working through the old RCA loyalists. It was a challenge to figure out how to meld the GE and RCA cultures, break down past loyalties, and make change happen quickly. RCA did not have the luxury of time. Even though RCA was the market share leader, it was facing stiff competition from the likes of Sony, Panasonic, and Hitachi.
>
> The way we initiated change was through forging a personal relationship among three key middle managers: the head of industrial design (an RCA guy), the head of national advertising (also from RCA) and myself, a GE guy. The three of us shared one thing. We believed that there was a huge opportunity for the merged companies and that we could grab that opportunity if we focused on the marketplace and not the internecine struggles.

So we formed an informal team and collaborated on a vision for the company that would be market-driven, data-driven, and independent of either GE's or RCA's traditional corporate culture or way of viewing the world.

We gathered a lot of market data to understand how RCA was perceived by consumers and channel partners in relation to Sony, Panasonic, and other competitors. Through market analysis, we identified opportunities for RCA to leverage its past to create a new RCA. We articulated a whole new vision for what RCA could become.

To represent this new RCA, we came up with the idea of Chipper. You're probably familiar with Nipper, the dog from the old RCA ads—"His Master's Voice," and all that. Nipper is an American icon. Well, we created Chipper, a pup representing the future; Nipper being the old RCA, Chipper representing the new. Nipper and Chipper became the symbol for the new RCA, representing the grand and historic past of RCA as well as its vision and hope for the future.

Nipper and Chipper were instant hits, both within the Company and outside. They were very effective in drawing out the residual goodwill towards the RCA brand and in telegraphing the new vision for the brand. They were the symbol around which the entire company could rally, transcending the GE or RCA roots. They were instrumental in building a coalition and a ground swell of support for moving the brand forward. The process was cathartic for the company.

And within a short time, RCA was revitalized and re-energized and became a significant player in the consumer electronics market again.

Let's think about the challenges Sunil faced and how he used his managerial skills to become an effective Translator:

- *Lack of Message.* When Sunil was put in charge of the "new RCA," there really was no new RCA. Sunil realized that his first challenge was to develop a Message that would work for RCA and also fit the long-term goals and objectives of the parent company—which were focused on growth and excellence in the consumer electronics marketplace.

- *Language gap.* People at the acquired RCA felt that their new chieftains from GE had nothing to teach them. After all, hadn't GE lagged behind RCA in consumer electronics? The GE and the RCA corporate cultures were very different. Would it be possible for these two groups to learn to work together?

- *Business stresses.* Despite its marketplace success, the company was not profitable, and challengers, especially the Japanese companies like Sony and Panasonic, were gaining on RCA's turf.

Sunil and his colleagues turned again and again to the data—the facts about the consumer electronic marketplace, customer attitudes toward RCA and GE, and the history of both companies—which had been gathered through objective research and could be accepted as valid by all concerned. This was crucial to building consensus and organizational support. Building the new Message around objective facts rather than around opinions or traditional views helped transcend emotional barriers that may have otherwise slowed down the process of getting the buy-in and support from both the GE and RCA folks, which, in turn, was necessary for mobilizing the organization and rallying it around a common and shared vision. The ultimate result was a language—and a Message—that everyone could support.

Translating Tribal Dialects

Of course, the role of the Translator isn't restricted to company mergers. Even people who have long worked for the same company or even in the same division or department may speak different languages.

You remember Steve Mummolo, the Linkmaker from US Search whom we profiled in the previous chapter. Steve is also called upon to be a Translator from time to time, even when talking to people who work on his own design team. Because the design projects Steve's group works on are generally Web-based, they require at least two very distinct sets of skills: programming skills, which are technical, scientific, and math-oriented, and design skills, which are graphic, esthetic, and image-oriented. These two sets of skills are occasionally combined in a single person (as they happen to be in Steve's case). But more often they are housed in two different people, usually combined with widely varying social attitudes, personal values, intellectual interests, and business languages. To manage both kinds of people, Steve has had to develop his linguistic skills to a high degree. "We're separated by a common language," is how Steve describes it (with a rueful laugh).

When talking with members of the techie tribe, Steve has learned to be very careful about how he uses jargon. "You have to be careful not to throw around their terminology unless you know exactly what it means to *them*," he comments. "Which may not be the same as what it means to you—or even what it says it means in a book or a dictionary."

When he violates this rule, Steve has found, his technical people tend to misunderstand him, and often respond to his questions by saying, "Oh, well, our system isn't designed to do that"—when in fact the system is perfectly capable of doing what Steve has in mind, except that he hasn't described it accurately. The only solution is for Steve to go back to square one and try explaining—in jargon-free, non-technical language—exactly what he would like to have done and let his techie team member figure out the jargon to describe it.

Working with techies can be challenging to Steve in other ways. He has one team member (call him Jay) who is especially valuable not only for his programming prowess but also for his gung-ho attitude. Jay loves a challenge—the tougher the better. Throw him a difficult assignment and he'll work night and day to get it done. The problem is that sometimes Jay loves challenges *too* well. "He'll go after the project that's the most interesting and the most difficult," Steve says, "and stick the day-to-day things that you need to get done on the back burner."

Steve's solution? To devote time specifically to talking about time management with Jay. "We meet about weekly and go over the priority list. 'All right,' I'll say, 'This is your number one, this is your number two. Let's talk about when you think we're going to have some progress on these.' And then I check in with him periodically to make sure he's staying focused on what matters. Generally it works out pretty well."

By contrast, the designers Steve works with pose very different translation problems. "Offering criticism is the biggest challenge," he says.

"Even a great designer can sometimes come up with a design that's just horrible. I've done it myself. And there were times when a manager tossed a design back onto my desk and just said, 'This stinks—redo it.' I happen to be very thick-skinned, and over the years I've learned how to separate my work from my art and to leave my art in my studio at home. So I'm okay with the blunt criticism. But most creative people hate it. Talk to them that way and you may lose them forever."

Steve's translation technique is based on appealing to a common goal—namely, the business objective for which the design is intended:

> The form has to follow the function. So when I'm talking with a designer, I'll start by asking, "What are our priorities for this ad? What's the action we want the viewer to take?" Based on that, we can figure out together what our priorities are, and that tells us what should be most prominent in the design.
>
> Once we've agreed on that, I have an objective basis for my criticisms. I can say things like, "This spot might be hard to read" or "The main selling point gets lost."
>
> Or I can give the designer some principles to work off rather than just vague artistic preferences. I can say, "Here are some loose guidelines we've developed and some objectives we have to meet. Does this design meet those objectives?" When I put it that way, a lot of times the designer will look at the piece again and respond, "Well, I really liked this image, so I guess I got carried away with putting the focus on the image rather than the caption." In effect, they can find the flaws in their own work rather than responding defensively to criticisms from me.
>
> Best of all is when I can point to a rule that can be quantified. For example, "We've tested a few different Web designs, and when we put the button on the right rather than the left, our click-through rate is X percent higher." This moves the conversation away from artistic integrity or good taste and onto results, which is really all that matters.

Notice the slightly ironic technique that Steve has developed for communicating with members of different tribes. When talking with techies, it's best for Steve to *avoid* technical language. Instead, he tries to describe in general, jargon-free terms the effect he hopes to achieve and lets the techies figure out how to explain it. Similarly, when talking with artistic types, Steve *avoids* couching his ideas in artistic terms. Instead, he focuses on business issues, practical functionality, and even quantitative measures of effectiveness (click-through rates), and lets the designer figure out an artistic solution to the problem.

Perhaps what this suggests is that one secret to talking with people from various exotic tribes—whether they be techies, artists, numbers people, financial types, marketers, PR or HR experts, or any other kind of specialist—is to stick to plain English rather than trying to "talk their language." A smart Translator like Steve Mummolo simply lets his listeners do their *own* translating. And why not? After all, who knows their language better than they do?

Translating Up the Pipeline

Communication is a two-way street. (Actually it's much more complex than that, but let's leave it at two ways for now.) It's not enough for the manager in The Middle to figure out how to translate the needs and concerns of top management to his team members lower on the corporate ladder. The manager in The Middle must also be able to translate information and ideas from his people into terms that the top brass can understand and use. In other words, the Translator must be able to send information effectively up as well as down the corporate pipeline. And that often requires a different set of skills.

Here are some of the circumstances that call for bottom-up translation of information:

- Finding and packaging information that management seeks about your operation or your people.

- Communicating the feelings and opinions of your team members about new business initiatives, strategies, or restructurings.

- Presenting and defending business proposals or ideas created by members of your team.

- Assisting team members when they deal with personnel issues, such as requests for raises, promotions, or transfers.

In all these cases, your role as Translator is not about passing along the thoughts and feelings of your team members without filtering, as if you were simply a neutral conduit for information. Rather, it's about translating your team members' messages into a language that management will understand and respect and that will, in the long run, enhance your standing and that of your entire team in the eyes of the company's leadership. This isn't always easy to do.

You can *never* be simply a neutral conduit of information because, whenever you pass along an idea, a piece of news, an opinion, or a proposal from someone who reports to you, that concept immediately becomes wedded to you—your image, your credibility, your standing as a leader.

Suppose the members of your team are up in arms over some company policy—a set of new and much more restrictive rules about travel expenses, for example. If you drop in on your boss and simply convey their feelings, the assumption will be that you share their attitude... unless you consciously and deliberately counter that assumption.

In a case like this, your first responsibility is to know how *you* feel about the controversial policy. Is it a necessary cost-cutting measure? An over-reaction to one or two cases of irresponsible employee behavior? A misguided act by some bureaucrat who doesn't recognize how it will affect people? A good idea whose presentation was mangled by a tone-deaf administrator? Or some combination of the above?

Next, you need to communicate to your people exactly where you stand on the issue and the degree to which you agree, disagree, or differ with their position. The more honest and transparent you can be about this, the better.

Finally, you need to decide about how you can most productively translate your team's concerns for the benefit of management. Much will depend on circumstances. Is the travel policy carved in stone, with virtually no chance it will be changed any time soon? Then complaining about it may be merely an exercise in venting that will benefit no one. Is it possible that the policy could be adjusted based on a thoughtful critique of its effectiveness? Then marshaling sound *business* arguments to support certain smart, specific changes may make sense. Is the policy merely a symbolic lightning-rod that employees are angry about because of a host of similar problems that have left them feeling under-appreciated and misused? Then a conversation with your boss about morale, in which the travel policy is not the focus but simply Exhibit A, may be necessary.

Above all, the Translator needs to apply her knowledge of the needs, goals, and problems of her boss to any bottom-up communication task. Think about how this message will sound to the boss. Does it represent yet another unwelcome headache? (If so, why haven't you taken care of it?) Is it an opportunity to solve an unrecognized problem and thereby improve some system or process in the company? (If so, present the solution along with the problem.) Couching the message in terms the boss can immediately understand improves the chances that the top-down response will be one that everyone can live with happily.

The same general principles apply when the bottom-up communication is in response to a top management request. For example, suppose your boss asks you to report about a particular activity in your department as part of some company-wide survey or analysis. It could be about anything from travel expenses (that again) to new-product initiatives to employee educational activities. Before responding, evaluate the information through your boss's eyes. Ask yourself (or, if necessary, your boss) questions such as:

- *What is the purpose of the request?* Is it to locate potential cost savings, to prepare data for a government report, to identify opportunities for revenue growth, or to look for corporate dead wood?

- *What would your boss* like *the answer to be?* If there is flexibility in defining the activities to be included in the answer, should we lean toward including more or including less?

- *Would more detail be helpful in this case, or detrimental?* What kinds of information will make our department or division look good? What kinds will make us look bad?

Don't misunderstand—I'm not advocating falsehood or concealment of material information. I'm just saying that, in your role as Translator, your goal should be to present the most favorable portrait of yourself, your department, and the people it comprises that you can *honestly* offer. Helping your people present themselves in a favorable light to your company's top management is one of your responsibilities as a Translator.

When the Message Is Unwelcome

Many times, the manager in The Middle must convey a message that no one wants to hear.

Sometimes it's a top-down message that you know your people will dislike: a freeze on salary increases, possible layoffs, and a merger that creates uncertainty about the future. Other times it's a bottom-up message that your boss, and her boss, will be unhappy about: a sales or production shortfall, loss of a key client or account, a rebellion on the part of one or a few key employees.

When you find yourself in this position—not *if* but *when*—here are some of the rules you must follow to play your roles as Translator *and* leader faithfully and well:

- *Don't sit on the information.* Conveying bad news is so painful that the temptation to hold off is great: "Maybe something good will happen so that I won't have to report the bad news... or at least I can present them together and soften the blow... or maybe tomorrow or next week will be a better time." But if you delay disclosure, you'll probably be sorry. Any important news has a way of traveling around organizations very quickly, and if people get the word from some other source before they get it from you, they'll start to wonder: Is he playing fair with me? Is he holding back? Is he even in the loop? Your credibility and reputation will take a hit, however small. And once such hits start to land, they tend to accumulate. If you have to eat crow, eat it warm now rather than cold later.

- *Think before you speak.* Emotions run high when bad news must be delivered—and that includes *your* emotions. Think through carefully what you will say and how you will say it. Jot notes or even a word-for-word presentation if necessary. Be certain the information is absolutely accurate, that you have answers to all the obvious questions people are likely to ask, and that you also know what you *don't* know and are prepared to say it honestly.

- *Deliver bad news in person.* Yes, it's easier to drop the hammer in a memo, an e-mail message, or even a phone call. Don't do it. A face-to-face conversation or meeting conveys the message, "I'm personally sorry that I have to tell you this, but I want you to know that I care and that I will do whatever I can to help you deal with it." It says you are *there* for them, literally as well as figuratively.

- *Don't try to deflect blame.* Those who receive your news may respond with anger. You don't have to accept their anger as fair, just, or accurate; there's no need to blame yourself for something that has gone wrong if you weren't actually responsible. But by the same token, don't try to shift blame onto someone else: your boss, the people who work for you, people in some other department, or the economy at large. Even when such attempts are subtle, they come across as cowardly and classless. When people express disappointment or anger, just respond honestly: "I understand how you feel. This is very bad news, and I'm disappointed [upset, worried, troubled] myself."

- *Give people time to absorb the news.* Many people—especially males, I think—are raised to be "problem-solvers," unwilling to accept the fact that sometimes bad things happen that can't be glossed over. As a result, when the news is bad, they often rush to offer consolation or partial solutions, even before people have had an opportunity to fully understand what has happened. Take your time. Give people a chance to think about the news and ask questions before you try to move on to solutions.

- *Don't sugar-coat it.* People can handle the truth. They respect leaders who are honest about the problems they face rather than pussy-footing around with words like "challenge," "issue," or "opportunity." Be frank about how bad things may be, and you'll retain some credibility for your future announcements when good news returns.

- *Offer hope for the future.* Once people have been able to fully absorb the bad news, you can and should begin to talk about what comes next. Let people know that you are at least two steps ahead of them—that you've begun thinking about ways of solving the current problems and getting the organization or department back on the right track. But don't just lay out your own plans; give people an opportunity to offer their own ideas. Let them participate in the solution so that it will be as much theirs as it is yours.

Above All, Clarity

People talk a lot about the communication styles of great leaders. All kinds of prescriptions have been offered. Some say that an effective leader is optimistic; others say he offers a vision; still others recommend humor, story-telling, humility, energy, emotion. All are important. But there's one quality that the Translator needs above all, and that is *clarity*—the ability to say whatever you are trying to say so that people simply *get it* rather than walking away misunderstanding, apathetic, or confused.

Of course, you can't have clarity unless you've thought long and hard about the Message, thoroughly mastered its meaning, and made it your own.

9

IGNITION POINT 4: THE LANDSCAPE

The Power of the Scout

One of the most common tendencies of any business is to become inward-focused. It's also one of the most deadly. "Navel-gazing" may be all right for Zen students who want to tune out the world and become more connected with their inner, spiritual essence. But companies that spend too much time navel-gazing are so enamored with and fascinated by themselves—their brilliantly-designed processes, their wonderful corporate culture, their admirable history, their fabulous products and services—that they gradually lose sight of the *purpose* of it all: serving customers.

It's understandable that this should happen. As a company grows, an increasing degree of self-consciousness is necessary and important. Managers need to take time to reflect on how the company operates, to develop systems that are adaptive and flexible, and to massage the culture so that positive traits are encouraged and negative traits are squashed. All of this requires some self-analysis. A company that can't perform such inward-focused analysis is doomed to grow willy-nilly, ending up with structures that make little sense and often don't work.

Furthermore, with increasing size comes growing complexity, which inevitably requires rules, standardization, and internal systems of communication. When a company has 6 or 12 or even 50 employees, ideas, strategies, plans, and methods can be shared by osmosis. Get much bigger, and you need ways of making sure that everyone is in the loop and on the same page. Such dreaded phenomena as the weekly staff meeting, the company newsletter, the procedures manual, and even (horrors!) the Human Resources department all come into being. Software systems to organize and link the multiplying parts of the company become increasingly complicated and important. With these phenomena comes a staff of people—small at first, but growing over time—to create, administer, and maintain them.

Here is where the risk of navel-gazing arises. As soon as internal systems become important elements in your company's functioning, one or two or a handful of your people will get the mistaken impression that they are the *most* important elements. These people become "keepers of the systems," their primary function enforcing the rules: "You need four copies of that form, not three." "You missed the deadline by two hours." "We can't solve your customer's problem because our system won't permit it." "We can't fix that mistake and save a boatload of money because *that's not the way we do things around here!*"

Sometimes we try so hard to get people to drink the Kool-Aid that, after a while, all we want is Kool-Aid.

You've looked at the roles of the Process Master and the Linkmaker in changing the systems or, when necessary, working around them to get the *right* things done in the company. But an equally important role is played by someone I call the Scout. The *Scout* is the ignited manager who understands the power of the fourth Ignition Point— the Landscape.

The *Landscape* is the outside world in which our companies operate— a world of customers, suppliers, competitors, and countless individuals and organizations that impinge on our activities in one way or another. It's a complicated, ever-changing world that no one person can completely master—because as soon as he did, some part of it would have already begun to morph beyond recognition. The best companies devote an extraordinary amount of time and effort to studying the Landscape. Many others, however, get lost in navel-gazing, sometimes to the point where they actually forget about the needs of those people in the outside world that the company actually exists to serve.

This is where the Scout comes in. The Scout knows how to study the Landscape, measure its contours, track its changes, and look for the opportunities, resources, pathways, and openings it contains. The Scout knows and cares enough about internal systems, processes, and communication methods to be able to use them effectively. But he isn't *focused* on them, and he never forgets why they were invented in the first place—not for their own sake, but to enable the company to do a better job of serving the world at large.

The Scout's chief way of staying abreast of changes in the Landscape is by constant interaction with the two outside groups with whom most companies have the strongest and most important connections—their customers and their vendors.

These relationships offer companies an amazing amount of untapped power. And it's up to ignited managers to make it happen. In terms of sheer person-hours, the connections with customers and vendors are nurtured primarily by front-line employees—sales people, service reps, the production and staff people who use the goods and services vendors provide and make the calls when problems arise. But front-line employees aren't usually well-equipped to act as Scouts. For one thing, they're too busy just getting their routine tasks accomplished to devote significant time to monitoring the environment, drawing conclusions from what they observe, and putting those conclusions to work on behalf of the company. They also generally lack the birds-eye view of the business that's necessary to draw meaning out of discrete bits of data.

So the manager in The Middle has the responsibility—and the opportunity—of making sense of the Landscape by operating as a Scout: serving as the antenna of the company and making sure that the rest of the organization never loses sight of the real world as it shifts and reshapes around them.

Knowing Why They Buy: Understanding the Customer Landscape

As Peter Drucker, arguably the most insightful management guru in history, famously stated, "The purpose of business is to create and keep a customer." It's a brilliant definition because it avoids the question-begging that weakens most of the alternatives. Is the purpose of business (as some would have it) to earn a profit? That leaves unanswered the obvious and crucial question: How? Is the purpose of business to produce excellent goods and services? That doesn't explain why. Nor does it define that key word "excellent." Excellent in what way? For what purpose? Measured by whose standards?

By contrast, the Drucker definition puts the focus squarely where it belongs—on the customer, the key person in any business person's universe and the most dynamic force in the most important Landscape every Scout needs to study. The Drucker definition encompasses what's essential from other definitions of business. Thus, a business that succeeds in creating and keeping a customer will inevitably make a profit (because, by definition, a customer is someone who will pay a fair price for what you provide her). It will also produce excellent goods and services (because, otherwise, no customer will be willing to buy). Creating and keeping customers includes, by implication, everything a business does: production, service, sales, marketing, distribution, all centered on the customer and her needs.

Unfortunately, however, not every company operates in accordance with the Drucker definition. Many behave as if customers are a nuisance, a mystery, or, at best, an afterthought. Even companies that pride themselves on their excellent service betray their real attitudes toward customers in subtle but significant ways. For example, they trim the ranks of customer-facing workers first when the company belt needs tightening. Or they measure and give incentives to the employees in their call-in centers based on the speed with which they zoom through service calls, rather than on the skill and accuracy with which they solve customer problems.

It's up to managers in The Middle to keep the company's eye on the crucial role of the customer—to connect customers to the company and make sure those bonds remain strong. And this begins with *knowing* customers: talking with them, observing them, listening to their concerns, making their problems our own.

When it comes to customers, the Scout is in the know. He or she devotes time every day to understanding the customers and their environment in a way that adds value to their company. He or she meets them on their own turf, watches them buy and use the company's products and services, and talks with them about how competing companies differ from his own. Then the Scout shares knowledge with others in the company via internal white papers, reports, memos, presentations, Web pages, and plenty of elevator talk. And he introduces key customers to colleagues and counterparts in various divisions of the company, making sure that everyone in the firm has the opportunity to actually see and interact with that fabulous beast—the customer—who remains for all too many in business a quasi-mythical creature like the unicorn or the yeti.

The Scout as Educator

Brian Monahan is a vice president and communications director at Universal McCann, the global media planning and buying agency. He manages 25 employees who share a fascinating challenge—to manage sales of the new interactive media, such as online advertising, within an organization that is a powerhouse of traditional media (television, radio, newspapers, magazines, and the like).

This assignment is designed to test Brian's ability to serve as a Scout on behalf of his company. He and his team are literally pioneers, exploring a new media Landscape about which relatively few people in advertising are knowledgeable. Not only must Brian be effective at understanding how this Landscape is affecting the company's customers, but he must also find ways to communicate what he learns in a meaningful, compelling fashion to colleagues who lack his comfort level with the world of new media.

Brian usually does not bring customers and clients who are deeply involved in online marketing into meetings with his agency colleagues as an educational tool. "There's a pretty big cultural divide there, and I don't want to make anyone feel uncomfortable or self-conscious about what they do or don't know." Instead, Brian, as Scout, must find ways to communicate what he learns about the online world to his more traditionally-minded colleagues.

In part, the challenge is generational. "Top management is older," Brian explains. "That means we don't have shared experiences. The music, the movies, the TV shows, the economics, the politicians—everything they grew up with is different from the things my team members and I grew up with. So if we're going to communicate our insights about new media to them effectively, it takes openness on their part and clear explanation on our part."

In other cases, the gap between some of Brian's colleagues and the ultimate customers—the audiences that both Brian's agency and its clients are trying to reach—is based on lifestyles, interests, and values. Brian explains:

> Getting other people excited about a new idea can be hard if they don't live it themselves. One example is Fantasy Football. Our agency spends millions of dollars on TV spots that are run during NFL telecasts. I've been pushing to carve off just a small share of that to sponsor the AOL Fantasy Football program. But the reactions from different people here at the agency are all over the map. Upscale, techy males usually get it immediately. But others who think that Fantasy Football is for geeks don't get excited about it.

One way Brian translates what he discovers as a Scout into terms everyone can grasp is by using the universal language of numbers:

> To educate our older managers about the Internet and the interactive programs we can sponsor there, I tell them about the quantitative results some of our clients have obtained. It's all about customers and their success, which is easy for anyone to understand. For example, I've made case studies illustrating the business results some clients have enjoyed through search marketing on sites like Google. The numbers prove that it really works, which demonstrates that we need to get really good at this capability or some other company will get the business.

Brian also reaches out to colleagues in many departments at the agency, spreading his insights and ideas around in search of allies and supporters who can help convert potential into reality. For example, when working on a promotional deal with *The New York Times* aimed at marketing to the fans of the paper's world-famous daily crossword puzzle—a devoted, or as some would say, addicted audience—Brian quickly recognized its cross-disciplinary implications. "This is a concept that should be online but in the newspaper, too. That means I have to reach out to another group, tap another budget, and get a different set of people involved in reading and analyzing the data and developing the program."

In the end, the primary driving force that Brian and other Scouts rely on to help them spread their insights throughout their companies is the pressure exerted by evolving customer demands. When the Landscape is shifting in fundamental ways that the Scout is the first to recognize, the competitive equation also shifts in ways that may ultimately threaten a company's very survival.

In Brian's world, the shift is about the increasing difficulty his agency's advertising clients are experiencing in reaching their goals. "The drumbeat of client dissatisfaction with TV CPMs is steadily increasing," he notes. (*CPM*, or *cost per thousand impressions*, is the most common measure of the relative cost and effectiveness of various advertising media.) "This is forcing agencies to look for other ways to have an impact. So advertising and relationship marketing have become more aligned, and there's now a greater emphasis on global coordination. And online marketing plays a big role in all of it."

This, then, is what gives the Scout his ultimate authority—the all-important voice of the customer, which the Scout is positioned to hear and interpret on his company's behalf.

Making Customers into Partners

At their best, Scouts are able to forge such close relationships with customers that they turn into partners, helping to design and shape company strategies and programs for everyone's benefit. Here are some of the techniques managers in The Middle have developed to make this possible:

- *Continually tap the insights of your front-line team members.* Not every manager has everyday direct access to customers. If you are not client-facing, make it part of your daily routine to seek the latest customer information from those who are. This takes tact and skill, because not every sales rep or customer service agent knows how to communicate the nuances of client concerns. When seeking customer feedback through your front-line people, avoid yes-or-no questions, which often push respondents toward particular expected answers. Instead, ask open-ended questions that promote ongoing dialogue, and listen, always, for the "message behind the message"—the unspoken concerns that underlie customer dissatisfaction. For example, rather than asking, "Are customers mainly complaining about the price of our products," ask, "What are some of the main concerns you hear customers talking about?"

- *Look for opportunities to bring customers in-house.* Periodic customer forums, thank-you parties, or open houses can be a great way to give customers direct access to the people at your company. Make sure that the company representation extends beyond the usual suspects from Sales and Marketing. Encourage people from Production, Finance, R&D, Human Resources, and other departments to attend as well. There are bound to be some eye-opening exchanges whenever managers get face-to-face with the real, live customers who ultimately pay their salaries.

- *Invite customers to help design your products, services, and client-facing systems.* Don't rely solely on your product designers or IT professionals to solicit feedback on your company's offerings. Encourage people throughout the organization to involve a cross-section of customers whenever they are developing any new product or service that will affect them. You may be stunned to discover that some of the fancy bells and whistles your engineers are most proud of are irrelevant to customers' real needs— while simple, inexpensive features that no one in-house has considered could add enormously to your offerings' appeal.

- *Spend part of every week out in the "real world."* You can't know the Landscape unless you are immersed in it. This means continually refreshing your awareness of what is happening in the competitive arena from your customers' point of view. Do you produce a consumer product that's sold through retail outlets? Try to visit one new store every week, looking for what is unique and different about that particular set of customers and seeking new trends they may represent. Are you in a B2B (business-to-business) industry? Spend time each week with one of your customers, watching how he uses your product or service on the factory floor or in his office, noting the features that frustrate or delight him and observing the unsolved problems he is grappling with—which your company may be able to fix.

- *Cherish complaints.* Every letter, call, or e-mail with a gripe about your company is a gift—because each one represents an untold number of other people who share the same complaint but haven't bothered to express it. Rather than blow off complainers ("This dope doesn't even know how to use our product!") or soft-soap them ("Send her a few coupons—that'll shut her up"), take them seriously. Delve into *why* their experience with your company has been unsatisfactory and look for ways you can change your product, service, systems, or processes to eliminate the problem or (better yet) turn it into a source of pleasure for the customer. Then *tell* the complainer what you've done and why—a respectful gesture that in and of itself is likely to transform an unhappy camper into a fan and booster of your company.

- *Learn from people who are not your customers.* There's often more to learn from those who don't buy than from those who do. Don't dismiss them with lines like, "They just don't get it." Instead, study the options people choose when they don't choose you, and make an effort to get inside those choices. That's the only effective way to change them.

You may be surprised at the simple elegance of some of the discoveries you'll make. When AM/FM Radio hired a fancy consultant to find out what clients wanted, the facilitator who ran dozens of focus groups boiled down the results into these basic propositions:

1. Run my spots as ordered.

2. Bring me ideas.

3. Make me look good in front of my boss.

Most companies like to talk about their closeness to customers. Few really achieve it. Those that do have talented and persistent Scouts who devote a significant chunk of their time to simply being with customers and really *listening* to what they have to say.

Learning from Your Vendors

After customers, the second great constituent group that many companies neglect is vendors—those people and organizations that sell you goods and services.

Virtually every company relies on vendors to make its own operations possible. They include not just the companies that sell you goods you resell or parts and components that go into your products, but also the companies that provide services of every kind that keep you running, from accountants and lawyers and business consultants, to marketing, advertising, and public relations agencies, and from shipping and logistics companies to suppliers of office services, temporary help, and even the people who mop your floors and water your plants.

Vital as our vendor networks are, most companies have unevolved relationships with them, often adversarial and price-centered: "Can you give us a two percent better deal next year than last? If not, we'll be signing up with your competitor—thanks for the ten years of service, and don't let the door hit you on your way out." Some market-dominating firms, like Wal-Mart, are famous for their willingness to squeeze every last cent out of their vendor deals, using their size and clout to leverage price concessions that improve their own bottom lines while making their vendor relationships antagonistic at best.

There's no doubt that price is always important. But if you think about vendors purely in terms of beating them down on cost, you're missing the boat. Vendors have a different perspective on your business and how you do it. In many cases, they work with your competitors and have information about the market, about customers, and about emerging trends that could be disruptive to your company. The closer and more positive your vendor relationships are, the better your chances of learning some of this information early enough to use it for your benefit.

Am I talking about corporate espionage here? Not at all—you don't want to put your vendors in the awkward position of having to say no to a request for confidential or proprietary information about another customer of theirs. But your vendors have a unique and often valuable point of view about your company based on their experiences, and you have much to learn from listening to them.

The Scout sees vendors as a vital part of his or her network. Among other things, vendors can teach you

- How to save money by streamlining or eliminating complex processes.

- How to improve products or services by borrowing (and enhancing) ideas developed elsewhere.

- How to solve problems you face that other companies have grappled with.

- How to think differently about your own business (and avoid the "drinking our own Kool-Aid" syndrome).

- Where the most skilled and knowledgeable employees, consultants, and service providers can be found.

- About alternative sources for goods and services on which your company relies.

Some vendors create incredible value for their customers in ways that go far beyond the traditional customer-seller relationship. A shipping company like UPS can offer remarkable expertise in logistics, warehousing, and customer service developed through decades of experience serving thousands of companies in every industry around the world. An auto parts supplier like Johnson Controls provides its carmaker customers with invaluable insights into auto design trends based on its own intensive research into the habits, needs, and wishes of drivers and passengers. The best advertising agencies are sources of enormous volumes of data and insight into consumer behavior derived from their extensive research studies. If you don't take full advantage of these kinds of resources, you are wasting a large portion of the money your company spends with its vendors.

Bose and JIT II—A Manager in the Middle Transforms Vendor Relationships

One of the most famous examples of an innovative and hugely beneficial vendor relationship is the JIT ("Just-in-Time") II supply management system developed in the late 1980s at the Bose Corporation, the maker of high-end audio equipment. Almost 20 years later, JIT II is still considered a powerful model for tapping vendor expertise. Remarkably, this breakthrough program was launched and designed by a manager in The Middle, a director of purchasing and logistics for Bose named Lance Dixon.

In Dixon's own account, the idea for improving Bose's supply management program originated when he observed something dysfunctional in his role as Scout:

> The Bose JIT II approach to supplier relations began in 1987 when I happened to look out my office door and noticed a top-notch salesman for G&F Industries, an excellent manufacturer of plastic parts and related items and a major supplier to Bose Corporation, talking to one of our best buyers. And I realized what they were doing.

> The salesman wasn't selling. The buyer wasn't buying. These two highly paid people were talking about day-to-day orders—administering the relationship.

> And I thought, "That isn't right." Neither of them were operating at the high end of their skill set.[1]

To remedy the problem, Dixon developed a system whereby Bose's suppliers were brought in-house. JIT II would require that key suppliers station a full-time representative at Bose plants to monitor inventory levels and to manage the demand forecasting, ordering, and replenishment processes between the two companies. Dixon selected plastics and printing to be the first two commodity groups migrated to the new purchasing regime.

The planned introduction of JIT II wasn't without controversy. Letting an employee of your supplier walk unhindered around your plant, observing everything, and even reading your business documents, was unheard of. Some Bose executives thought that JIT II would make the company totally reliant on a few selected suppliers. It was uncertain how

---

[1] Lance Dixon, "JIT II: A New Approach to Supply Management." *Center for Quality of Management Journal,* Autumn 1992, page 15.

fair negotiations and prices could be guaranteed in an arrangement where the supplier had full access to confidential Bose information. Dixon himself wasn't sure how to make JIT II attractive to his selected vendors—after all, wasn't there a danger that the supplier representative stationed at Bose would become "captive" to the customer's interests?

Understandably, Dixon had a tough job convincing top management that his plan made sense. They had the traditional mentality regarding vendor relationships, which focused on squeezing suppliers on prices. But Dixon realized that the costs associated with managing suppliers, ordering, and warehousing parts—not to mention the losses incurred when Bose was out of stock on a vital component—far outweighed the cost savings Bose could reach through tough negotiations.

Dixon pushed ahead. The supplier representatives were brought into Bose's facility in Framingham, Massachusetts. They wore Bose badges, sat in on Bose meetings, and placed orders for the companies' products using Bose purchase orders. Basic purchases using standard parameters required no special approval; larger orders outside the conventional framework needed the signoff of a Bose purchasing supervisor.

Within five years, seven major suppliers were participating in JIT II. Bose reported savings of about $1 million a year on overhead alone. And with some key vendors, the new efficiencies were enormous. Dixon noted, "On parts from G&F Industries, moreover, the new system has allowed a reduction in inventories to one-seventh or even one-ninth the already low levels we had reached with our conventional Just-in-Time program."

Soon other companies, from IBM and AT&T to Honeywell, Motorola, and Johnson Wax were adapting JIT II for their own purposes. Current business trends, from increased outsourcing to the use of the Internet as a powerful communications medium, have only enhanced the usefulness of this now venerable program. For example, the Foxboro Company, a Massachusetts-based maker of automation systems, has worked with Sun Microsystems and Dell Computer to create customized Web sites that allow Foxboro and its suppliers to communicate globally in real time about their need for parts and components, current price points and specifications, and other data, all of it monitored and used by in-plant vendor representatives.

Close vendor relationships like those facilitated by the JIT II system don't just lead to increased efficiencies (valuable as these are). They also produce many other benefits:

- When a new product is being designed, on-site vendor reps can participate in the discussions, offering ideas for the use of cost-saving standard parts adapted for the new purpose.

- Vendor reps can alert their home companies in advance about new components that may be needed, permitting time-saving "concurrent engineering" of new product designs.

- When the transition from drawing board to manufacturing plant is under way, the vendor rep can anticipate problems related to the handling of parts on the assembly line and solve them in advance.

- When a vendor firm anticipates supply shortages or heavier-than-normal demand for a key part, the on-site rep can warn the host company and make sure that adequate supplies are available.

- Quality control and consistency problems related to parts and components can be fixed much more quickly and easily.

JIT II is a brilliant example of how strong vendor connections can enable a Scout to vastly improve the intelligence level of his company, facilitating smarter, faster decisions and saving time, money, and energy. But you don't have to go the JIT II route to enjoy many of these benefits. Just working hard to create and maintain close, positive relationships with vendors and constantly monitoring the ever-changing Landscape in which they operate can yield most of the same results. These results are a lot more meaningful than the savings you can enjoy simply by beating up your suppliers when it comes time to negotiate the next contract.

Using the Internet to Scan and Master Your Landscape

As you've seen, the Scout adds value to the company by the breadth, depth, and currency of her knowledge of the Landscape in which the company operates—in particular, the competitive arenas where customers and vendors live and work.

At one time, Scouts gathered their knowledge of the Landscape primarily through personal, often face-to-face communication—breakfasts, lunches, phone conversations, and general "schmoozing." All of these are still important. So are the traditional media of mass communication—trade journals, business magazines, newspapers, and television and radio broadcasts that focus on business trends. But today, the Internet has taken on enormous importance for the savvy Scout.

While always a brilliant research tool, an explosion of user-generated content on the Internet now available in blogs, social networks, and video sharing takes us to the front lines where we can listen, learn, and interact with consumers directly.

Blogs, originally known as weblogs, have inspired a whole new breed of citizen journalist, given platforms to new stars such as celebrity gossiper Perez Hilton and given us guides in the form of BoingBoing.com, specializing in wonderful things, or Techcrunch, a site profiling Internet companies and products.

Social networks such as MySpace and Facebook have allowed people to connect with friends, and the friends of their friends, to share their passions as well as likes and dislikes. In social networks, users join groups around their interests. These interest groups might give you insight into a particular market, such as the couple hundred who joined the "Once I start itching my eye I can't stop" group, or you may actually find your own brand being discussed. A quick search revealed dozens of groups mentioning Nordstrom's, groups for employees and customers. One group in particular shares their passion for Nordstrom's branded salad dressing.

Video networks such as YouTube, Metacafe, and Break.com have given filmmakers, speechmakers, and aspiring tastemakers a place to share their polished productions or webcam videos. Humor plays a big a role, but so does education. You can learn how to pay for one Coke but get three from a vending machine—something the vending guy needs to see right away—or you can also learn how to run your iPod from a 9-volt battery. The opportunities to see your consumers in action with your brand or talking about your industry seem endless. A quick search under customer service featured recorded customer service calls from Apple and AOL. None too complimentary. The consumer is now empowered and driving the conversation that ultimately defines what a brand is and how you, in your job, should be serving them.

All of this threatens the old and traditional rules of corporate communication, which focus on a consistent message and a spin that's approved at the top and pushed down and out. You've probably encountered the slightly paranoid approach that many traditional companies take toward public communications: "It's a reporter on the line? Call our P.R. guy—no, make that our lawyer—and whatever you do, *don't say anything!*" When this is the prevalent attitude, the wide-open atmosphere of the blogosphere is understandably frightening.

Occasional horror stories about consumer-driven blogs reinforce the anxiety. In September 2004, a maker of bicycle locks named Kryptonite was blindsided by a series of postings on blogs frequented by bike lovers that claimed certain models of Kryptonite locks were vulnerable to picking simply by using a plastic pen. Initially disregarding the furor ("It's just a few techies, so no big deal"), Kryptonite soon found its products being pulled off the shelves of bike stores and its sales plummeting.

The company has since recovered, introducing a new line of locks with the design flaw remedied. And they have also made monitoring of the blogosphere—and participation in blog forums about biking—a regular part of their public-outreach efforts. Other companies who worry about being hit by a similar nightmare ought to adopt the same policy.

There's no doubt that getting involved in blogging requires a mindset adjustment. When a company allows or even encourages its employees to create blogs about their products, services, or industry, it is saying, "We trust you and your judgment enough to give you freedom. We believe that, in the long run, all of us—employees, customers, and the company itself—will benefit from open communication."

This is a confusing time for many companies, and it no doubt feels a bit like the Wild West. That said, burying your head in the sand is no answer to the growing power of user-generated content and online communities.

With over 50 million active blogs, 100 million registered users at MySpace, and over 100 million videos viewed each day on Youtube.com alone, we're in for a new world of communication and a new way for you to gain competitive advantage. If you're just beginning to explore this, here are some ideas to help you become more deeply engaged:

- *Find existing blogs that are relevant to your company and industry, and visit them often.* It's a virtual certainty that there are already blogs focused on your business—and perhaps even on your company. A topical search via Technorati, a search engine dedicated to the blogosphere, or your favorite search engine will uncover a few; each blog you find will lead you to others via embedded links, which virtually every blog has in abundance. Bookmark the most lively blogs you find, keep adding to the list, and visit them often. If you've begun to explore RSS (really simple syndication) and have an RSS reader set up, you can subscribe to multiple blogs and have them aggregated into one destination for viewing. Regardless of how you organize your blogs, you'll learn a lot about what people are saying about your industry and your company—including, at times, valuable inside information about your competitors.

- *Consider participating in blogs, including those aimed at your customers and vendors.* Smart businesses are using blogs as a way of talking with people who matter to them. Within your industry, there are probably a couple of companies blogging and dozens of individuals blogging on even the most seemingly minor issues. When you have something interesting, relevant, and honest to say about a topic that is under discussion on one of these blogs, log in and comment about it. If you see a partner of yours disparaged in a blog, and you can speak up in support of them, consider doing so. You'll be representing your business, reaching out to customers, and responding to their needs and concerns—all vital parts of your role as a Scout for your company. However, before you do any of this, find out what the policies are at your company and either follow their guidelines or begin using your influence as an ignited manager to educate those around you and raise your company's dialogue with consumers.

- *Consider launching your own public blog as a company representative.* A company-authorized blog can be a useful public relations tool—a forum for customer questions, a bulletin board for news of interest, an exchange for new ideas about how to use your products and services. Microsoft has several hundred bloggers sharing their work and collectively humanizing their company's corporate image. But be aware that it takes time to maintain a good blog. If you hope to attract regular visitors, you need to create fresh content at least once per week. So don't get involved in blogging unless you're comfortable with that kind of commitment. When it comes to technology, companies like Google's Blogger.com make setting up a blog pretty easy.

- *Join a social network.* We've talked about linkedin.com and that's a no-brainer for business neworking, but Facebook, My Space, and other social networks have the groups, and the groups are where you'll find consumers connecting and sharing their thoughts. As a member you can join these groups and even start groups. Keep in mind, however, that the spirit in these communities is just like that of the Internet—open, sharing, and free from commercialization within public forums. Sure, the last point gets violated often, but it's also among the greatest complaints of the user base as zealous bands and side-show hucksters over-promote their wares to the wary. Instead, join a community where you've got something to contribute. According to my friends in this business, the best model for community interaction is to seed the discussion with interesting ideas and contributions, listen intently as the conversation evolves, and then demonstrate your listening by responding with ideas crafted from their input.

- *Register at a Video Network.* With registration you'll gain the ability to tag the videos of interest and collect them for later viewing. You can also rate the videos, share them with friends, and contact the creators. After the Coke/Mentos videos that dazzled us all and generated millions of viewings, Coke reached out to the creators, Fritz Grobe and Stephen Voltz of eepybird.com, and partnered for the EepyBird Challenge. Your brand may be lucky enough to have a community of users who find great pleasure shooting your product into the air or you may have to take it upon yourself to create your own videos to demonstrate, in a less dramatic way I'd imagine, how to use and enjoy what you sell. Regardless, these video sites empower the sharing and the sizes of their audiences make their role going forward undeniable.

- *Think through your message before you hit the Enter button.* Digital communication is notoriously *easy*. It takes just a few seconds to type a message and send it wheeling through cyberspace where anyone can read it. Before you commit yourself, force yourself to think carefully about what you want to say, how you want to say it, and whether you want to publicly acknowledge the message as a representative of your firm. If in doubt, hold back! You can always revisit the idea in a few hours or tomorrow morning and send out the message if it still makes sense to you.

Of course, as savvy web users and multitaskers, you're probably surfing the web to explore some of this now. However... know that we've got you covered as well with a list of Internet resources at www.BeIgnited.com.

Today, blogs are among the hottest and most rapidly-evolving forms of communication in the world. Tomorrow, there will undoubtedly be some new way of tracking people's changing attitudes, interests, and ideas, perhaps using some technology we can only speculate about today. Whatever it is, the Scout will be among the first to discover it and develop its full potential for the benefit of the business, as well as his or her own career.

10

IGNITION POINT 5:
THE STRATEGY

The Problem with Strategy

Strategy is one of those big concepts that people in business feel obliged to pay homage to. In part, it's a matter of hierarchy and power. Corporations today pay millions to the men and women in their very top echelons, the folks who breathe the rarefied air of the C-suite. And what exactly do they do to earn those big bucks? Their central focus is usually the overall direction of the firm—in other words, its strategy.

But the truth about strategy is that strategy is often more pull than push. Traditional strategy is shaped in the boardroom, but real strategy—often called *emergent strategy*—takes shape on the street. You open a cafe decorated with gorgeous art and find that your customers would rather pull their chairs outside to eat. Traditional strategy gets you to first base. Emergent strategy gets you to home plate.

Experience shows that top-down strategy has an inherent weakness: It tends to be divorced from the realities on the ground. The same kinds of problems arise in every field of human activity—just ask any historian who has studied the missteps of "the best and brightest" when they crafted top-down strategy for the American war in Vietnam... or our more recent struggles in Iraq.

The problems with traditional strategic planning are incredibly costly. Author and consultant Laurence Haughton reports that the average big company spends as much as 25,000 person-days on planning for every billion dollars in sales. This amounts to $1.2 billion dollars' worth of planning at a company like Ford.[1] "Yet the extraordinary reality is that few executives think this time consuming process pays off," conclude authors Eric Beinhocker and Sarah Kaplan. One executive comments, "[It's] like some primitive tribal ritual. There is a lot of dancing, waving of feathers and beating of drums. No one is exactly sure why we do it, but there is an almost mystical hope that something good will come out of it."[2]

The Power of the Pilot

Strategic planning, then, often occurs in an abstract vacuum, where a hands-on knowledge of the company's real-world challenges and opportunities is absent.

That's the bad news. The good news is that, at many companies, great strategies get developed and implemented anyway—even when they are not handed down from the mountaintop. Instead, they take shape in response to ground-level market conditions and are implemented by managers in The Middle. When the behavior of customers, competitors, vendors, regulators, and other players in the arena make the company's "official" strategy ineffective, these managers make mid-course corrections on the fly. They modify product and service offerings, improvise new marketing and sales techniques, assemble task forces to respond to unexpected challenges, speed up or slow down or cancel long-planned initiatives, and quietly shelve the cherished programs of the top brass in favor of projects suggested by their people in the front lines.

Often, when the dust settles and the financial results are tallied, it is the *ad hoc* tactics developed by the managers in The Middle rather than the grand strategies of the central planners that spell the difference between loss and profit in any given year. And often those *ad hoc* tactics become the basis for the following year's corporate strategy—if the leaders in the C-suite are smart enough to recognize the value of the strategic

---

[1] J. Hope and R. Fraser, Who Needs Budgets. Cited in Haughton, 2005.
[2] E. Beinhocker and S. Kaplan, "Tired of Strategic Planning?" *The McKinsey Quarterly*, cited by Haughton.

thinking that's going on in their company's field offices, factories, warehouses, showrooms, and departmental meeting rooms.

Management experts have long recognized this paradoxical reality about business and the importance of emergent strategy. Here's how one of today's leading strategy thinkers describes it:

> Henry Mintzberg, author of the classic management text *The Rise and Fall of Strategic Planning,* has studied what really happens under the guide of strategic development. His findings are eye-opening. . . .[F]ully 90 percent of the results projected in most companies' formal strategic planning processes never come to fruition. Instead, they fall by the wayside, vanishing into the limbo of "unrealized strategy." ...
>
> But what is the source of the other 90 percent of what companies do? Mintzberg calls it "emergent strategy." This describes the series of ad-hoc initiatives, reactions, decisions, and choices that managers make in response to daily pressures, without guidance from any overarching strategic concept. Taken together, they amount to the *real* strategy that most companies follow.[3]

Here, then, is the strategic role of managers in the middle—not simply to execute the strategy dictated by the top executives of the firm, but to supplement it with creative ideas, initiatives, and inventions of their own, driven by their first-hand knowledge of developments in the competitive arena, their own capabilities, and the openings for profit they perceive. The manager who understands this challenge and rises to meet it is what we call a Pilot—someone who spots the pathway of opportunity and steers the company (or the part of the company he controls) in that direction.

The Pilot is the maker of emergent strategy and therefore, in a profound sense, a shaper of the company's destiny. He is, then, the progenitor and champion of the fifth Touchstone—the *real* Strategy that actually drives the future revenues, profit, and growth of his firm.

The Pilot can:

- Identify new competitive threats in the market, measure their strengths and weaknesses, and test responses

---

[3] Willie Pietersen, *Reinventing Strategy.* New York: John Wiley & Sons, 2002, pages 44-45.

- Recognize new trends among customers, vendors, and other players and experiment with ways to turn those trends into opportunities

- Spot process innovations or creative concepts developed by front-line workers, recognize their broader potential, and help disseminate them throughout the company

- Launch small-scale programs around new products, services, marketing methods, inter-company partnerships, and other initiatives

- Change the entire course of a company by creating a strategic breakthrough

As an ignited manager, you need to spend some part of every week focusing on your role as Pilot, looking for threatening shoals and promising open sea lanes, and working to steer your company away from the former and toward the latter.

Updating a Legacy for the Twenty-First Century

One of the most fascinating strategic challenges that is shared by many incumbent firms is figuring out how to update a rich corporate legacy, transforming what might be a dead weight of tradition and history into a powerful competitive advantage for today's marketplace. It's a challenge that is being conquered by one of America's most historic businesses, the Rawlings Sporting Goods company, by using its century of experience and expertise in crafting high-quality gear for baseball and other sports as the basis for a set of valuable tools for twenty-first century athletes. And the process was launched not by a strategic planning department or an outside consultant, but by an ignited manager named Andy Pawlowski, who saw the potential for a powerful emergent strategy and ran with it.

Andy joined Rawlings in 2002 in the role of promotions manager, charged with running the company's co-op marketing programs and dealing with the outside firm that managed the Rawlings Web site. Just 26 years old with a freshly-minted MBA, Andy was a bit of a maverick in the Rawlings culture. Founded in 1887, the St. Louis-based firm was dominated by male ex-jocks in their forties who loved sports and were deeply passionate about the Rawlings gloves, bats, and other gear they remembered from their own playing days. For them, the Rawlings tradition of excellence was close to perfect and needed no updating or improvement.

Andy shared his colleagues' appreciation for Rawlings' history. He was impressed by the stories he heard about the company's contributions to sports—for example, the fact that almost all of the performance features that baseball players take for granted in their gloves, from leather fingers to padding to the webbing used to snare balls, were originated by craftsmen at Rawlings. But he also sensed that the company needed a fresh approach to compete in the twenty-first century. Companies like Nike had entered the baseball marketplace, bringing with them a hip brand image and innovative product designs. Rawlings needed a new strategy if it was to remain relevant to new generations of athletes and retain its market leadership. But where to begin?

Market research gave Andy the insight he needed. A survey revealed that nearly three quarters of customers planning to buy new equipment for baseball or softball conducted online research before shopping. The Internet, then, could be the key leverage point for building a new Rawlings image, one that made the company's unmatched heritage into a valuable component of its selling proposition.

Andy spent months working with colleagues from throughout the company to develop a unique array of content and online tools for the Rawlings Web site. He researched the company's history for a remarkable survey of baseball gloves from 1906 to today, highlighting the contributions made by Rawlings to the improvement of sports equipment and of the game itself. Technical experts created Web pages designed to answer every conceivable question about baseball gloves, such as an explanation of the thirteen different kinds of webbing design and the advantages of each. And Andy worked with Rawlings' product and R&D teams to develop an interactive tool to help customers choose the perfect glove for themselves or for a child, based on a series of questions about age, gender, position played, "feel" desired, budget, and other factors.

Most impressive of all, if the tool doesn't return a solution for the consumer, it allows them to e-mail a member of the Rawlings design team to describe a unique need not currently met by the company's product line. "On several occasions, we've modified our production plans to manufacture a new kind of glove to meet a demand we didn't know existed," Andy says. "For example, until we were alerted by e-mail requests, we didn't realize that there was a market for left-handed, youth-sized, fast-pitch softball gloves. Now we're making and selling them. At how many market-leading companies can you contact a technical expert via e-mail and not only receive a prompt response, but also actually get a new product made to your specifications?"

The innovations have won acclaim in the industry. Rawlings' retail partners report that customers are visiting their stores armed with accurate information and product specs, and are excited about buying the new glove or bat they've researched online. Some observers are shocked to find such cutting-edge technology coming from a company they'd long viewed as tradition-bound. A buyer at one major retailer told Andy, "Frankly, I would have expected this kind of leadership from Nike or Adidas—not Rawlings." But, as Andy points out, neither Nike nor Adidas nor any other sporting goods company could have created a Web site like Rawlings', because no other company has the depth of history or technical expertise required.

Since being promoted to brand director, Andy has driven his emergent branding strategy into other marketing areas as well. For example, there's a new partnership with Electronic Arts, the leading sports-themed video game company, which not only features Rawlings products in its new college baseball game, but actually integrates them into the competition. Players can win virtual Rawlings gear as they play the game, and when they use their new gloves and bats, their fielding and hitting actually improves—a subtle but powerful validation and reinforcement of the great Rawlings brand.

Partly as a result of Andy's innovations, the venerable Rawlings name is now being perceived as cool by a whole new generation of sports enthusiasts. And in 2005, Rawlings' sales grew significantly—no mean feat in a flat overall market.

Andy Pawlowski's creative role in reshaping Rawlings' image illustrates the positive impact that Middleshift managers can have on their companies' strategy. And you don't have to wait until your boss invites you to join the strategic planning team. All you need is a great idea and the willingness to make it happen.

Being Cassandra

Championing emergent strategy sometimes means bucking your company's establishment—which, naturally, has vowed allegiance to the top-down strategy formulated by the company's highest leaders. Sometimes this puts you in the awkward position of having to emphasize what's *wrong* with the company line—for the greater long-term good of the company, of course.

In the classic management memoir *Only the Paranoid Survive* by Intel's legendary CEO Andy Grove, he talks about the Cassandras in every organization. In Greek mythology, Cassandra was the Trojan seer who uttered truthful prophecies—including warnings of danger—which were never believed. In business, a Cassandra is a bearer of bad tidings—someone within your company who warns you of an imminent threat, such as a dangerous new rival, a disruptive technological innovation, a shift in customer preferences, or a growing internal weakness.

In most companies, Cassandras get short shrift. They're called "pessimists" or "naysayers" or "doom-and-gloom types" and they're told to "cut out the negative thinking." But Andy Grove learned to listen to Intel's Cassandras:

> Although they can come from anywhere in the company, Cassandras are usually in middle management; often they work in the sales organization. They usually know more about upcoming change than the senior management because they spend so much time "outdoors" where the winds of the real world blow in their faces....
>
> Because they are on the front lines of the company, the Cassandras also feel more vulnerable to danger than do senior managers in their more or less bolstered corporate headquarters. Bad news has a much more immediate impact on them personally. Lost sales affect a salesperson's commission, technology that never makes it to the marketplace disrupts an

engineer's career. Therefore they take the warning signs more seriously.[4]

One of Intel's Cassandras warned Grove in the early 1980s about the need to move the company from manufacturing memory-chips to focusing on microprocessors. It was a radical move that many in the industry questioned. But this shift positioned Intel to benefit enormously when the personal computer business boomed over the following decade.

As a Pilot, there may be times when you can't personally bring about the strategic change your company needs to make. The necessary shift may be too large-scale, too costly, or too dramatic for a manager in The Middle to undertake alone. When this happens, your responsibility is to be a Cassandra—a messenger bringing prophetic insight to those who need to hear it. Other times, your job is to *listen* to the Cassandras around you—those who work on your team, or those who come to you because they can't get a hearing elsewhere. Sometimes the worry-warts will be wrong. But the times when they are right may affect your company's fate for decades to come. Better be sure before you choose to ignore them.

Nobody likes to hear bad news. When you play Cassandra, it's important to be prepared with plenty of hard facts to support your argument about the need for strategic change—sales figures, financial estimates, demographic data, whatever. And unlike the original Cassandra, don't just offer the downside; suggest a positive response your company can make to transform the danger into opportunity. If appropriate, offer to launch a pilot program to test your idea. Make it clear that you are ready to do what you can, personally, to solve the problem you've identified.

Even so, don't expect to be welcomed with open arms. A Cassandra should expect resistance. If you're sure you're right, be persistent. And if and when your prophecy is proven right, resist the temptation to gloat. But *do* find ways to claim credit for your prognostication, and use your new-found credibility to gain a hearing for your ideas as to what the company ought to do next. You will have earned that much.

---

4 Andrew Grove, *Only the Paranoid Survive.* New York: Doubleday, 1999, pages 108-109.

Making the Pieces Fit: The Manager in The Middle as Strategic Linchpin

You may never have heard of InterVarsity Christian Fellowship. Because it operates in the religious non-profit sphere, it flies under the radar of many business people. Yet it's a large, complex organization with a challenging mission and a management structure that gives managers in The Middle an enormously powerful—and difficult—role to play in juggling a range of concerns in service to an overall strategy that is only broadly defined at the executive level.

InterVarsity Christian Fellowship/USA is an evangelical campus ministry serving more than 32,000 students and faculty on more than 560 college and university campuses nationwide. (Think of those students and faculty as the "customers" of InterVarsity.) Incorporated in 1941 and headquartered in Madison, Wisconsin, InterVarsity is part of a global movement currently active in some fourteen countries, as well as 48 of the United States, with some 1,200 employees in the U.S. One of them is Greg Jao.

The complexities of Greg's job begin with the fact that he isn't purely a manager. He estimates that he spends about one quarter of his time as an individual contributor, helping to develop campus ministries at specific colleges, speaking at conferences and meetings, writing program outlines, and so on. The rest of his energy is devoted to managing front-line managers, a job he's been learning to do by doing it.

Like many organizations, InterVarsity has a complicated management structure. "InterVarsity exists at three levels simultaneously," Greg explains:

> At one level, we're a 501(c)3 organization [the specific not-for-profit designation that covers this group in the federal tax code] with twelve hundred employees, a seventy-two-million-dollar budget, and all the legal and financial and managerial requirements that any corporation that size would have. And those are the issues our national staff has to deal with—things like human resources, insurance, staff training, headquarters operations, and so on.

At another level, we're a movement of God among students and faculties at universities. At this level, InterVarsity is really thirty-three thousand students, fourteen hundred faculty members, and the activities and ministries they're all involved in. That's the work our front-line people are focused on.

And in the middle is where managers like me operate. At this level, we're a community of staff and colleagues, working together and supporting one another. Our job is figuring out how all the levels intersect so that the organization attains its goals, serves the people we're here to serve, and grows and maintains itself in a strong, stable way.

The challenges, of course, arise when the interests of the three levels of the organization come into conflict. Sometimes the needs of students on campuses clash with the needs of InterVarsity's management—for example, when a beloved organizer of campus ministries and community life gets pulled off the front lines to join the headquarters staff or a managerial team at the middle level. On the other hand, sometimes the sales staff may have to forgo a desired benefit because of a conflict in funding priorities, with the student work getting higher billing than internal needs. And on still other occasions, initiatives that would serve both the front-line staff and the campus operations may be vetoed because of issues at the headquarters level, such as insurance, risk management, or national budgetary concerns that, beyond a certain point, become unbudgeable.

These kinds of conflicts aren't unique to InterVarsity—instead, they're commonplace in any national or global organization. Greg sees managing them as the heart of his role as Pilot: "Middle management," he says, "is where those realities intersect the most. And what makes one middle manager successful while another is unsuccessful is the ability to negotiate them successfully."

Greg points out that all three levels need to be outwardly focused, consciously working to coordinate their goals and efforts:

To the extent that any group inside the organization refuses to own all three realities, we tend to get ourselves in trouble. For example, whenever a particular state or local unit gets too self-absorbed and starts saying, "Forget about what's happening nationally, we're just going to focus on this exciting project we've got going," inevitably they run astray and get into trouble. Whenever the national movement gets a little too obsessed with risk management or organizational requirements, then the entire system starts to seize up.

And when managers in the middle get too focused on themselves, then the work suffers. Sometimes you hear a manager saying, "I'm primarily in this because I've got such a great team of people to work with." That's a warning sign. When people are too concerned with enjoying one another, they often stop producing the work that's needed and serving the people we're here to minister to.

For Greg Jao, then, the job of the manager in The Middle is to fit the broad concerns of top management into a coherent whole together with the specific tactical objectives of individual campus ministries as well as the organizational interests of staffers and managers in between the two. Only if this juggling act is successful can the organization's overall strategy be carried out effectively at the grass-roots level. "The successful middle manager," he says, "can understand the unique concerns of all three realities, figure out how to integrate them, and help people align their interests together."

Without managers in The Middle playing this vital connecting role, top-level strategy is nothing but a collection of papers gathering dust on the shelves back at headquarters.

Luckily for Greg Jao, InterVarsity's top leaders recognize this reality. (Not all corporate chieftains do.) Greg observes:

> If you were to ask our people at the CEO or the vice-presidential level, "Do you feel like you're running things here?" they would say, "Only barely." They know that the vast majority of the work is what happens on campus and that almost all of the initiative has to come from there.
>
> In fact, when I was talking to one of our vice presidents several years ago, he said, "You know, I've found I can get one issue, one

idea, one mandate across each year. And that one is the only chance I'll get during the year to make any real change in the organization. So that means if I don't choose my one issue carefully, I can blow an entire year really quickly."

That's an unusually astute observation by a top executive. Creating major movement in any big organization is terribly hard. One such movement per year is a lot to accomplish. It means that life at the C-suite level can be pretty frustrating. But it also means that ignited managers have an extra responsibility. They're the ones who, as company Pilots, have to launch and shepherd all the dozens or hundreds of *little* changes that make up a company's total strategy and that determine whether a given year will be a roaring success or a dismal failure.

Creating Business in the White Space

Paraag Lal is a Strategic Relations Manager for the media, entertainment, and hospitality industry at a Fortune 500 technology company. Paraag has found a successful niche for himself driving strategic change from his mid-level position by finding and pursuing business opportunities in what many at his firm call *white space.*

The concept of white space originated during a time when his firm was financially and strategically challenged. It was clear that business as usual would not be enough to revive the company—innovative thinking would be required to find new business opportunities, expand markets, develop new uses for products, and increase revenue from existing customers. Therefore, while his company continued to assign specific, clearly defined areas of responsibility to individual managers and staffers, the company also created a new, deliberately *undefined* responsibility—the "something more" needed to propel them into a more successful future. This is white space—"Undefined stuff," in Paraag's words, "and it's our responsibility to define it."

How does white space fit into Paraag's traditional job description? Here's his explanation:

> My first responsibility is to meet with my customers in the hospitality and entertainment sectors to ensure they are using our

products and solutions, as opposed to the competition's. That's a requirement for any sales job. It's also, frankly, the basic responsibility of the job. It's about hardware and it's talking chips, bits, and bites. White space is something else. It's about understanding our customers' industry even better than the customers themselves, to enable us to add new value.

Paraag is the first to admit that understanding the customers' industry better than they do is a tall order—"Our customers live it day in and day out," he says. "But we try to become experts in the industries we serve, and that's how we find and go after the white space."

As an example, let's look at the hospitality industry—the business of managing hotels. Why would a hotel chain want to talk to a company that manufactures computer chips and processors? Paraag and his team came up with an answer:

> When we studied the hospitality industry, we learned that their success is determined by the number of heads in beds, which in turn drives revenues and profits. Then we asked, what can we do to promote this goal? What can we offer that would attract customers to a specific hotel chain and help in their goal of retaining customers and increasing profits?

> We realized that one way we could provide hotel customers added value was wireless connectivity. Business travelers and even vacationers want to be able to surf the Internet and read their email from anywhere in the hotel—not only in their own rooms, but also in the lobby, the pool, or the restaurant. Therefore, three years ago, we launched a major initiative around installing wireless hot spots in public areas, coffee shops, and the top two US hotel chains. As a result, hotel guests will have more freedom and be more apt to choose our client's hotel chain over another.

> That's a perfect example of a white space initiative. We found a way to create new value for hotel customers, while enhancing revenues and profits for our client, and our own firm. It's not just doing the same old business better; it's creating a new business.

One white-space project has a way of leading to others. Since the success of this wireless initiative, many of Paraag's other corporate clients have installed wireless service for their customers.

Paraag's other big industry space is entertainment. Here he is pursuing a different white-space initiative, another one he believes has home run potential. But it started, as so many opportunities do, with a problem:

> Five years ago, our company was paying minimal attention to the media and entertainment business. Although the potential for increasing our presence in entertainment was evident, getting attention paid to the opportunity was very tough in the early years—as the initial revenue opportunity appeared small when compared to other industries, such as healthcare and financial services.

The firm's focus on media and entertainment was finally galvanized by a shock to the system—a painful business loss that was actually covered in the media and entertainment press. One of Paraag's customers, a large movie studio, decided to partner with a competitor for its digital technology. "It was a wake-up call," Paraag admits. "While I wish we had not lost this key account, the loss did bring about positive change to our organization."

Beyond providing standard data center products and solutions, the key opportunity for the firm in the newly burgeoning digital entertainment business became the ability to provide technology that allowed ease of content production and distribution, ultimately leading to the same-day distribution of film to both theaters and direct to consumers. Hitting this home run requires putting several solutions in place, including a new digital media device for the home in addition to developing trusting relationships with the studios and leading content providers. This is where Paraag's role as Pilot is crucial:

> I think what we bring to the table is relationships, especially in the digital media and entertainment space, where your Rolodex is your gold mine.

> Next is an understanding of the economics and business models of the industry and the ability to decifer where technology can be applied to create success. We're now in the process of

trying to establish an important role for our firm throughout the production pipeline, from development to distribution. In the past, our products were primarily relevant in the post-production process—editing and rendering. Now the level of conversation revolves around an end-to-end digital pipeline that has huge value for producers and opens up new ways to reach the consumer.

Paraag has become deeply immersed in the possibilities of this new initiative. When we interviewed him, he was working with a producer shooting a film in Prague in the Czech Republic. Thanks to his firm's technology, sharing the dailies (footage from one day's shooting) with his partner in the States no longer requires courier service via air. Instead, the producer is sending the footage directly from the set via the Internet using a wireless-enabled laptop. At the time of this interview, it was a movie-industry first—"and it'll save them a fortune," Paraag reports.

It's clear that managers in The Middle, like Paraag, are doing more than just selling their firm's products. He's creating new strategies for his company, developing entirely new lines of business, opening up new markets, and shifting the perception of his firm from being a high-tech company of interest only to IT departments, programmers, and manufacturers to being a digital company whose unique creative capabilities can empower those in many walks of life. This is emergent strategy at its best.

It's easy to see that Paraag is energized by this way of doing business. The new streams of revenue and profit he is creating for his company are winning him notice as a rising star in the industry. And he loves the relationships he is forging with people throughout the worlds of entertainment and hospitality, which will serve him in good stead in his future career, whether he stays with his firm or moves on to another company. "White space," he says, "is about fulfilling my company's goals and objectives as well as my own."

Creating Your Own Strategic Space

His firm's "white space" philosophy gives managers like Paraag plenty of room to follow strategic opportunities wherever they appear. That's not the case at every company. Many managers in The Middle feel they are so hemmed in by job descriptions and the demands of their stakeholders that they probably wouldn't even recognize an emergent strategy, let alone have time and energy to pursue it.

However, smart managers can find ways to overcome these obstacles. In their article "The Trap of Overwhelming Demands," authors Heike Bruch and Sumantra Ghoshal tell the story of Thomas Sattelberger, a human resources manager at Lufthansa who somehow—despite the usual array of horrific day-to-day business challenges—managed to realize his personal dream by creating the first corporate university in Germany.[5]

Circumstances were far from ideal for such an ambitious concept. Sattelberger describes joining Lufthansa: "I thought that I would enter an intact HR department and would have wonderful conditions to start building the pillars of the temple that would become the corporate university.... What I actually found was a complete mess."

He spent two years cleaning up his dysfunctional department, reorganizing inefficient systems, speeding up the response time to employee queries (which had stretched out to as much as six months), and even correcting typing errors in contracts. It was an arduous task that took nearly all of his time, forcing him to delay implementation of the bigger opportunity he saw—Lufthansa University. But he knew that doing a superlative job at fixing the problems was an essential first step:

> "I cleaned the pigpen," he recalls. "Nobody anticipated that I would cope with these draining issues. They were obviously surprised, and that was the moment for me to suggest new standards and new ideas. I wanted to transform the HR role and transfer it to a level that was higher than what they had ever imagined. It was a true innovation because no other company in Germany had such comprehensive business-driven HR processes." Had he instead tried to present his ideas before doing the dirty work—and gaining management's appreciation—no one would have accepted his ideas. As it was,

[5] Heike Bruch and Sumantra Ghoshal, "The Trap of Overwhelming Demands." *Harvard Business School Working Knowledge*, May 17, 2004. Online at http://hbswk.hbs.edu/item.jhtml?id=4128&t=career_effectiveness&noseek=one.

Sattelberger's bosses began to see and treat him as the expert and believed in his commitment to create something really special. "I demonstrated to them that I would develop a means to support their business strategy, developing corporate entrepreneurship in a former state-owned company and maintaining change momentum after the crisis had eased off," Sattelberger said. "I addressed their concerns and showed them how we could jointly create new ways of solving their problems."

Thus, the first thing Sattelberger had to do to win permission to step outside the box of his job was to exceed expectations *inside* the box. Fixing the HR systems, of course, also benefited Sattelberger by gradually freeing up his time to pursue his long-range goal; after all, the less time he and his staff members had to spend tracking down misfiled papers or placating angry employees, the more time they could devote to planning the university.

Sattelberger also maintained his own motivation by squeezing out time for his strategic vision, even in the midst of the daily grind:

> "Sometimes I felt guilty when I blocked about half a day every month for work on the corporate university," he recalls. "But I needed the time to make myself believe that my agenda was still valid, and that I was not being drowned in the operational HR work—although it occupied me more than 99 percent of time."

Sattelberger's dream has come true: Not only is Lufthansa University a going concern, it has won awards for its innovative collaborative strategies and been named Europe's best corporate university.

If you'd like to play the Pilot role in your organization but still need a little more inspiration, consider the story of Gary Thompson.

In a glamorous industry—casino gambling—Gary Thompson started out with one of the less glamorous jobs. He was director of communications for Harrah's Entertainment, which meant that he spent his time editing the annual report, writing press releases, and answering questions from newspaper reporters about the company's quarterly earnings. It wasn't always exciting, but he liked his job, and he enjoyed working with the people at Harrah's.

But when he left the office, Gary had another love. It was the game of poker—in particular, the variation known as Texas Hold'em that Gary had first learned to play in the early 1980s and which had gradually become, in the early years of the twenty-first century, a major obsession for millions of Americans.

You might think that poker and Gary's job at Harrah's fit together naturally. But poker actually played little or no role in Harrah's casino business, which was built around other games (craps, blackjack, roulette), and especially its highly lucrative slot machines. So when Gary shelled out his own money to play in the famous World Series of Poker starting in the mid-1980s, he figured it was just a fun, fascinating experience—not one with particular relevance to his career.

That changed one Saturday morning in January, 2004. Gary opened up the newspaper to learn that Nevada state gaming regulators had moved to shut down Binion's Horseshoe Casino the night before, as a result of a dispute over required payments to certain union pension funds. Gary's eyes got wide. Binion's owned the rights to the World Series of Poker, which had been played at the Golden Horseshoe every year since its inception in 1970. With Binion's in trouble, the rights to the World Series were up for grabs. And Gary instantly knew this represented an emergent strategy opportunity for Harrah's.

As the company's corporate communications guy, Gary wouldn't normally be involved in launching strategic conversations. But this time was different. As a poker lover who'd actually played in the World Series of Poker, he knew he was in a better position to appreciate the allure of the brand than anyone else at Harrah's. Gary picked up the phone and called Chuck Atwood, Harrah's CFO. He explained the situation and the opportunity it represented, and Atwood immediately got it. Atwood and his team lost no time in entering negotiations with the owners of Binion's, and within four days they had made a deal to buy the World Series of Poker.

The next three months were a blur. With the next World Series scheduled for April, Harrah's moved quickly (prodded by Gary) to announce that the tournament would go off as planned in its traditional venue at the Horseshoe, which had been purchased by a third party called MTR Gaming, but was being managed by Harrah's. In a period of twenty days, Howard Greenbaum, Harrah's vice president of specialty gaming, pulled together a team to organize and manage the dealers, info systems, surveillance, security, and financial personnel required to run a tournament involving some 15,000 players—and make it not only a fun and exciting event for the participants, but also a colorful, highly rated spectacle for ESPN, which owned the TV rights.

As this massive effort was being pulled together, Gary Thompson found himself deeply involved. At first, he felt a little hesitant. "I almost felt that I was sticking my nose in where it wasn't needed. After all, Howard and his team were involved in operational and marketing issues, which are nowhere near my area of expertise." But Gary's background as a player made him a unique source of information as to the nature of the strategic opportunity represented by the World Series of Poker. He knew what motivated the participants—"the opportunity to win a lot of money, and the chance to compete on ESPN, just like the jocks we all grew up watching on TV." And he knew the kinds of marketing, advertising, and publicity that would attract the attention of poker fans like himself. Howard and the rest of Harrah's team pulled Gary into most of their meetings, and his suggestions helped shape the successful outcome.

The payoff for Harrah's has been big, and it's still building. The super-fast transfer of the tournament and the brand name from Binion's to Harrah's in 2004 culminated in a highly popular and profitable tournament that April. By the following year, the number of participants in the final event had actually *tripled*. The television contract with ESPN, which Harrah's had inherited from Binion's, was renewed at a significant increase in value. And a whole new audience of gamers—the millions of avid poker players around the country—had been introduced to Harrah's, a casino company they had formerly spent little of their time or money in.

As for Gary Thompson, he has an impressive new job title: Director of Tournament Operations. Modestly, he calls it "kind of misleading," saying that he leaves the gaming details to the experts—people like Howard Greenbaum, Ken Lambert, and others with years of experience running such operations. Gary's job is to coordinate brand strategy for Harrah's in the poker arena, making the most of the publicity, marketing, and licensing opportunities that come with hosting the world's most famous card-playing tournament.

That's a pretty exciting outcome for a manager in The Middle who just happened to be in the right place at the right time—with the right strategic idea.

Not every corporation will make it easy for managers in The Middle to play the role of strategic Pilot. In some places, managers must battle to create their own strategic spaces. But if you see an opportunity to benefit your company that no one else sees—the way Gary Thompson did—the battle is well worth waging.

11

IGNITION POINT 6:
THE STORY

The Power of the Bard

In ancient times, the Bard was the poet, storyteller, and historian of the tribe. The Bard entertained the people with tales of the old days while they were gathered around the fire at night or during long journeys to the next hunting ground or settlement. But the Bard's tales weren't merely for entertainment. In the Bard's keeping were the traditions of the tribe, the stories of its great leaders, the triumphs and tragedies of the past, and the values that united the tribe into one people.

Today, for many of us, the company is the tribe—the focus of our days and the center of our dreams and struggles. Yet the traditions and values of the corporate tribe are often unclear. Here is the where the Bard comes in. The contemporary Bard is the manager in The Middle who acts as guardian and transmitter of our sixth Touchstone—the company's Story.

Wise managers don't view their company's past as a mere collection of old stories that are irrelevant to today, or as the dead hand of tradition that must be shrugged off in the name of progress. They understand that what is valuable in a company's core values must be preserved even as new insights, innovations, and improvements are being created and as new people join the tribe. They know and act on the wisdom in historian George Santayana's oft-quoted dictum, "Those who cannot remember the past are condemned to repeat it."

You probably haven't thought of yourself as a Bard, a historian, or a story-teller. But if you think about the people you've worked with over the years—especially those you found most inspiring as mentors, guides, and advisors—you can probably identify the ones who played the Bard's role. The contemporary Bard uses methods a little different from his ancient counterpart. Rather than singing songs by the campfire, the corporate Bard shares anecdotes about the company's history on airplane flights to the next sales call, in the corporate hospitality suite during a convention, over lunch in the company cafeteria, or during the annual holiday party.

When you hear the Bard's stories, you may not even think of them as fragments of company history. They just sound like great stories—memorable, surprising, and often funny. You know the kind. They start something like this:

> "That reminds me of the time good old Joe came up with a bright idea to salvage a $2 million deal just before it went south. We thought he was nuts at first, but by God it worked. It happened like this..."

> "You think we're working hard today? This is nothing. Back in the old days, we sometimes worked around the clock—no exaggeration—to finish a customer's order by deadline. Why, I remember one time..."

> "Did you know this company almost went bankrupt ten years ago? Bob and Sue actually took out a second mortgage on their house to meet payroll. And the very next day, their first really big contract came through. It all started with this phone call..."

As a younger employee, you may have rolled your eyes when the old-timers started swapping tales like these. But you listened. And consciously or not, you absorbed lessons about your company in the process—how it got started, grew, faltered, recovered, and triumphed; what drives the people there, what makes them tick; and what's unique about your company and its spirit. Eventually, you may have caught yourself retelling some of those same stories to new team members, and perhaps adding a couple from your own experiences. Guess what? You've become a Bard.

Change for the Sake of Change

The past sometimes gets a bad rap—especially in America, the land of eternal optimism and endless new beginnings. Turn on the TV, surf the Internet, or open any magazine, and the cult of newness is much in evidence: "The ten new ideas that are revolutionizing business!" "Hot new opportunities that will change your world forever!" "The new thinkers who are overturning conventional wisdom!" When we want to criticize something, our favorite slur is to call it old-fashioned: "Ho-hum," "Same old same old," "Been there, done that," "Tell me something I don't already know." We live by the assumption that change is constant, rapid, unpredictable, and essentially *good*—and that our greatest imperative, especially in the business world, is to *keep up*: to change as fast as the world around us, if not faster.

But change always carries a price. When we discard the old ways, we discard not only the outmoded and outgrown, but also the tried-and-true, the tested, the reliable. In our eagerness to explore the uncharted brave new worlds of the future, we toss overboard the compass of experience and hard-earned wisdom.

During the dot-com years, many managers believed that the way to move forward was to throw out the rules of the past and start from scratch. You remember those days. Traditional management concepts and real-world experience were viewed as liabilities rather than assets. Twenty-two-year-olds were running huge companies. (As I write these pages, it's happening again.) Familiar measurements of corporate success such as customers, revenues, and profit were derided as "old-think," and anyone who expressed doubts about new values such as "eyeballs" and "click-throughs" and "network advantages" was dismissed with the vague but devastating sneer, "He just doesn't *get* it!" Eager to prove that they got it, big corporations invested billions to buy or launch dot-coms of their own. And Wall Street responded by assigning the digital upstarts street values far greater than their bricks-and-mortar counterparts, even when the "old-fashioned" companies had actual customers, revenues, and profits, while the upstarts didn't.

This radical rejection of the past led to a few great new ideas—eBay, Amazon, AOL, not to mention foosball—but it also caused countless catastrophic failures. Did someone say Pets.com? Turns out that, even in the digital age, a realistic business plan with an actual profit model is still a nice thing to have.

The dot-com frenzy, of course, was unique. But even in less chaotic times, companies often invoke "change" as if it were a mantra with magic powers. As managements turn over and market conditions evolve, companies are often looking to escape their past and redefine themselves. Sometimes it makes great sense; other times companies simply lose their way.

We see these efforts at corporate redefinition in ever-changing public relations and advertising campaigns. Just recently, Visa shifted its slogan from "It's everywhere you want to be" to "Life Takes Visa." Other recent examples include Nike putting less focus on "Just Do It" and VW moving past "Drivers Wanted." And how many slogans for Coke, McDonald's, and Gap can you recall? They've been turning over so quickly in recent years that few, if any, have gained traction.

Many of these reinventions are driven by internal company dynamics rather than customer needs. A new CEO wants to put his stamp on the organization; a new ad agency is determined to prove it's smarter than its predecessor; a new marketing director decides his people need a shake-up. The fastest way to make it happen (and get publicity and attention, at least inside the industry) is to announce, with much fanfare, "The New Company X!"

Ironically, the effect on most customers is negligible. The truth is that no one out in the real world pays as much attention to our ads, PR efforts, and corporate announcements as we do. (Why should they? They have lives, after all.) So even if a company's CEO and marketing director are bored to tears by the current two-year-old ad campaign, that doesn't mean the world at large is also bored. In fact, the world at large has probably barely gotten around to *noticing* the campaign. So change for the sake of change is usually a costly, pointless distraction from your company's *real* needs.

The American cult of newness is also related to the cult of youth—the ingrained assumption that people under 30 have access to some invisible source of power (energy? hipness? sex appeal?) to which all must bow. If change is inexorable, then surely young people, who are naturally plugged into the spirit of the future, must be our leaders. Which means our older people are fit for nothing except to be gently put out to pasture.

Of course, it wasn't always this way in American business. *The Wall Street Journal* columnist Jonathan Kaufman accurately captures the shift:

> Turning 50 has always been tough for managers. It is the age most of them plateau. But a generation ago, most managers in their 50s had security. They were seen as a company's institutional memory, mentors to younger workers. These were the years many managers spent more time with their families and, with the company's blessing, became more involved in community activities.
>
> No longer. Middle-age managers are still plateauing, but there is no resting. They must keep changing—reinventing themselves, learning new skills, mastering new technologies—even as nothing much changes for them.[1]

Young people *are* great—idealistic, hopeful, full of fresh perspective, and fun to be around. Change *is* inevitable—and often good. But when crunch time comes—when a company is facing a financial crisis, a tough marketing dilemma, a devastating accident, the advent of a scary new competitor, or any of the other challenges that are part of daily business life—it's nice to have someone around who has lived through such challenges in the past and learned a thing or two from them.

Youth and change are necessary. But so are experience and continuity. That's where the Bard comes in.

The Value of Memory

The Bard is an ignited manager with the ability to record and pass along organizational history—occasionally in a formal, written fashion but more often informally, embodied in "campfire stories" and the evocation of relevant facts and comparisons from past events when current decisions are being weighed. Institutional memory makes possible a

---

[1] Jonathan Kaufman, "Gray Expectations: A Middle Manager, 54 and Insecure, Struggles to Adapt to the Times." *The Wall Street Journal*, May 5, 1997, page A1.

future empowered by its history. A company gifted with such memory doesn't have to continually reinvent the wheel. Instead, it can build on the wisdom of the past while avoiding the errors of the past.

Understanding your company's roots can help you

- Recognize its strengths and weaknesses, making it easier to identify potential bumps in the road ahead as well as opportunities to build on your core capabilities

- Trace the evolutionary path that has brought you to your current situation, which may suggest new options for future growth that would otherwise be easy to overlook

- Celebrate and reinforce its central values, helping current and future employees make the right decisions to benefit the company and its customers through the inspiration they derive from the past

- Navigate hard times by remembering how the company has survived and rebounded from similar challenges in the past

- Discover old ideas (from once-discarded project concepts to long-forgotten research reports) that may suggest new applications that are more appropriate today than they were yesterday

In this book, I've talked a lot about the importance of escaping the influence of groupthink and really connecting with new ideas and concepts. In that effort, history can play a vital role. History may not be new, but the lessons it has to offer are easy to forget. An episode from your company's past may well contain a seed of insight that can help you solve a current dilemma in a fresh and powerful way.

Some companies with particularly rich histories make a deliberate effort to draw on the lessons of the past when facing new challenges. When Johnson & Johnson was hit with the most serious crisis in its history— the Tylenol poisoning cases in 1980—the company management deliberately turned to the firm's decades-old credo for guidance. Following the values mandated in that historic document—put patients first, do nothing to jeopardize public safety, be utterly transparent—Johnson & Johnson handled the crisis brilliantly, saving its threatened Tylenol brand and emerging with its corporate reputation greater than ever.

By contrast, companies that forget their history often make serious missteps. Hershey Foods, maker of the classic chocolate bar and other candies, was founded by a deeply religious entrepreneur named Milton S. Hershey, who envisioned a company dedicated to serving its community and particularly the students of a school for orphans that he founded (and to which he dedicated the proceeds of a trust that managed practically all his Hershey stock). For decades, the company's management remained true to the founder's vision. But in 2002, the firm got a black eye when it suddenly revealed secret plans to sell the company, potentially threatening the future of Hershey, Pennsylvania, and the founder's beloved school. So great was the public outcry that the company had to back away from its plans and is now trying to relearn the lessons of its own past.

During my years at AOL, I found that company history played an important role in keeping managers focused on the important things. This may be surprising, since AOL, founded in 1985 as Quantum Computer Services, is a relatively young company. But AOL predates the frenzied Internet boom of the mid-1990s and, by dot-com standards, is a venerable firm. Whenever we faced significant marketing or growth decisions, founder Steve Case—still youthful (he was born in 1958) but a hero of the "early days" of computing to many younger managers—would recap the company's story and conclude with the crucial reminder, "It's not a sprint, it's a marathon." The lesson: Make choices for the benefit of customers and for the company's long-term health, not for an immediate spike in sales or stock price. It was an historical truth all of us needed to remember.

Using Stories to Motivate and Inspire

Here's another anecdote from my time at AOL that illustrates a different use of storytelling.

In August 2002, Jon Miller was named the new CEO of AOL. It was a tough time to be taking over the business. Two years before, AOL had acquired Time Warner in one of the most controversial mergers in history. In the months that followed, the stock had taken a beating, hurting not only company shareholders but the pension plans in which much of the managers' retirement funds were invested. So by the time Miller took over, employees of the old Time Warner companies (such as Time Inc. and CNN) were feeling resentful and bitter, a reaction worsened by their perception that AOL's previous management had been arrogant and unconcerned.

In this charged atmosphere, Miller was called on to address these managers. As the crowd assembled in a large conference room, speculation was high. What could Miller say to alleviate their anger and start the relationship on a positive note? Would he apologize? Defend the company? Promise reform? Lay out a strategic vision? Ask for renewed dedication? There were serious risks in each of these alternatives.

Miller decided to start his speech with... a story. But not just an off-the-rack joke like those used by many speakers to break the ice. Instead, he told a story artfully designed to send exactly the right combination of messages to his new team. Based on the recollections of those who were there, here is what Miller said:

> Ever have your car towed here in New York City? Let's see a show of hands. [A few people ruefully responded.] If you have, you know it's a hideous experience. You go to get your car from a parking spot on the sidewalk and you discover it's gone. All kinds of emotions hit you—anger, anxiety, rage, frustration. But then you realize that your car has probably not been stolen but instead towed, because you were parked in the wrong place at the wrong time.
>
> So you call the police department and listen to a recording that tells you what to do. You have to go to the place where they take impounded cars—a dreary warehouse way out on the end of a pier in a godforsaken neighborhood on the far west side of Manhattan. This kills half a day or more. And when you get there, you find a line of 50 people just like you, waiting to pick up their cars. You sigh and get on the line. It moves really slowly, which gives you plenty of time to get more and more steamed about the unfairness of it all, and especially about the huge fine you know you're going to have to pay just to get your damned car back. And all the while, as you creep slowly toward the front of the line, you're looking up at this little booth with a little guy

sitting in it, the guy who has the power over you and your car, and you're getting more and more upset.

By the time you reach the booth, you're ready to let this guy have a piece of your mind. But what do you see taped to the chicken wire on the front of the booth? You see a little slip of paper with the following handwritten message: "'THE PERSON HERE DID NOT TOW YOUR CAR, HE IS HERE TO HELP YOU GET IT BACK. IF YOU COOPERATE, YOU WILL GET YOUR CAR BACK SOONER."

Naturally, the execs in the room burst out laughing. Miller let the laughter subside. Then he continued:

As I look out across this audience today, I want you to know that *I* am the guy in the booth. Our company has been through some really hard times. But I am here to help you get it back. So please be nice to me.

Just like that, Miller had the Time Warner managers in his corner.

What is it about Miller's story that made it so effective?

- *It enabled the audience to identify with the speaker.* Not everyone has had their car towed. But everyone has had the experience of dealing with a faceless bureaucracy. Miller's story was one that everyone could identify with, which instantly made every listener care about him and about what he went through.

- *It expressed the speaker's empathy for the emotions of the audience.* By comparing the Time Warner managers to a person who has had his car towed—an experience that Miller himself had faced—Miller was saying, indirectly, "You feel as if you've gotten screwed, and I understand that feeling. I get it."

- *It distanced the speaker from the mistakes of the past.* Miller was in a tricky position. As a new CEO, he doesn't want to start his tenure by denouncing his predecessor—that would stir up old controversies, anger too many people needlessly, and create a combative mood rather than a conciliatory one. Yet Miller wanted to send a signal that he knew that change was needed and that he wasn't wedded to old policies. The car-tow story sent that signal. Miller was telling his audience, "I didn't tow away your company. I'm sorry it happened. Now let's move forward together and make things better."

- *It told the audience members that the speaker shared their goals, and appealed for their help and support.* The handwritten note taped to the car-tow booth spoke for Miller: "I'm here to help you get your company back—the great old Time Warner that you remember and miss. Please work with me, not against me, and together we can make it happen."

- *It achieved all this with a light touch.* If Miller had straightforwardly expressed the same message without using a story, his speech would have been much less effective. His funny, mildly self-deprecating anecdote set just the right tone: "We're facing a situation that is very frustrating, and I understand what you've been going through. I'm here to help. But I don't take myself or our problems too seriously. Let's put the situation in perspective and realize that, if we pull together, we can get through this all right. And maybe someday we'll even look back on it and chuckle."

As this episode illustrates, a well-chosen story can achieve many goals at once. It's the world's most powerful method of communication. This is why most of the great leaders of history have been skilled storytellers. Lincoln was famous for using homespun frontier yarns to persuade juries and win the support of voters. Ronald Reagan told tales drawn from Hollywood pictures and his boyhood in Illinois to convey the basic American values he stood for. Even Jesus relied on stories—we call them parables—to teach theological and ethical truths, and the movement he built on those stories ended up spreading across the globe.

After a four-year run, Miller has departed AOL. He has been widely credited with putting the company on a winning track.

Muscle Memory and Thinking in Time

Understanding and connecting with your company's story is also an important element of sound decision-making.

Muscle memory is the ability to do something automatically, without thinking about it consciously. All of us have muscle memory in regard to such everyday activities as walking, eating, and getting dressed (although, of course, it must be redeveloped in people who suffer strokes or other debilitating medical conditions). And skilled athletes, artists, craftsmen, and performers develop muscle memory for many highly advanced activities. An excellent baseball player at the top of his game doesn't have to consciously think about his batting stance, his grip, the position of his feet, or the timing of his swing—it's just, "See the ball, hit the ball." Something similar happens with concert violinists, master painters, and expert diamond cutters.

Companies also develop a kind of muscle memory. Certain patterns of behavior become so familiar and so deeply ingrained in their people that they become second nature and are performed almost unconsciously, without much effort or awareness. At a company with a great tradition of customer service (like the retailer Nordstrom or the Four Seasons hotel chain, for example), experienced employees don't need to be reminded to bend over backward to solve customer problems—they do it as automatically as they brush their teeth in the morning. At other companies, muscle memory drives deeply ingrained behaviors in areas such as process efficiency (think back to Southwest Airlines and its "balletic" turnarounds at the gate), product quality, sales, and even budgeting. There are companies where the managers practically do spreadsheets in their sleep.

Muscle memory can be a powerful ally. It's wonderful to *know*, deep in your bones, that you and your team are capable not merely of pulling off a particular task but of acing it—and what's more, of doing it without a second thought. But it can also be dangerous. Things done without consideration may be ill-timed or inappropriate. There's a constant temptation to revert to the easy and familiar, even when it may not be the best solution to a new problem. In companies where the managers do spreadsheets in their sleep, they sometimes pull out their Excel templates at times when creative brainstorming might be more effective. As the saying goes, to the person whose only tool is a hammer, everything looks like a nail.

That's why muscle memory must be supplemented by *conscious* memory, and why important decisions must be tackled deliberately and head-on, with the help of data, analogies, case studies, and reference points drawn from company history. It's hard to make smart decisions unless you know what Hollywood calls the *backstory*—the sequence of events that led you to the current moment, together with the assumptions, wishes, aversions, fears, and desires that drove your past choices. The more conscious all of these elements can be, the smarter your current decision-making process.

Historian Richard Neustadt teaches this lesson in his brilliant book *Thinking in Time: The Uses of History for Decision-Makers.* Although aimed primarily at government policymakers, the book applies equally well to business leaders. Neustadt shows how the best decisions generally get made when the people in the room follow certain principles for understanding and using history, and he illustrates these principles with reference to some remarkable episodes—for example, the Cuban missile crisis, which Neustadt (like most historians) regards as highly successful because President Kennedy managed to avert the imminent threat of nuclear war.

Neustadt's principles include

- *Consider historical comparisons—but examine them closely rather than taking them at face value.* For example, during the Cuban crisis, some of Kennedy's advisors said that an unannounced attack on Cuba would be like "Pearl Harbor in reverse." Former secretary of state Dean Acheson thought this analogy was absurd, and explained the differences between Pearl Harbor and Cuba at length. But in the end, the group decided against a "sneak attack" for different historical reasons—because it wouldn't be in keeping with American traditions, as revealed in two centuries of U.S. wars.

- *Put today's problem in historic context.* Kennedy made sure to include foreign policy veterans with long experience in dealing with Cuba and Russia on his working team—including two members of the opposition Republican party. He repeatedly asked them to compare the immediate crisis with past crises and to discuss how Russia might respond based on their previous experiences. He never assumed that the future would be the same as the past—but he wanted to consider the possibility and prepare for it.

- *Test assumptions against historical precedents.* When some members of the task force urged "surgical air strikes" against the missile bases, Kennedy challenged the assumption that such strikes would work by turning to former defense secretary Robert Lovett, who had been in charge of U.S. air forces during World War II. Lovett said that his observations showed that surgical strikes rarely worked and called for a naval blockade instead—the option Kennedy ultimately chose.

- *Think about the historical impact of your decisions.* In the end, Kennedy chose the conservative, cautious path of a naval blockade rather than an invasion or attack on Cuba in part because of his concern over how his administration would look to future historians. He wanted to be sure that he would be remembered as having tried everything possible to avert a nuclear war.

This last principle is worth applying to any major business decision. How will your decision affect the company's reputation ten years or fifty years down the road? Will it uphold the best elements of your company's traditions or undermine them? Will it be viewed as a proud moment in your company's history, or a moment to be forgotten or hidden? Taking an historical perspective will help you make choices you can live with, both individually and as an organization.

Deploying history to inform and guide decisions is an important aspect of the role of the Bard.

Reconnecting the Threads of History

Not every company has a series of intact links from its founding days to the present. Particularly in today's world, where mergers and acquisitions are a common fact of life, many companies have gone through a series of incarnations, taking on fresh names, identities, and business missions. After several such reinventions, even the people who work at the company may be uncertain what it stands for, what its values are, and "how we do things around here." In such cases, the role of the Bard in preserving institutional memory is especially important. The Bard can help to make sure that the company backstory isn't forgotten altogether, and with it the crucial lessons of history.

This problem may sound abstract and high-minded, but its implications are surprisingly concrete. Consider, for example, the nuts-and-bolts exercise of developing an annual budget for a company or one of its divisions. A budget is usually based on an extrapolation from the previous year's numbers. But how can that be meaningfully done when the thread of continuity from one year to the next has been broken due to the reshuffling of business units, mergers or spinoffs, profit and loss restatements, or changes in the fiscal year?

Furthermore, how often do the managers charged with developing next year's budget ground their discussions in an analysis of history and its lessons? How often do they ask questions like, "How close did we come to making our revenue numbers each of the last three years? If we fell short, what happened and why? Have we gotten into the habit of pre-booking sales late in the year so as to meet the budget numbers? If so, what impact is that having on the first quarter of the following year? Which members of our team are consistently over budget? Which members are under budget?" and so on.

Questions like these could uncover historical information that would inform more realistic, accurate, and effective budgeting for the future. Unfortunately, in too many companies it's almost impossible even to track down the data needed to answer these questions. Here is where the manager in The Middle must step up to speak on behalf of the institutional memory. After all, the only way an individual can get better at a task is by learning from experience—and the same applies to an organization.

In April 2005, Time Warner and Comcast jointly purchased Adelphia Communications, one of the nation's largest cable operators. The $17 billion deal created a shuffled leadership lineup that threatened to sever the historical threads that made the budget numbers meaningful.

During subsequent discussions about the following year's projections, Tim Young, Time Warner's regional sales VP in Los Angeles, told me about working on budgets with Adelphia's marketing team. After reviewing the figures they submitted, he decided to ask a rather probing, indelicate, yet vital question. "I'm curious about something," he said. "We all know that over the past couple of years, your company was getting dressed for sale. Under the circumstances, how much did they ask you to cut your spending budget, and what has the effect been on your department?"

The leader of the Adelphia unit was startled by the question. But she was obviously pleased that a reality check was being invited. "Wow," she replied, "I'm so glad you asked that. We had to make some big cuts, spread out over the last several quarters. It's been really tough on all of us."

The Time Warner manager pushed a little harder. "Did the cuts hurt your effectiveness?"

"Well, I hate to complain. Naturally, we adjusted. We even came to accept the reduced spending as the 'new normal.' But there's been a lot of business-building that we couldn't do because we just didn't have the resources."

In most companies, this exchange would never have occurred. The Time Warner manager would have taken the Adelphia budget at face value, and the marketing division of the newly-merged company would have limped into the next year without the tools it needed. But with the backstory on the table, both of these managers in The Middle could have a realistic discussion about what marketing *really* needed to fuel growth. Soon they agreed on a new budget that reset the department on a path to prosperity.

What Kind of Movie Are You In?

Notice that I've described the manager in The Middle who uses the power of stories not as a historian or datakeeper but as a Bard—a poet or minstrel who entertains the tribe even as he reminds them of their deepest values. The great storytellers bring a touch of poetry to the tales they tell—meaning not rhyme or rhythm or the other technical qualities of poetry, but rather the ability of poetry to touch the emotions of an audience. Jon Miller's story about having his car towed exemplifies the power of the Bard because it evoked feelings of frustration, sympathy, anger, and, ultimately, forgiveness and reconciliation from his audience. That kind of emotional connection is what the art of the Bard is all about.

Miller's story also clearly (if indirectly) conveyed to his audience his vision of the story of AOL Time Warner and where they all were in the unfolding of that story. "Your company has been taken away from you by mindless forces beyond your control," he was saying. "Now we have the opportunity to take it back and restore the natural order of things. Let's do it!" This is another powerful attribute of the company Bard: the ability to convey a clear vision of the corporate story and help others understand where they fit into that story.

One way to think about this challenge is to ask yourself, "What kind of movie are you in?" As you probably know from a lifetime of watching movies in theatres or on TV, there are just a relatively small handful of classic storylines that skilled authors, playwrights, script writers, and directors have reworked and modified over the years, creating from these basic plots a seemingly endless series of fascinating and compelling variations. Four hundred years ago, Shakespeare took the classic story-line of "The Hero Doomed by His Excessive Ambition" and turned it into *Macbeth*. In the 20th century, movie makers transformed the same basic storyline into such films as *Citizen Kane*, *Wall Street*, and *Scarface*.

The same is true of the storylines that underlie the businesses we work for. Most follow specific, often familiar patterns. Understanding the story of your company includes recognizing the kind of movie it might make.

Here are a few examples:

- *A Boy and His Dream.* This is the story behind such companies as Disney, Virgin, and Microsoft. If you've ever worked for a firm built around the creative vision of a young entrepreneur, you've lived the Boy and His Dream story.

- *The Tale of Education.* In this story, a company must pass through a series of changes as it learns from experience, ulti-mately emerging wiser and stronger at the end, yet with its fundamental nature intact. IBM, for example, has gone through several incarnations, its most recent being as a provider of information services, while remaining a high-tech firm driven by intelligence and discipline. Today, BP is reinventing itself from an old-fashioned oil company into an environmentally-friendly energy company—another kind of education tale.

- *The Tale of Redemption.* This story describes a company that has been through a near-death experience, perhaps because of a serious mistake, but has recovered by returning to the values that originally made it great. Apple has gone through a redemption drama, its share of the computer marketplace having shrunk due to insularity and arrogance, only to rebound thanks to an infusion of new creative energy in the form of the iPod music player.

- *Stranger in a Strange Land.* This is what's sometimes called a picaresque drama, in which the hero passes through a series of disconnected, often colorful and amazing, sometimes mysterious adventures in a weird, unknown country (think *Easy Rider*, *Planet of the Apes*, or *Being John Malkovich*, for example). Some companies that go through a series of incarnations and flit from market to market live through this kind of movie.

- *The Tale of Revenge.* Sometimes a company is driven by the desire of its founders to outcompete another organization that is viewed, for some reason, as "the enemy." Some companies grow for years fueled by this form of energy. Some independent Hollywood producers, for example, revel in thinking of themselves as feisty upstarts challenging the hegemony of the big studios.

- *The Action Adventure.* Just as some movies are built around a series of hair-raising escapes, each more exciting than the last, some companies seem to lurch from one business crisis to the next, living off the adrenaline generated by sheer danger. We see this pattern in the software industry, where companies are repeatedly betting their business on creating the "next big idea" and hoping the "bad guys" (i.e., the competition) won't get there first.

- *The Tale of Testing.* Some companies, especially those created by high-minded founders, go through repeated periods of testing, in which their adherence to high standards of ethics and professionalism is challenged. Johnson & Johnson lived through this movie when the Tylenol poisoning crisis tested its moral values—and the company passed with flying colors, achieving both ethical greatness and business success as a result.

Of course, this isn't an exhaustive list of the master storylines that define businesses. Maybe your company fits some other narrative pattern. (Some, like the Enrons of the world, embody tragic tales that end in destruction and despair. Hopefully that's not the kind of story you are living through.) The important thing is to begin thinking about the shape of your company's story and where you fit into it. Ask yourself questions like these:

- What kind of movie is my company in? Who is the hero? Who is the villain? What is the central conflict?

- What stage of the story are we now experiencing? Are we in the early days of the company's story, in the midst of a crisis, or approaching the denouement? Is a new story (a sequel) about to be launched?

- What role do I play? Am I the rising hero, the loyal sidekick, the misunderstood prophet, the gadfly, the unexpected hero, the comforter, the redeemer, the secret agent, the mysterious stranger?

- What actions are my team and I being called on to perform to advance the plot? What do the next few pages of the script dictate? Can we do anything to rewrite the script to make the ending more satisfying?

One of your jobs as an ignited manager is to understand the movie you and your company are living through and convey that understanding to the people you work with—not necessarily in those exact words, but through the stories you tell, the comparisons you draw, the challenges you set, and the feelings you evoke.

Finding Your Roots

If you've been with the same company for a number of years, you've probably absorbed a lot of history by osmosis—through the stories people swap and the anecdotes recounted in speeches by the top brass. If not, you may need to go out of your way to learn about your company and its backstory.

Sometimes company history is captured in documents: old sales materials, company presentations, annual reports. If your company has a library or an archive, spend an afternoon browsing there. (Whoever is in charge will be thrilled with the attention and will probably become an ally and helper whenever you need to research some obscure bit of company data.) In other cases, the Internet may be a trove of historical materials. Eye-opening discoveries are possible. Some companies are actually reviving old slogans, ads, or historical images for their inspirational value. For example, Bank of America has focused in recent television commercials on the bank's historical role as a supporter of female investors and entrepreneurs—including Mary Pickford, the 1920s movie star who helped found United Artists.

More often, history is captured in stories that express the central values, mission, goals, and aspirations of the company and its people. Often these stories aren't written down anywhere. Discovering them is a matter of asking questions—especially of your firm's veterans, those who may be retiring, and people leaving the company—and listening closely to the answers.

Older employees can be a little-used source of surprising wisdom. Connect with them and turn them into mentors. Meet regularly with them, keep them up-to-date on what you are learning, and share with them the challenges you are facing. Many times they'll have been through the same problems before and have insights to share with real practical value.

If you consciously play the important role of Bard—company historian, storyteller, and keeper of values—you'll find yourself eventually acting as mentor to a younger generation of employees who will appreciate the wisdom and insight you've developed.

12

IGNITION POINT 7:
THE SPIRIT

The Power of the Healer

Bad managers ignore the emotional dynamics of their teams. They try to fix most problems by employing fear ("Get this project done on time or else!") or incentives that are simplistic and ham-handed ("Get this project done on time and you'll earn a bunch of brownie points!"). A manager like this induces spasms of eye-rolling and behind-the-back joking from his team members—as you know if you've ever had the misfortune of working for one.

By contrast, smart managers treat every situation as a unique circumstance—not just from a business standpoint, but also from a *personal* standpoint. They recognize that business problems can't be defined solely in terms of profit or loss, sales or inventory, salaries or bonuses or productivity. They understand the emotional, psychological, and even spiritual sides of the issues their people are grappling with, and they recognize the impact these "soft" elements have on the hard results they achieve.

Rather than treating people like anonymous cogs in a machine, smart managers empathize with the struggles and aspirations of their team members. They realize that each one is an individual with strengths, weaknesses, and emotions that must be understood fully. This is the power of the Healer—the ignited manager who knows that motivating people is, in part, about nurturing their hearts and minds.

Understanding the emotional currents at work gives a manager enormous power. Emotions are informative. If we know what drives people emotionally, we know how to motivate, inspire, guide, strengthen, and support them.

The Healer uses his sensitivity to the organization's emotional climate to

- Guide the company in establishing wise, productive policies in regard to compensation, training, scheduling, workplace conditions, and other "people" issues

- Coax high performance from his people when others fail because of morale problems, life/work imbalance, perceived problems with fairness, or the inability of team members to understand or commit to corporate objectives

- Inform management about what is actually possible and impossible to achieve, shaping strategic plans and operational targets that are realistic and appropriate

- Anticipate people problems before they threaten productivity, and develop methods for avoiding or minimizing them

- Attract and retain the smartest and most capable people, and find gentle but effective ways of moving people out of jobs where they don't belong

- Help make the organization a place where people can grow and thrive, not just financially and professionally, but also in personal and human terms

Developing these skills takes more than managerial know-how. It also takes sensitivity, maturity, and the courage required to communicate openly.

Getting Serious About Motivation

The Healer understands the soft side of leadership—the emotional and spiritual elements of motivation and commitment without which no company can achieve lasting success.

None of this is to say that hard factors—things like salary, bonuses, titles, and perks—aren't important. They're very important. But they don't substitute for being challenged, acknowledged, recognized, and nurtured as the individuals we are. Though often ignored or misunderstood, these soft motivators are just as important.

Knowing how to combine the various kinds of motivation can be tricky. And when you mess it up, you can pay a big price—both in terms of morale and in terms of pure economic loss.

Remember Michael Drake from Freddie Mac? (We told part of his story in Chapter 4, "Managing Your Emotions.") When we interviewed Michael, he recounted a clash with his superiors over what it would take to reward and motivate some of his most valuable employees.

Michael went to his boss at the time and said, "I have a couple of people I really want to reward—people who've been working night and day for weeks to help clean up some of the systemic problems we inherited from past management. I want to show them that we appreciate their extra efforts and recognize what they mean."

"Fine," said his boss. "How about throwing them an ice cream social?"

"A what?" Michael responded.

"You know, make-your-own sundaes and sodas and such. It's fun and tells people you really care."

Michael was silent for a few long seconds. "Uh, that isn't exactly what I had in mind. I was thinking more along the lines of a cash bonus."

"How much?"

"Fifteen thousand dollars. Apiece."

Now it was his boss's turn to be silent. Finally he choked out, "Did you say $15,000?"

"That's right."

"No way. We can't do that. It's just too darn much." And he walked away, leaving Michael speechless.

There's no doubt that $15,000 is a lot of money. But Michael had done the math. The people he wanted to honor were earning $50,000 or

$60,000 a year each. And during this painful time of retooling, Freddie Mac was draining them dry, soaking up their energy, emotion, intellect, and talent. If these key employees left—which they would soon do, if conditions didn't improve—they would have to be replaced in the short run with independent consultants who would probably cost the equivalent of $1 million a year. And in the long run, hiring permanent replacements—factoring in recruitment costs, training, and lost time as the new people got up to speed—might cost double their salaries during year one.

"I wanted to save us all that," Michael says. "But the company balked spending at $15,000."

The alternative suggested by Michael's boss—an ice-cream social—was the wrong idea at the wrong time. It's not a simple matter of "money talks." Non-financial rewards can be very meaningful when they build on an existing basis of mutual trust, respect, and commitment. (I've written heartfelt thank-you notes and seen them posted in people's offices weeks later because they *meant* something to those who received them.) In an organization where people have a sense of camaraderie and shared goals, then a spontaneous ice-cream social on a Friday afternoon—or equivalent gestures like a beer blast, poker party, or movie outing—can be a great way to blow off steam and thank the team for a week of hard work. But when people have been putting in long hours for uncertain rewards and with little clear sense that the organization understands their sacrifice, a small act like an ice-cream social feels condescending. They know their work is worth millions to the company; to be rewarded with pennies is insulting.

This was a case of being dollar-wise and heart-foolish. Freddie Mac is still struggling to learn how to constructively use the personal understanding that managers like Michael Drake bring to their jobs. Until they do, they will expend money needlessly and unproductively, struggling to overcome the problems caused by excessive turnover and plummeting employee morale—all in the name of economy.

The manager in The Middle usually has a limited ability to control the financial rewards his team members receive. Salary increases and bonuses must be approved by those higher in the chain of command, and strict guidelines are usually established at the C-suite level. But the Healer owes it to himself or herself and to the people he or she leads to be extremely sensitive to the importance of such rewards and to be a strong, vocal advocate for fairness.

If the compensation program at your firm is inequitable or fails to provide what it takes to truly motivate your people, fight to change it—not to prove that you are a "nice guy" but because it's one of the prerequisites for building a high-performing team. And if getting to fairness proves to be a long-term process, tell your people the truth about where you are in that process. They'll appreciate knowing that you "get it" and that you are pushing for what's right.

Making Positives Out of Negatives

In the workplace, money is certainly a sensitive, emotional button. But other factors can be equally powerful—and equally problematic for managers. One manager who has developed a thoughtful sensitivity to the emotional climate of the workplace and the leadership challenges it can pose is John Sherrard, associate director of vendor contracts at SBC, the long-distance, Internet, and communications company recently purchased by AT&T.

In his 20 years as a manager, Sherrard has led people through some tough corporate times—periods of downsizing, for example. "Many say that middle management is hit the hardest" at such times, he acknowledges. Sherrard has survived, and helped his people to adapt, by using his communication skills—less as a transmitter than as a receiver:

> Actually, I find you have to be prepared for a lot of venting during hard times. And I invite it. When I know people are worried or suffering, I get together with my team and ask them to tell me what's on their minds. Venting can be very therapeutic.
>
> Sometimes I can affect the situation in a concrete way—for example, when the company is struggling, I may be able to convince the firm to reduce the number of layoffs or shift people into other jobs. Other times, there's nothing I can do except help ease people's transitions by giving them references and contacts. But I can always express empathy for what they're going through. I can talk about what I've done to try to fix the

problem. And I can show them how the pain is being spread around, at least to some degree.

Most important, I can make sure to provide venting sessions that are a safe environment for my people, where they'll never have to face retribution for speaking out. And it's not only the people who are directly affected that have to vent. It's also the people whose jobs aren't touched but who will now have to do twice as much work as before, and with greater uncertainty hanging over their heads.

The fact that I let them get their feelings off their chests makes a big difference to the emotional climate here. After a venting session, people can say, "Okay, you know how we feel. Now, how do we now move forward and deal with reality?" Just the fact that they see that you share their concerns and care about their problems may help them cope with the situation.

"I'm trying to be a leader," Sherrard says. "But you can't be a leader without followers. And I find that people are more willing to follow you if you give them the opportunity to talk about their feelings, their concerns, and their needs." Leadership, as Sherrard has found, isn't about exalting the leader—it's about caring for all the people.

The need for emotional sensitivity may be extreme in times of corporate upheaval, but it's important every week of the year. For example, nothing could be more mundane than the traditional performance appraisal. But many business leaders find that delivering honest, sometimes negative, performance feedback is profoundly stressful—perhaps even more so than *receiving* negative feedback.

Here, too, John Sherrard has developed an approach that works for him and his people:

> Having had twenty years' practice now, I really don't find it difficult to have to give feedback to people. Of course, I always try to make my criticism constructive—to tell people what they can do to improve rather than just tell them what they are doing wrong. But one of the keys to doing it well, in my mind, is to be just as quick about providing positive reinforcement as you are in providing criticism. Managers tend to assume that, if

people do something well, there's nothing to talk about—isn't that what they're supposed to do? I think that's a big mistake.

Instead, I try to stick to a ratio of four-to-one. You need four positives for every negative in order for people to feel like your comments are balanced. If it's one-to-one, people will feel that you're being too negative. It's because people tend to remember negative feedback much more. So when I stick to a four-to-one ratio, people actually hear what I'm saying rather than over-reacting.

Sherrard also works hard to make sure that people understand the *reasons* behind his feedback, positive or negative:

When I'm doing the first evaluation for a new person on my team, I try to make it clear that I am here to help them be more successful. To achieve this, I am going to provide them with positive feedback and, if needed, with criticism as well. And I literally ask for their permission to provide them with constructive criticism if needed.

In a sense, this is just a formality. What are they going to say? They are not going to say no! But I think they appreciate being asked. It's a gesture of respect for them, their dignity, and their feelings—all of which are important to me.

So when something doesn't go well on the job, I ask, "What can we learn from this?" And I think that I've been able to create a culture around that kind of question among our team members.

Finally, Sherrard makes sure that the scheduled performance appraisal session isn't the only time his team members get feedback:

We have four formal feedback sessions a year, but I talk about performance with my team every week. Once you create that culture, then it's just a natural part of how you do business. When people get both positive feedback and criticism often, it's more acceptable to them. And, of course, when I see signs that they've managed to turn around or improve on a weakness, I'm very quick to praise that.

Maybe the most important thing John Sherrard has to teach us comes from his use of the word "culture." As a manager, Sherrard is keenly aware of the impact of his words and behavior on the emotions of the people around him. Praise or criticism from a boss carries a lot more weight than the same comments from someone of lesser stature. And the emotional overtones generated by the boss's words, actions, gestures—even his facial expressions and body language—produce ripples that affect the entire office, sometimes for days to come. Thus, the tone the boss sets by his demeanor and his communication style creates a culture that influences everything that happens in the organization.

If you create a culture of mutual respect and caring, the people who work with you will imbibe it and imitate it. The result will be a workplace where people pull together in pursuit of common goals and where people stay on an even keel no matter how tough the obstacles.

Business is tough enough. We've all gotten wounded on the job. The role of the Healer is to minimize the inevitable hurts that come with working in today's ultra-competitive environment and help people press forward.

Insight and Courage

An ignited manager like John Sherrard illustrates the kind of intelligence and sensitivity required to play the role of Healer. But those aren't the only qualities needed. Two others are equally important: street-smart insight into the impact that organizational constraints can have on the emotional climate, and the courage to buck those constraints, even when that means challenging the power structure in a potentially self-threatening way.

Author and consultant Harold J. Leavitt tells a story that vividly illustrates the kinds of psychological binds in which managers in The Middle often find themselves. It involves an off-site sensitivity training workshop Leavitt conducted that included members of five levels of management from the same company—first-line supervisors who had risen from the ranks of blue-collar workers right on up to the CEO, including several layers of management in between. The group had been selected with sensitivity to the problem of having direct reports interacting in such a potentially charged environment; almost none of the lower-level managers had their bosses in the room. However, avoiding such conflicts was impossible at the narrow top of the corporate pyramid, so two vice presidents with direct reporting ties to the CEO were present.

The session began smoothly. Leavitt moderated a general discussion of business issues, including the current economic climate, strategic challenges facing the company, and changes in market conditions. Everyone participated eagerly, from the CEO on down through the vice presidents, divisional managers, and the front-line supervisors. But then, with Leavitt's guidance, the conversation began to shift gears. More sensitive topics surfaced: alleged mistreatment of workers by managers, ethical lapses, and accusations of cover-ups. With the emotional temperature in the room rising, Leavitt noticed a curious change in the conversational pattern:

> As these more sensitive topics entered the discussion, the decibel level decreased. Those just below the CEO were among the first to drop into near silence, followed by the next level down and so on, until the meeting became pretty much a two-way talkfest, with first-line supervisors laying it on the line and the CEO responding. The others, sandwiched between the two ends, sat mostly silent, almost frozen in their seats.

Later, Leavitt reviewed the session with the CEO, who was delighted with the experience. "He was feeling heroic," Leavitt recalls. "He had shown himself to be one of the good-old boys, duking it out with the real working folks. It was fun, like doffing his suit and tie and climbing into a gray (not pink!) jumpsuit—for one afternoon."

As for the managers in The Middle who'd basically stopped participating, what was the CEO's diagnosis of their silence? He was dismissive. As far as the CEO was concerned, they'd revealed themselves to be timid, "ivory-tower" paper-shufflers, unable to comprehend the feelings and attitudes of the "real" people at the bottom of the hierarchy, while also being too protective of their own perks and privileges to speak boldly and honestly in the presence of the big boss. "They cover their tails," the CEO said scornfully.

Viewing the scene from the more objective position of an outsider, Leavitt offers a very different analysis:

> [The CEO] was certainly right about one thing. Those middle levels, especially the upper middles, *were* covering their tails— for good reason. I thought the middle folks had shut up because they were just plain scared by the presence of their close bosses, especially the CEO. If the in-betweens had argued with first-line supervisors, they would probably have been called to the boss's office the next morning. The first-line supervisors, however, didn't need to feel afraid. The CEO was too distant, too far up the hierarchy to scare them. The chief executive of a large organization wasn't likely to go after a veteran foreman, four levels down the hierarchy. Besides, if these old-timers pointed to things that were going wrong, who was likely to be held responsible? Certainly not the top boss! That was middle managers' territory.[1]

The CEO in this story was well-meaning. His willingness to talk openly with the front-line managers was admirable, and it's likely he learned some valuable truths from his interaction with the troops. But his attitude toward the managers in The Middle of his organization showed a fundamental blindness to the realities of life in corporate America. It's scary to challenge your boss—especially the boss you work with every day, the one who doles out your job assignments, hands out perks (like that training program on a Caribbean island in February) and booby prizes (like that mid-summer sales trip to rural west Texas), appraises your performance, and recommends salary increases and end-of-year bonuses. And it was unrealistic of the CEO to expect his direct reports to violate or ignore this iron law of organizational life.

Leavitt's story is far from unique. In fact, it's useful mainly because the dynamic it describes is so *typical*—one that most experienced managers can replicate from their own work histories. So what are the lessons about leadership and life that the aspiring Healer can take away from this small but revealing anecdote?

---

[1] Harold J. Leavitt, "The Plight of Middle Managers." *Harvard Business School Working Knowledge,* December 13, 2004. Online at http://hbswk.hbs.edu/ item.jhtml?id=4537&t=leadership.

First, always be aware of the powerful emotional constraints that everyone in business is operating under at virtually all times. Working people are extraordinarily dependent on the organizations that employ them—not just for their livelihoods but for their social status, their sense of self-esteem, even (to large measure) for the meaning of their daily lives. And being so dependent induces in most people a high level of vulnerability and sensitivity. In this kind of environment, either giving or receiving any kind of negative message is deeply stressful—something that most people will do almost anything to avoid. This is one reason bad news takes so long to migrate up the corporate communication ladder (if it ever does)—it's just too darn frightening to deliver an unwelcome message to the person who holds your fate in his hands.

All kinds of business communications labor under the limitations imposed by these constraints. So for managers at every level in the organization, finding out what is really going on is tremendously difficult.

What can the ignited manager do about it? In his role as Healer, he can constantly be aware of the emotional barriers to openness and honesty, and work to help team members overcome them when tough corporate challenges *demand* clear communication. Necessary tactics to achieve this include

- *Acknowledging the constraints.* ("Hey, I know it's hard to talk about this stuff with your boss. I feel the same way with *my* boss.")

- *Establishing an important business context and purpose.* ("We've got to get to the bottom of this problem. Otherwise there's no way we'll make our sales targets for this year.")

- *Recognizing the crucial role of the team member.* ("We can't fix this without your help.")

- *Creating a separate space where it's safe to be open.* ("Let's go get a cup of coffee and hash this out, one on one. And let's agree that nothing we say will be shared with anyone else without the other person's permission.")

- *Rigorously avoiding any form of recrimination or retribution for negative or "politically incorrect" statements.* ("I appreciate your honesty. There are no hard feelings. Now let's figure out how to solve the problem together.")

Second, the would-be Healer needs to model open communication in times of stress—including the kind of upward communication of negatives that requires special courage (which the managers in The Middle in Leavitt's anecdote were unable to muster). This means taking such bold steps as:

- Speaking frankly about problems in the company when no one else is willing to do so

- Admitting your own mistakes without trying to blame other people or outside circumstances

- Recognizing the flaws and weaknesses of the organization as a whole and honestly discussing what's required to fix them

- Acknowledging the role that morale, emotions, motivation, and other "people" facts play in the company's performance

- Being willing to say, "I don't know," "I don't think it's possible," "We goofed," "That would be a mistake," and other such often-taboo utterances

If one of the managers in The Middle in Leavitt's account had been willing to play this role, the story might have ended very differently. Emboldened by the example of their Healer colleague, other managers might have stepped up with their own honest statements. The front-line supervisors would have heard the perspective of mid-level managers on the problems they were griping about—and perhaps would have discovered that the problems were more complex and more intractable than they'd realized. The CEO might have recognized that his management team was capable of much more than merely "covering their tails." And the organization as a whole might have begun to get a handle on the *real* sensitivity problems that had been holding them back.

Is this easy to do? No way. (That's why it's called courage—because it's so hard to do.) The help of an outsider like Leavitt can be important, both to read the organization's emotional climate objectively and to provide a "safety valve" by expressing uncomfortable truths that others in the room would like to reveal but can't.

Yet *someone* must be willing to play the role of Healer—to recognize the impact of emotional cross-currents on life inside the organization and take the steps needed to prevent those cross-currents from making the company absolutely dysfunctional. When this doesn't happen, the results can be catastrophic—even genuinely tragic—as the managers at NASA discovered.

When Emotional Deafness Can Kill

On February 1, 2003, the space shuttle Columbia disintegrated during reentry into the Earth's atmosphere, killing the entire seven-member crew. The accident was caused by damage sustained during launch when a large piece of foam broke off the main propellant tank and struck the leading edge of the orbiter's left wing. A thermal protection system panel on the wing was damaged, which allowed the hot gasses of reentry to penetrate and weaken the wing structure, ultimately causing it to fail. The vehicle then became uncontrollable and was destroyed by the extreme heat of reentry.

This terrible human tragedy was a technical failure, of course. But it was an even greater management failure—one that was precipitated by the inability of the managers in The Middle at NASA to recognize and effectively manage the emotional constraints within the organization. In the end, the dysfunctional culture at NASA helped to kill the astronauts.

Similar chunks of foam had fallen off on at least three previous shuttle flights, but those incidents had caused no serious damage. The euphemism used by NASA management to refer to this phenomenon was "foam shedding." As with the O-ring erosions that had doomed the Challenger shuttle back in 1986, NASA management seemed to grow complacent when no serious consequences resulted from these earlier episodes.

Video taken during Columbia's lift-off was routinely reviewed two hours after the launch and revealed nothing unusual. However, the following day, higher-resolution film that had been processed overnight revealed that a piece of insulation foam fell from the external fuel tank 81.9 seconds after launch and appeared to strike the shuttle's left wing, potentially damaging the shuttle's thermal protection. The exact location where the foam struck the wing could not be determined due to the low resolution of the tracking camera footage.

Here is where the managerial missteps began to accumulate, as NASA failed to recognize the relevance of engineering concerns for safety.

Engineers made three separate requests for higher-resolution Department of Defense (DoD) imaging of the shuttle in orbit to more precisely determine damage. But NASA management did not honor the requests and actually intervened to stop DoD from assisting. NASA's chief thermal protection system engineer was also concerned about left-wing TPS damage and asked NASA management whether an astronaut would visually inspect it. NASA managers never responded.

Throughout the risk assessment process, senior NASA managers were influenced by their belief nothing could be done even if damage was detected. As a result, they decided to conduct a what-if study more suited to determine risk probabilities of future events rather than inspecting and assessing the actual damage.

In the wake of the Columbia tragedy, two managers at NASA named Bill Parsons and Wayne Hale began to look inward at the culture that had spawned the accident. They recognized that the agency's militaristic, macho mindset, which didn't tolerate doubt or "negativity," had discouraged engineers and others from speaking up when they were uncertain or worried about possible design flaws or mechanical problems that could scuttle a mission. Now they're working to transform the culture just enough to prevent such tragedies in the future. They don't want to lose the gung-ho, high-achievement orientation that has always characterized NASA and led to some of the space agency's greatest triumphs. But they want to temper it with a greater encouragement of open communication, even when the message is one of uncertainty and confusion.

Making such change happen in a proud agency with a tradition of accomplishment isn't easy, as reporter Marcia Dunn explains:

> The flight director who guided the Apollo 11 moon landing and the Apollo 13 rescue finds the space agency's new, soft, mushy approach distasteful—and flat-out wrong.
>
> "Look, these people are professionals. They're being paid a professional wage. If they have a problem, I expect them to stand up and speak up. Period," says Gene Kranz, the subject of the

recent History Channel documentary, "Failure Is Not an Option." The title is borrowed from his 2000 autobiography.

"We've got 19- and 20- and 21-year-olds over in Iraq right now who have to make daily decisions. It's no ambiguity. I don't think we should expect anything less of the people who are working in the space program. Daily decisions, no ambiguity," the 70-year-old Kranz says, his words clipped as short as his lifelong crewcut.

Kranz isn't the only old-timer complaining about the New Age NASA.

Retired space program veterans from the 1960s and '70s are asking Hale how he, as chairman of the mission management team for all future shuttle flights, will make potential life-and-death decisions if there is an overload of opinion, gut feelings and hunches—and no consensus.

Do what we did, they tell him.

Hale shudders at the thought.

"They were dealing with all-white males, and there was a lot of in-your-face, militaristic almost (communication)," says Hale, 49, a former shuttle flight director.

Soft-spoken and bald with a storyteller's voice and a fondness for space-motif and stars-and-stripes ties, he says: "I'm still a student at this, but if you want to inhibit communication, that's a good way to do it these days."[2]

Kranz's old-style management technique wasn't all wrong. He understood the importance of managers in The Middle to making crucial decisions correctly:

The opinions of technicians and engineers, no matter how low on the ladder, were not only respected, but sought by flight directors like the legendary Kranz. He practiced "defense in

---

[2] Marcia Dunn, "Post-Columbia NASA Managers are Sensitive Guys." Associated Press, October 13, 2003.

depth," so that if a technical problem slipped past one group, it would be caught by the next, or the next. He demanded toughness, competence, confidence.

He contends the NASA of yesteryear would not have allowed the Columbia accident. The system would have fixed the recurring launch problem of breakaway fuel-tank foam, he says.

Midlevel management—gutted during the 1990s to save money—is where Kranz would turn to hear about workers' gut feelings. If two or three workers had the same hunch—even without data to back it up—then that would be enough for Kranz to call a halt and investigate, and to collect more data.

The framed plaque from that era still hangs in the Mission Evaluation Room at Johnson Space Center, downstairs from Mission Control:

"In God we trust, all others bring data."

With Columbia, engineers had no data, just a sick, sinking feeling when they saw the video and film images of the chunk of foam smacking the ship's left wing during liftoff in January. Their repeated requests for spy satellite pictures were ignored or overruled, so no one knew Columbia had a mortal gash that would let in scorching atmospheric gases when the spacecraft headed home.

It's possible to diagnose some of the problems that led to the Columbia disaster by reading between the lines of this account. Kranz professed (no doubt sincerely) a respect for the "gut feelings" of his managers in The Middle, and he relied on them to express those nagging doubts forcefully. But over time, Kranz's other mantra—"In God We Trust, All Others Bring Data"—seems to have taken pre-eminence. It seems that NASA engineers came to feel that they *shouldn't* express their doubts unless these could be backed up by "data"—hard facts that would prove the validity of those doubts. This sense led to silence about the damage to Columbia's exterior, and in turn to the deaths of the astronauts on board.

The lesson of the Columbia disaster is clear: It's not enough to respect the ideas of your people. You also need to respect their feelings, even when they're inchoate, unclear, and seemingly based on very little—and encourage them to do the same. It's especially true when crucial decisions that affect lives, or the future of your company, are being made.

Leading with the Heart

Unfortunately, too many companies today still manage to follow old-fashioned, emotionally tone-deaf leadership styles. In August 2006, newspaper headlines told the world that Radio Shack laid off 400 employees... and had notified the unlucky ones via email! Talk about an embarrassing corporate black eye. It seems likely that Radio Shack is in desperate need of managers with Healer skills.

Managers like NASA's Bill Parsons and Wayne Hale—as well as CBC's John Sherrard and Michael Drake of Freddie Mac—represent the challenges and the promise of Healer leadership. Middleshift managers who respect the power of emotions embody the enlightened future of business... a world in which feelings aren't suppressed or lied about, but recognized as our most powerful drivers of achievement.

Reforming organizations in which a macho-style, emotionally deaf, quasi-military model of leadership still dominates won't be easy. Each of the managers we've talked about in this chapter has faced enormous challenges. But in the long run, they'll succeed—because they *must* succeed if tomorrow's organizations are to survive and thrive in the ever-escalating competition for human talent, energy, and commitment.

PART III
GET MORE SUCCESS

13

SELLING FROM THE FULCRUM

Shift Happens

Congratulations! Whether you've realized it or not, by getting solid with your team and style in the first part of this book ("Get More Power") and by adding unique and clear value to your company by working the Ignition Points in Part II ("Get More Purpose"), you've created a shift—a shift that has taken the fulcrum point you live on between management's vision and the demands of the field and elevated it to a new and higher platform.

You've become an ignited manager.

To confirm the change, simply redraw your Manager's Universe and consider your portfolio of projects. Have you expanded your universe and made your relationships more meaningful? Have you gained traction against serious issues that only you, with your unique vantage point and skill set, have the ability to solve? These are indications of the kind of change you've begun to make.

Part III of this book is about more success. In this chapter, you'll discover a system for getting your ideas sold and ensuring that you achieve the success and recognition you've earned. In the next chapter, you'll examine the meaning of success and learn about tools that will help you discover and pursue it for yourself.

Success Is a Verb

As an ignited manager, your job is to add value by uncovering and solving problems. In some cases, everything will fall into place in support of the solution. However, most problems that are really worth solving require people to change their ideas, their behaviors, and their ways of working, and creating that change is quite challenging.

Here is where the importance of selling becomes evident. The ignited manager needs to be skilled at selling because creating change depends on the ability to successfully convince other people of a new point of view. And this, in turn, requires that you bring to the table a persona and a style that have credibility and can attract followers.

Let's begin with some honest self-evaluation.

Who are you today? And, equally important, how are you perceived? What is the meaning of the Brand of You in the eyes of your colleagues, your team members, your boss, the C-level executives, and even the people in your company who may know you only by rumor and reputation?

We all know that people tend to get tagged and labeled. It's terribly unfair, but it happens. The tag you wear may be based on first impressions, the things you did or said during your first crucial days with the company or in your first managerial position. Or it may be based on your behavior during some moment of truth: the big presentation at the annual meeting, the make-or-break sales pitch before a major client, the 60-second interview on CNN.

Maybe you pulled it off beautifully—you appeared smart, articulate, upbeat, passionate, funny, and likeable. Now you are tagged for a while as a winner, a reputation that will help you survive future mistakes and missteps (up to a point). But maybe you stumbled, saying or doing something that you realized (instantly or days later) was cocky, thoughtless, or just plain off-base. Now you are carrying the burden of a mixed reputation—a stereotype hard for people to get past.

First think of the following labels assigned to your peers. Then think about how you may be perceived. Does one of these images sound uncomfortably familiar?

- *The whiner,* who sees only the dark side of any situation and is forever spouting visions of doom and gloom. The whiner thinks he is doing good by only pointing out the bad. Somehow he believes pulling the fire alarm is enough. However, after a while, people stop listening to the complaints of the whiner, even when they are dead-on accurate. (Tennis great John McEnroe was a classic whiner. Ironically, a recent review of close shots from his matches reveals that McEnroe's complaints about judges were often right! Perhaps if he'd whined less, he'd have won more arguments. Of course, he was pretty fun to watch.)

- *The politician,* always looking for an angle, sucking up to the powers that be, jumping on bandwagons and deserting sinking ships. The politician may just think he is being opportunistic, but without an acknowledgment of the current reality and a connection to all involved, politicians leave people feeling that behind any idea that they propose is nothing but selfish motivation.

- *The victim,* the passive, helpless, suck-it-all-in guy, who takes everybody's crap and never complains. The victim is simply trying to stay the course without rocking the boat. However, the victim often gets passed over for promotions and plum assignments because people consider him weak and ineffectual. As Malcolm Forbes once said, "If you don't ask Why often enough, people will ask Why You?"

- *The wise guy,* who is too clever for his own good—constantly sounding off with "great ideas" and "brilliant insights" that are invariably half-baked and not-quite-ready-for-prime-time. The wise guy may in fact be brilliant, but without a clear plan and buy-in, the wise guy gets dismissed.

- *The schmoozer,* inevitably charming, attractive, and oozing sincerity, believes that being liked is the clearest path to success. The problem, however, is that the schmoozer spends all of his time on the personal issues and none of his time on the work. A great lunch date doesn't make up for missing the deadline. So while the schmoozer is pleasant to have around, people quickly learn not to count on him.

If you've ever suffered from one of these labels, it's because your sales pitch has failed. Whether you realized it or not, you were selling—and they weren't buying. Instead of seeing the value of you and your offer, the labelers focused on your lack of substance and tagged you.

I remember attending a meeting with one of my mentors. We were working on problems, and I found myself jumping in and offering solutions to everything. I felt inspired, banging out solutions as fast as Federer's serve.

After the meeting, I turned to my mentor and said, "Wow—I thought that was a great meeting!"

He turned to me and said, "Of course you did. You talked the whole time." It was a simple yet hard-hitting comment that made it immediately obvious to me how oblivious I'd been to my failure to connect with those around me.

Maybe you've had a wake-up call like the one my mentor gave me. The good news is that your failure to connect with others doesn't have to be permanent. If you've become trapped in a losing stereotype, the process we will explain in this chapter will help you escape. But fair warning: It's not about putting on a fresh façade or deploying a better spin. It's about doing the work that is necessary to build substance and genuinely changing the behavior that has put you in the box you're in today.

First, Examine Your Motives

Every business has thousands of problems to solve. Some are mundane and relatively straightforward (the broken door in the restroom, the crummy quality of the printouts produced by the brand-new photocopier), others are significant and complex (the flawed revenue-tracking system, the inaccurate information being provided by some of the customer service staff), and still others may be big and hairy enough to threaten the entire company (the ill-conceived marketing strategy, the questionable ethics of some of the members of the sales force).

When you apply your time and talents to solving the problems that plague your company and its people—especially those that are complex and significant—you are potentially operating at the very highest level available to a manager in The Middle. You may well be the *one* person in your organization best positioned to notice, understand, and address a particular problem, and in so doing you may be able to save your company thousands or even millions of dollars, to say nothing of incredible headaches and heartaches. But before you jump in with both feet, a little self-examination is in order—starting with your *motives* for acting.

For many of us in business, half the time we're bent out of shape. It's just a function of our roles. As managers in The Middle, we catch grief from all directions—from customers, front-line staffers, suppliers, partners, and of course from those who are higher up the chain of command. We have our fingers in dozens of processes and have to make connections with divisions and departments throughout the company. So when things go wrong, we're the first to know it and feel it. The internal results include stress, anxiety, confusion, resentment, and anger. When people and processes throw us for a loop, we want to strike back. We want to expose the injustice, correct the errors, challenge the stupidity.

From our central vantage point, what needs to be done seems so *obvious* that's it's hard to understand why everyone else can't see it, too. We find ourselves questioning their good intentions: "The only reason for such a monumental screw-up must be that they're deliberately trying to undermine us! Nobody could be that dumb!"

Your initial impulse is to jump on your white horse and charge. But slow down. Remember the lesson from Chapter 4, "Managing Your Emotions"—when strong emotions drive your actions, you are likely to lose control, with results that are the opposite of the ones you seek. With anger and self-righteousness as motive, you're casting yourself as part of the problem, not the solution. Your emotional involvement undermines what you are trying to do. Yes, it seems unfair that trying to fix a problem should create a downdraft. But sometimes stating the negative—even when the negative should be obvious to all, and when your ultimate goal is to change the negative to a positive—often makes people regard you as a threat, not a helper.

Before you take any problem-solving action, you must really examine your motives. Are you looking to expose (and perhaps humiliate) those behind the failure, or do you want to work with them to develop a better solution? Are you jumping up to pull the fire alarm just because you like the excitement and the attention, or do you have a well thought-out plan for fixing the emergency? Are you eager to prove how clever you are (and make those around you look foolish and ignorant by comparison), or are you genuinely focused on improving the way your company serves customers, enriches shareholders, and creates opportunities for employees?

If your motives are self-serving, your problem-solving venture is likely to fail. People will sense what is driving you and they will avoid getting involved. Others with equally selfish motives will align themselves against you, transforming a problem-solving mission into a war over turf, power, authority, and reputation.

Start by looking at yourself in the mirror. If powerful, negative emotions are driving you, take a deep breath. Apply your emotional intelligence. Don't start developing plans until you can strip away the raw intensity, distance yourself from it, and refocus on the good of the company and all those associated with it.

Bring your boss into the loop. Make sure he or she shares your concern and agrees with your priority. Get confirmation that your boss sees your intentions as sound and honorable, and is willing to back you in your quest for a solution to the problem. This goes a long way toward establishing that your motives are good and that your effort will truly deserve the support of others in the organization.

Once you confirm that your motives are pure and dedicated to a real solution, you can get to work.

Problem-Solving Mode: Being an Internal Consultant

One key to successfully solving problems and building a new and higher platform for yourself is to leave your perspective in The Middle and rise in your thinking high enough to view the organization as a whole. This is challenging. We often have a hard time separating what's good for us and our teams from what's good for other teams within the company and for the company at large. But learning how to do this is essential for anyone who aspires to "think like a CEO" and develop the 30,000-foot perspective that goes with a broad-based, aerial view of corporate realities.

The first step toward developing an objective take on any problem is to go into an information-gathering mode. Take a step back from your personal point of view and think about the problem with fresh eyes. Begin asking some basic questions about the nature of the problem you perceive:

- Who is involved in the problem? (Consider creating a Manager's Universe chart, like the ones we looked at in Chapter 2, "The Manager's Universe," to map the key relationships that affect the problem.)

- Who is driving the problem—that is, who is in charge of the business area within which the problem resides?

- How did we get to this point? What is the history behind this problem?

- What are the goals, interests, fears, and aspirations of the people involved? Do they have reasons to feel threatened by an effort to examine, expose, or resolve the problem?

- What would a solution to the problem involve? Whose behavior might need to change?

- Who would benefit from a solution to the problem? Who might suffer?

- Is there a way to solve the problem while allowing those involved to achieve their goals as well? If your tentative solution creates some losers, is there a way to help them find a win?

The answers to some of these questions may be unclear, especially at the start of the process. To find answers, you need to assume the role of consultant. This means coming to the problem as an outsider, temporarily abandoning your personal and professional agendas and simply *listening*.

Ginny Shanks, a senior vice president at Harrah's, talks about the "Tall Poppy Syndrome." In most business workshops or problem-solving meetings, there's one person in the room who is the Tall Poppy—someone who keeps raising his hand or jumping to his feet to offer answers and solutions, even before the problem has been clearly and thoroughly defined. (Does this remind you of someone?) The Tall Poppy's conclusions may be good or bad, but they are usually incomplete and rarely win the needed support from the entire organization. By driving the group toward closure prematurely, the Tall Poppy stifles exploration, limits the group's creativity, and discourages team-building.

If you tend to play the role of Tall Poppy, work on breaking the habit. Slow down and give the group a chance to work before offering answers. Make participation by everyone the goal. When faced with a Tall Poppy, don't let them drive to a premature solution. Table the good ideas and keep thinking. Many of us raised in the U.S. school system were led to believe that there is always one right answer, and when we get it we need to move on. In reality, there may be several right answers, and true success comes by fully exploring them and combining their best features.

With your Tall Poppy under control, you're ready to begin exploring the nature of the problem in depth.

When you start working on a complex problem, begin by arranging one-on-one visits with the people involved (including anyone who appears on the relevant Manager's Universe map). Ask them to explain the problem as they see it. (You might start with the list of questions we provided a page or two ago.) Then simply listen. If they define the problem differently than you do, don't correct them or argue with them. Just follow up each answer with another question to get greater detail. Probe with questions like: "How exactly does the process work?" "Who specifically is affected?" "How often does this happen?" "Can you give me an example?" "Can you show me what happens?" Your goal should be to understand the problem at a granular level of detail, so that the solution you develop will be practical and grounded in reality.

As you go through this information-gathering process, keep your own perspective and interests at bay. Avoid suggesting solutions prematurely. And when the conversation evokes emotional reactions, don't let yourself get carried away. If you find yourself listening to people offer complaints, accusations, or anger, be empathic—but not sympathetic. In other words, use language that shows you are listening to and absorbing the message ("I can understand how that would be a problem for you," or "It sounds as if you've spent a lot of time working on that") rather than taking sides ("You were wronged," or "That was totally unfair"). Remain as neutral as possible.

Only after devoting time to gathering all the relevant information for as many points of view as possible are you ready to develop a proposed solution to the problem.

Working the Plan

Working the plan means developing a solution that is solidly grounded in everything you've learned while in information-gathering mode and that you have a reasonable chance of selling to the key decision-makers in your organization. To make this happen, I recommend a four-step process:

1. Define the problem.

2. Explore the costs of failure.

3. Explore the benefits of success.

4. Outline a solution.

Before we jump into these steps, however, let's examine a project that spun into a complete disaster and then look at how the four-step process could have enabled managers to find a path to success.

With the passage of the Health Insurance Portability and Accountability Act (HIPAA) in 1996, states around the Union began working to upgrade their Medicaid systems, first to comply with the new rules governing patient privacy and then to upgrade to Web-based services that would enable better claims processing. The ultimate payoff would be more efficient systems, benefiting the medical providers and helping the states to remain in compliance with rapidly-changing Medicaid policies.

The State of Maine knew this would be no small task. With nearly 120,000 Medicaid claims per week, the state had been using 1970s-era mainframes that were not up to the new demands.

After several years of analysis and planning, in April 2001, Maine issued a request for proposals (RFP) and received two bids—one priced at $30 million from a company that had some experience working on Medicaid systems, and another at $15 million from a company without such experience. Maine selected the lower bidder and set to work.

In January 2005, Maine's healthcare department cut the ribbon on its new system. Within a few days, the workers there found themselves facing serious problems. The system began rejecting claims for no clear reason and putting them into a "Suspend" file. The phones started to ring. By March, 300,000 claims had been suspended, and some of Maine's 262,000 Medicaid recipients were being turned away from their doctors. In fact, several dentists and therapists were forced to close their doors while some physicians had to seek loans in order to stay afloat. With Medicaid representing nearly 30 percent of the state's budget, Maine's finances were in shambles.

Meanwhile, four dozen contractors were working double time to try to fix the bugs, and the state's director of information technology was manning phones himself. Despite the effort, they just couldn't catch up. The demand was crushing and emotions were boiling.

Fingers were being pointed everywhere. The contractors claimed that when building the system they'd been forced to follow the initial Medicaid specs because they couldn't get the time they needed with Maine's state health officials. Could it be that the RFP specs had been unachievable to begin with? Others pointed to the great discrepancy between the bids and the fact that there were only two. Still others blamed the fact that, in the rush to make deadlines, the system hadn't been properly tested.

A year and a half later, the project failure had cost Maine an additional $30 million, and the problem had yet to be solved. Key players resigned, and the failure emerged as an issue in the governor's race. Maine is now the only state not compliant with the rules laid out by HIPAA.

The story of Maine's HIPAA disaster offers a clear warning about the price you and your organization may pay if you try to tackle a problem without the proper foundation. This is the importance of our four-step plan. Each step is important, and each requires you to drill deep. Otherwise, you'll probably be lacking a key element that you'll need to put the solution over the top.

Let's consider how this process might work in relation to a smaller and more typical managerial dilemma.

Suppose your company has launched a program in which you've agreed to help manage inventory of your products for several major clients.

Maybe they are large manufacturers whose products incorporate parts that you make, and you've offered to monitor their inventory levels and alert them whenever they need to replenish their supplies to avoid out-of-stock situations and factory down times. It's a valuable service that should strengthen the connection between your two companies and encourage clients to think of you as the supplier of choice.

So far, so good. But here is the problem: As manager of sales, you've begun to get feedback from a major customer (say, Acme Machines) that the inventory control system isn't working. They've suffered a couple of stock outages without being notified in a timely fashion, which forced them to shut down their assembly lines while waiting for parts. As a result, Acme's purchasing manager's hair is on fire.

Here's how you might apply the four-step process to this problem:

1. *Define the problem.* Start with a thorough information-gathering process. Speak with all the people involved: your key contacts at Acme; the salesperson in charge of the Acme account; the person or people charged with monitoring Acme's parts inventories; the person who is supposed to communicate with Acme whenever inventories are low; and any customer service rep, warehouse manager, order handler, or other person who might be part of the chain that links Acme to your company. Armed with the facts you gather, try to identify what exactly is going wrong and where the problem is localized. Are your people failing to monitor Acme's inventory levels frequently enough? Is there some uncertainty about how to count or record inventory levels? Are parts being used up in an irregular pattern so that a seemingly ample supply of parts may disappear in just a day or two? Is there a communication breakdown at a specific link in the chain? The more accurately you can answer questions like these, the more likely you'll have pinpointed the *real* definition of the problem.

2. *Explore the costs of failure.* Understand clearly with the help of all involved what failure is. Define it in both quantitative and qualitative terms, and lay out the specific negative impacts that the problem is producing. These might include costs that affect your

company and the people within it as well as other people and organizations. In this case, the costs created by the inventory control problem include the financial losses Acme has suffered due to down time on their assembly lines; the frustration and waste of time and energy experienced by Acme's managers, your sales and service staff, and others who have been struggling to rectify the problem; the potential cost to your company if you lose the Acme account as a result of continuing snafus; and the possible loss of sales commissions, bonuses, and even jobs by your team members if the Acme business disappears. Clearly identifying all of these costs is an important step in marshalling the attention you'll need to get the problem taken seriously and convince people to invest energy and money in solving it.

3. *Explore the benefits of success.* Now focus attention on the other side of the coin—the concrete benefits that will result from solving the problem once and for all. These might include improving the satisfaction level of Acme and its managers, thereby retaining the company as your client for years to come; saving the time and energy of the service staff who have been trying to solve the problem without success; increased levels of sales and profits from the Acme account, and consequent improvements in the sales commissions, bonuses, and other rewards earned by your sales team; and, perhaps best of all, the development of a foolproof system for inventory control that can be offered as a benefit to other potential customers, thereby attracting them to your firm and away from your competitors. Success is why we work, but without an examination and vision of success our work has less meaning. This is especially crucial during tough times.

4. *Outline the solution.* Finally, list the specific steps that need to be taken to solve the problem. Naturally, these steps will depend on the exact nature of the problem as you've defined it, based on the facts you gathered. If the problem was caused by unpredictable bursts of demand for your parts from the assembly lines at Acme, your solution might include assigning an employee to check in with the Acme plant manager once a day to find out how their production plans for the next two shifts will affect parts inventories. If the problem was caused by a

communications breakdown, you might need to shift responsibility for sending the crucial e-mail from a particular overworked staffer to another person with more time and a better understanding of the importance of the task.

Outlining the solution is obviously the most important step in the process, and the most challenging. Don't feel you have to solve everything on your own. Check with the real experts—the people on the ground who will have to carry out whatever steps you are envisioning. And don't assume that you know what is feasible, impossible, easy, or difficult. Quite often, tasks that seem simple from an outsider's perspective turn out to be almost impossible—and vice versa.

This was clearly the issue in regard to Maine's Medicaid system. With 20/20 hindsight, it's obvious they didn't understand the scale of the problem they were dealing with.

Think about your proposed solution from the point of view of everyone involved. Whose life will be made simpler? Whose will be made more complicated? Who might feel upset over having the boundaries of their job redefined? Whose workload will change?

The best possible solution, of course, is one that turns all of today's losers—those who are suffering from the impact of the existing problem—into winners, without imposing unacceptable costs on anyone else. In the real world, unfortunately, it's not always possible to devise such a solution. Sometimes, someone has to pay a price they won't be happy with. When that's the case, you need to creatively explore your ability to offer alternative forms of payback, reward, or recognition.

One manager found herself pushing for a solution to a problem that would unfortunately define a clear and specific loser. She strongly favored decentralizing a centralized marketing team that was led by a friend in the corporate office. Centralization had been a good way to start the business, but after several years of growth, the talent was really needed in the field and under regional leadership.

This plan was opposed—understandably—by the manager who headed the centralized team. Our manager had great respect for the leader of the centralized team, but they disagreed about what was best for the company.

After a year, our manager's plan prevailed, to the ultimate benefit of the firm. But it made the centralized marketing manager into a "loser," which did not make her happy at all. Fortunately, she and her manager kept their lines of communication open, and by championing the centralized manager on other initiatives, she made certain that everyone understood and recognized and appreciated her talents. Within weeks, the displaced manager from the centralized team was put into a new role with equal scope. What could have developed into an unfortunate battle with long-term scars remained on high ground and set the stage for a win/win result.

Selling the Plan

Up to this point, you've been the investigator, the problem-definer, the solution seeker. Now it's time to sell your plan—to leverage your personal brand value and communications skills into an effective process for winning approval for your solution and hopefully benefiting everyone affected.

There's that word: *sell*. It's a word that I've found many managers are uncomfortable with. I think they feel this way because of the many common misconceptions about selling. I want to take a moment to address those.

As it happens, I have an extensive sales background. Sometimes when new acquaintances hear about this, one will say, "Oh, I could *never* be in sales." Here is the first misconception. The fact is that if you work in business, you are selling all the time. Whenever you present information in a way people find interesting and convincing, whenever you make a suggestion other people agree with, whenever you make an offer people accept, whenever you lay out a plan people follow—whenever you do any of these things, you are selling. You couldn't have a job in management unless you have some degree of sales experience and expertise—perhaps without realizing it.

Other times, when I talk about the importance of selling skills in the everyday work of management, people respond, "I guess I can sell something I believe in. But I can't sell something I don't." They think of the typical salesman as being a huckster, trying to pawn off worthless goods on unsuspecting suckers, and naturally they don't want to have anything to do with this.

Fortunately, as an ignited manager, there's no reason why you should ever have to sell a product you don't believe in. In the situation we're addressing—trying to sell your solution to a problem that plagues your company—you've followed a process that has helped you understand the problem in depth, figure out its implications, and develop a solution that maximizes the benefits for everyone. So now you are trying to sell the solution because it will make winners out of everyone—not just you. Isn't this a product that's easy to believe in?

Finally, there are managers who tell me, "I suppose I can sell. But I hate the idea of closing. I feel so uncomfortable asking for a commitment."

This is the third big misconception about selling. In the first place, *closing* is the wrong word to use. It implies that the deal is done and over. In truth, any deal worth doing creates a *relationship*, in which there will arise a natural cycle of attention, reconsideration, and reselling. Making an initial commitment is simply part of that cycle—the part in which both parties say, "We want to work together, and we're ready to get started. Let's see how things develop."

The same thinking applies to selling a business solution. Asking for commitment is just a matter of saying, "Can we get started on this solution?" If your idea has been well researched, carefully planned, and clearly presented, it should seem unnatural *not* to make that kind of commitment.

The Wrong and Right Ways to Sell

None of this is to say that having to sell something isn't intimidating. Every salesperson has a couple of stories to illustrate how challenging it can be—and mine help to fuel me.

In 1993, I took a job selling advertising time at a television station in Monterey, California. For my first sales call, I went to visit a small nursery called Graeber Gardens out on Highway 68.

I found Tom Graeber, the owner of the nursery, in the back of his shop arranging some flower pots. I greeted him, "Hi, Tom. I'm Vince

Thompson from KCCN-TV. I came by to talk to you about television advertising. Did you know the television is the perfect way to expose your business to local consumers?"

Tom gazed back at me, blank-faced and silent. A little puzzled, I pressed on. "You see, Tom, with a television commercial, you can educate people about the great offerings you have and demonstrate that you are different from the other nurseries in town."

Still I got no response from Tom. I babbled on about TV advertising for a few more minutes until I finally gave up. Wearing a big, fake smile, I shook Tom's hand. "Well, thanks so much for listening. I'll come by again soon and bring you some research that shows how television can grow the business for local nurseries."

I was halfway back to my car, wondering what I'd said or done wrong, when something amazing happened. Tom called out my name. Thrilled, I hurried back. "How can I help you?" I asked.

"You forgot to ask me something," Tom said. "Ask me if I have any co-op dollars available for advertising." (That's money provided by manufacturers to help local distributors advertise their goods.)

Well, I was game. "Okay. Do you have any co-op dollars available?"

"Nope." Finally, Tom was smiling. "I just didn't want you coming back here to ask that question later."

In an instant, I saw the world the way Tom Graeber saw it. Besieged by media salespeople, he was fed up with people interrupting his work to try to get his money rather than finding out what *he* wanted or needed. And I had been no different—just another guy trying to earn a commission.

It was my first lesson in how *not* to sell.

A few days later, I went to call on a gentleman named Mr. Z., a jeweler who was a big buyer of local TV time.

"Hi, Mr. Z. I'm Vince Thompson with KCCN-TV."

Mr. Z.'s response was brief and sarcastic: "Congratulations." The message was very clear: The local television station I represented meant absolutely nothing to him. Once again, if I hoped to earn any of his valuable time and attention, I'd better learn something about his business and figure out how to meet some of *his* needs, not my own.

What I learned is this:

> *A solution is not a solution until it addresses a problem that someone cares to solve.*

If I were going to call on Mr. Z. today, I would do the following:

I would start by trying to understand the problems that Mr. Z was facing. I assumed he wanted to sell more jewelry, and that base assumption was probably correct. But businesses don't get too excited about base solutions, because they are generally focused on the many little problems that challenge their big mission. Mr. Z's problems could have been specifically related to selling more silver in the run-up to Valentine's Day. Gold was where the demand was, but silver had the margin. How could he get more consideration for silver during his biggest sales day? A smart salesman would have dug to uncover that specific problem, then offered a real solution for it.

Tom and Mr. Z. taught me an invaluable lesson about selling. Prospects are worried about *their* problems, not mine, and those problems are specific. To be successful, a salesperson must be perceived as someone offering solutions that are backed by expertise and ideas, not a bag of products. This approach—often called *consultative selling*—takes a lot more work. But it pays off in valuable ways.

After I adopted the consultative model, I achieved a record-setting level of new business during my first year selling television time in the Monterey Salinas market. I also gained pride in my role, as I wasn't just selling stuff, but rather helping people solve their problems.

Trying to sell when you *don't* have a true solution to offer is not a very satisfying experience. And it's not likely to be very successful. Fortunately, as a manager in The Middle selling solutions to business problems to your colleagues and your boss, you never need to be in that position.

Building Value for the Solution

In order to sell your plan, it's important to understand where the value lies and how to bring it forth. You've already explored the implications of failure or success, which serve as great motivators. But they don't explain how to tell the story of value.

Value is all about benefits *versus* costs. Let's face it, most business solutions are costly. They require an investment of money, time, or energy—often all three. That's why stirring people to action—getting them to accept and implement your solution—isn't easy. To make it happen, you have to show people the value of the solution—its quality, its utility, and the service it provides.

The Value Equation captures this basic relationship:

$$PV = \frac{PQ + PU + PS}{Price}$$

Translation: The perceived value (PV) of anything is its perceived quality (PQ) plus its perceived utility (PU) plus the perceived service (PS) it offers, divided by the price.

As a solution seller, your job is to build the top line in the Value Equation to the point where the price in the bottom line seems fair or even low. The more value you can demonstrate for the quality, utility, and service you are providing, the more your customer will be willing to pay.

Let's consider a simple example. Suppose you have a problem getting high-quality, inexpensive, timely color copies for your work in the marketing department. The current system is to send copy work out to a nearby copy center via e-mail. Every afternoon, Susan, who works in the front office and is in charge of the black-and-white copiers there, takes a walk to pick up the finished color copies. Under this system, it may take several hours to get a couple of copies for an important client presentation.

Your solution is to buy a color copier of your own. You're convinced that this would produce a series of benefits. It will help you get copies faster, allow you to use color more frequently, and help you create better presentations for your customers and vendors.

But this plan has to be approved by Susan in the front office and her friend Becky in Finance. They are convinced that a color photocopier is a ridiculous expense. What's more, Susan expresses concern that the new copier will be noisy, will create extra heat in the summer, and will give her one more machine to buy supplies for and to fix when it jams.

Now, getting color copies for presentations is only 1 percent of your job. But making copies is 50 percent of Susan's. Clearly the costs of getting a color copier will loom large in her mind, giving her a strong incentive to fight you.

To sell the concept, you need to build up the top-line value of your solution. You'll need to demonstrate PQ (perceived quality) by showing that the overall appearance and professionalism of your client presentations will increase. You'll need to demonstrate PU (perceived utility) by showing that having high-quality color copies available quickly and easily will offer productivity benefits to your department. And you'll need to demonstrate PS (perceived service) by showing that Susan will have *less* work to do—no more daily trips to the local copy center, because marketing folks will be able to make their own color copies.

Finally, you'll talk about the price difference of in-house *versus* outsourced copying. If you've really built the top-line value, then the price of the machine will seem nominal given the high level of quality, utility, and service it provides.

Now, you may be saying, "All this is well and good. And Becky in Finance might be impressed by the Value Equation. But Susan in the front office still has her reasons for fighting tooth and nail against the color copier."

True enough. We have to remember another of our selling principles: Find ways to make the losers into winners. Let's alleviate Susan's fears by officially putting her in charge of the new machine. She'll choose it, meet the vendors, and monitor usage. This may not be a complete win for her, but at least we can acknowledge that she is still running the world of copying. And maybe we can find a few bucks in the training budget to send Susan off for an all-day seminar on digital color imaging, helping her develop a bit of marketable expertise while increasing her value to the company at the same time.

Suddenly our solution is looking like a win for all involved.

Let's not forget the team in Maine who failed to make a case for the higher bidder or an entirely different Medicaid system. Had they fully understood the cost of failure and demonstrated the utility, quality, and service inherent in the best solution, they would have likely raised the value to a point where a winning option would have gained support. In the absence of perceived value, the low bidder always wins.

Here are some other tips for managing the selling process:

- Remember the CAVE people from Chapter 1, "Action with Traction"—the Citizens Against Virtually Everything? These are the people who can be counted on to oppose any new initiative. Your selling strategy: Avoid them. If you don't engage the CAVE people, they usually rant and rave in their own quiet corner, ignored by most other people (who have learned over time to take their complaints with a great big grain of salt).

- Go first to your support faction—the people who are likely to be on your side. Explain the Value Equation inputs and elaborate on both the costs of failure and the benefits of success. You will be giving your supporters the ammunition they need to join the argument on your side.

- Then go to the probable detractors. You've already met with them during your information-gathering process. Now pay them the courtesy of a visit, tell them about your proposal, and explain how you propose to make them winners (even if you can only offer half a loaf). Seek their buy-in. But understand that some will choose to oppose you. Some may immediately start working against you. Be prepared for this.

- Give people an opportunity to participate in shaping the solution. Legend has it that, back in the 1950s, the Betty Crocker company found sales of its new instant cake mix lagging. As it turned out, they'd made the process *too* easy. When they changed the formula to require customers to add an egg to the mix, sales improved. People like to feel they've contributed to the process—so let your customers "crack an egg in the cake" and watch as their buy-in and commitment increases.

Once again, it helps matters if your motives are right. If they are, you will be less likely to react with anger or defensiveness. Instead, you will be able to push your solution whole-heartedly for the good of the company, defining the best in the best terms. If you encounter evil motives—and sometimes you will—don't ignore them. At the same time, don't stoop to that level. There will be a time and place when you are asked about your detractors' comments. You can dismiss them by simply saying, "Consider the source." If they are truly out to cause trouble, those who hear your words will understand them and follow your lead.

Will you win every battle? Of course not. But you will end up feeling good about yourself, no matter what happens. Fighting for what's right is so much better than lying to people in the hallway about what you are doing and why.

Selling to the Top

If you are tackling a complex problem, the last step in the selling process is likely to be seeking buy-in from your company's senior-level or C-suite executives. It's usually the most intimidating part of the process. But it doesn't have to be. Start by realizing that a senior executive is fundamentally a human being like you or your colleagues, and that the same kinds of appeals that work with you probably work with him or her. If you've mastered the facts and thought through your proposal as we recommend, you will probably find that the senior executives are responsive to its inherent strengths and to the benefits its offers the company.

However, senior executives do have some special characteristics that you ought to be aware of when you communicate with them.

First, remember that these are very, very busy people. Swamped by too many decisions, they relish simplicity. So before you approach a C-level exec, master the elevator version of your story—the 30-second description of the problem, the costs and benefits associated with it, and your proposed solution. The executive is likely to want more details *after* hearing the elevator version, but he can ask for those specifically. Don't lay them on to begin with—keep it simple.

Here are a couple of examples of elevator presentations, each one built around the same basic structure—problem, costs and benefits, solution:

> "We have a problem with our marketing presentations. Only 20 percent are in color. The work is good, but the appearance is poor. For 500 bucks a month in additional expense, we can get all our copies in color. It'll make us look more professional and upscale when we're competing against other companies."

Or like this:

> "Our system for monitoring client inventories is broken. The clients are mad, and our sales are suffering. If we hire a specialist to focus on tracking inventories and keeping customers informed, we can retain more clients, increase our sales to them, and attract additional customers because of our first-class service."

Or like this:

> "We can turn outsourcing into a big win with our employees and the community by outsourcing a phone room to a local charity that provides jobs to the homeless. The quality will be as good as India, the costs will be only 20 percent more, and we'll get positive coverage in local media instead of being criticized."

Do you notice anything unusual about the vocabulary used in these presentations? That's right—there's nothing unusual about it at all. One of the big mistakes managers make when talking to senior execs is trying to impress them with consultant-speak, business school terminology, technical lingo, and similar forms of BS. Don't scatter your sentences with buzz phrases from the latest *Harvard Business Review* article. Just say it plainly, which is how most CEOs themselves prefer to talk. And if you're called up to make a formal presentation about your idea, don't over-prepare. No one wants to see a 40-slide PowerPoint presentation or a stack of 15 graphs and charts to demonstrate your point. Again, those details can always be provided later if a specific question arises.

If possible, try to talk face-to-face rather than making your pitch via phone, memo, or e-mail. If you've built a relationship with the person and with his assistant, this will be possible. You don't need to be golfing buddies, but if the executive vice president of finance or marketing at least knows your name, you will be able to call his assistant and say, "I need ten minutes with Mr. Harrison sometime tomorrow. Can you pencil me in?"

It also helps if you have one true fan on the C-level team. This is where a strong and positive mentoring relationship can be invaluable. If you've nurtured a real connection with any one member of the top executive team, the others will use him for check-in whenever your name comes up in conversation: "What do you know about this guy Vince? Is he on the ball?" This is why it pays to meet the needs of the senior executives. They will become your supporters when you need them.

Finally, when a problem is complicated and has *not* yet hit the radar of the executive decision-maker, consider presenting it in stages. It's very hard to get someone to become aware of a problem, its implications, and a potential solution all in a single meeting. It's just too much for most people to absorb. Instead, try to present the problem and its implications in one meeting, say you are working on a solution, and then come back a few days later with the solution. In the interim, the exec will have mulled the problem, perhaps gotten a bit of further information about it, and will be fully prepared to evaluate your solution when you return.

Above all, don't be afraid to talk to your senior execs. The smartest ones are well-aware that a good idea doesn't care who it belongs to, and they're eager to get insights from anyone and everyone.

David O'Reilly, CEO of the big Midwestern retailer O'Reilly Auto Parts, says it well: "If any manager has an idea, I'm totally open to them just bouncing it off me. I don't expect them to have all the answers. I know they've got jobs to do, and I certainly don't want them knocking themselves out on an idea before it gets vetted. So I'd rather hear an idea, even if it's half-baked. Then, if it's worthwhile, I can encourage them to go for it."

That's the attitude most CEOs have. After all, they didn't get to the top by refusing to listen to good ideas.

Follow the tips in this chapter, and you'll find that your reputation among your fellow managers—all the way up to the C-suite—is that of a smart contributor and a positive problem-solver—not a whiner, a politician, a victim, a wise-guy, or a schmoozer. You'll also find that the power and purpose you've developed through this book is manifesting itself in ways that you know are right and can feel great about.

14

YOUR OWN SENSE
OF BALANCE

What's It All For?

A corporate executive on holiday in a small Greek seacoast village was strolling by the docks and drinking in the local color. He complimented one fisherman on the quality of his catch. "How long did it take you to get all those fish?" he wondered.

"Not very long," answered the Greek. "An hour or two."

"Then why didn't you stay out longer to catch more?"

Shrugging, the Greek explained that his catch was sufficient to meet his needs and those of his family. The executive asked, "But what do you do with the rest of your time?"

"I sleep late, fish a little, play with my children, and take a nap with my wife. In the evening, I go to the village to see my friends, dance a little, play the bouzouki, and sing songs. I have a full life."

The executive said, "I have an MBA from Harvard. I can help you. You should start by fishing longer every day. You'll catch extra fish that you can sell. With the revenue, you can buy a bigger boat. With the extra money the larger boat will bring you, you can buy a second boat and a third one, and so on, until you have an entire fleet of trawlers. Instead of selling your fish to a middleman, you can then negotiate directly with the processing plants and maybe even open your own plant. You can ship fish to markets all around the world. In time, you can then move to New York City to direct your huge enterprise."

"How long would that take?" asked the Greek.

"Twenty, perhaps twenty-five years," replied the executive.

"And after that?"

"When your business gets really big, you can sell stock and make millions!" exclaimed the executive with zeal.

"Millions? Really? And after that?"

"After that you'll be able to retire, live in a small village near the coast, sleep late, play with your grandchildren, catch a few fish, take a nap with your wife, and spend your evenings singing, dancing, and playing the bouzouki with your friends."

Achieving a true sense of balance isn't easy in a world where balance is talked about but not rewarded. We live with the banging pots, filling slots in command-and-control hierarchies where goals like making the boss look good, covering our collective asses, and acting busy too often take precedence over real accomplishments—to say nothing of living a rich and meaningful life.

Living in Quake Country, under pressure 24/7, we tend to think of existence as a series of steps in a process—graduating from college, landing the first job, earning the first promotion, getting the big bonus, making VP, making SVP... At times the process becomes its own justification, as it did for the businessman on holiday. And in the midst of the daily grind, sometimes it's all we can do to focus on one year, one week, one day at a time—the next meeting, the next report, the next quarter's sales figures. A kind of myopia sets in, as if we are wearing blinders that only let us see one moment at a time.

It's ridiculous and ironic. Consider Lily Tomlin's take: "The trouble with the rat race is that, even if you win, you're still a rat."

The context in which we operate is certainly part of the problem. But even in today's imperfect, frustrating business environment, where it's hard to think about long-term happiness, you need to focus periodically on the end game—your ultimate purpose. Otherwise, like that businessman, you'll fail to recognize the good life even when it's staring you in the face. And this means finding your own definition of success and building around it a life and career that you can be proud of, regardless of whether or not you ever make VP, attain the corner office, or take a company public.

I once heard a speech by Ted Turner, the flamboyant and brilliant entrepreneur who founded CNN. Here's what he said about success:

> I've got great kids, and for that I'm very grateful. And I can tell you this: You may be really successful in your career, but if you don't have good kids, you won't feel very successful. But you can be moderately successful in your career, and if you've got great kids, you'll feel really successful.

Sure, we all know family is important. What makes Ted's statement powerful is his concept of choice. We'd all clearly choose great kids over material and ego-based success, but are we really doing that? Do our dreams for our families take precedence over everything else, or do we behave as if we think that the halo of our material success will somehow help our kids be better people?

Money, status, and the other trappings of conventional success may be important. But in the end, the old wisdom is correct—they don't bring you happiness.

The corporate world may never give you credit for developing and pursuing your own definition of the good life. And if impressing other people is the most important thing in your life, you may want to skip the rest of this chapter. But if impressing *yourself* is what ultimately matters to you, read on.

The Keys to True Balance

In my role as a sales manager, I've managed a drummer, a screenwriter, a singer, an actor, a book publisher, a race car driver, a marathoner, and a sharpshooter—none of whom ever imagined that they'd find themselves selling advertising.

Let's face it: If most of us pursued our dream jobs, we wouldn't be doing what we're doing. We'd be bartending in a beach shack in

Costa Rica, coaching a pro baseball team, or greenlighting films in Hollywood. The fact is that somewhere along the way we decided we needed to pay the rent and keep the lights on, and the careers we're in seemed either complementary or a means to an end.

At the same time, no one is getting any younger, and the concept that we'll work for a few years until we cash out our millions and pursue our dreams is not realistic for most of us. Instead, we need to fill our souls while putting family first and moving toward the balance we so desire.

We've talked about white space and demonstrated how your passions can play a role in your business life. Steve Jobs found a place for his love of calligraphy, and Gary Thompson made his poker dreams come true. The key to creating the environment for these kinds of successes is your own personal plan to work towards a sense of balance that fulfills all your needs.

Here is a five-step program that can help you get started.

The first step in achieving true balance is to *know what your goal is.* Where do you want to go? What do you want to accomplish in your life and work? Do you want to master accounting and then move into operations? Do you want to rise to the C-level within your company? Do you want to start your own firm, build it up, and then sell it? Do you want to go freelance and work independently? Or would you be content to find a comfortable, productive niche as a Middleshift manager driving your company through your unique ideas and training the future generation?

There's no one right answer to this question. Those who are hyper-competitive and those with more modest aspirations can both be equally happy (or unhappy). The key is knowing what you really want—not what your spouse or your parents or your mentor or your best friend might want—and pursuing it with gusto.

Your goal should also include life objectives beyond work. Try to define what a balanced life means for you. Is it getting home from work by six o'clock every night? Is it having weekends free to coach your kids' soccer team? Is it being able to take a month off in the summer to sail the Mediterranean? Is it working within five minutes of your favorite gym so you never have to miss your daily workout? Is it restricting your time on the road to no more than two weeks a year? Again, there's no single right answer to this question. Only you can define what constitutes balance for you—perhaps in consultation with the people in your life who matter most to you.

Which leads us to the second step in achieving balance: *develop a plan for reaching your goal.* Think realistically about what it will take to get to the level of accomplishment you are dreaming about. Do you need more formal education? If so, think about classes at night or on the weekend, or consider whether you can take time off to pursue that advanced degree. Do you need a broader range of experience outside your current job description? Ask about the possibility of a lateral transfer or, if need be, consider changing companies to get the background you need. Does a different industry hold greater promise for achieving the career growth you seek? If so, use your networking skills to identify contacts in that industry who may be able to advise you about how to get a foothold in that arena.

Understand that there are a lot of ways to get to bingo. Be flexible in pursuing your plan. Always look for new and faster paths. And when you find yourself in a rut (which almost everyone eventually does), don't kvetch—fix it or climb out.

Third, *develop a scale of measurement that is yours alone.* If you measure yourself by others' standards, you're likely to fail. It's human nature that, when we pick people against which to measure ourselves, we focus on the most visible, admired, accomplished, and successful people we know. If you measure your own success or failure by this kind of comparison, you'll probably always feel slightly inadequate.

What's more, the fact that we judge other people by *exterior* signs of success means that our judgments are always somewhat misleading. We see the big house on the hill; we don't see the jumbo mortgage and the maxed-out credit cards. We see the well-dressed spouse and the three kids attending Ivy League schools; we don't see the late-night tirades or little Susie's problem with cocaine.

Get away from measuring yourself against the Joneses, Gonzales's, or Patels. Instead, gauge your progress toward your personal goal. And in the short term, set intermediate goals for yourself and pat yourself on the back when you achieve them. For example, you might decide, "This year,

I want to launch at least one initiative from my project portfolio... I want to increase the value of the relationships in my Manager's Universe... I want to take a course in Web design so I can create an interactive site for our business next year... I want to get two of my best people promoted." It doesn't matter what anyone else would think about these benchmarks—if you believe in them, then they are the right ones for you.

You'll find that movement towards your own goals is a calming force. Take time to appreciate your work and be thankful.

Fourth, *create and work with your personal board of directors*—an informal guiding council of people you respect and trust to help you stay on course. They may or may not meet as a group; what matters is that you keep in touch with each member of your board, share honestly with them everything significant that happens in your career, and take their advice seriously. Your board members should include your mentor(s), one or two good friends who know you well and are prepared to talk frankly with you about your strengths and weaknesses, and perhaps a couple of professional acquaintances who can provide an objective perspective on your industry, your company, and your role.

The third-party point of view that your board of directors brings to the table can serve as a valuable corrective when you get out of balance.

Fifth, *care for yourself as needed to stay on track*. Many managers are so consumed with their responsibilities—to their team members, their companies, their families—that self-care becomes an afterthought, usually neglected. Don't make this mistake. If you don't care for yourself, in time you'll become unable to care for anyone else.

This means nurturing both your physical and your psychological well-being. On the physical side, you know the drill: Eat right, exercise, get enough sleep, visit your doctor, and take his advice seriously. Don't fall into the trap of abusing your body as some kind of macho proof of how tough and valuable you are: "Hey, I work 80-hour weeks and haven't taken any time off since 1989!" Some people may be impressed, but that doesn't include the people who know you and love you the best—and how impressive will it be when you drop dead of a heart attack at age 49?

On the psychological side, there are many paths to balance. Some managers use prayer or meditation; others recharge their batteries by walking in the woods, doing painting or sculpture, or practicing yoga, tai chi, or pilates. What matters is that you periodically clear your brain of information and your heart of stress, so that both can be filled and refreshed with silence and light. Otherwise, you'll eventually drive yourself crazy, either literally or figuratively. And no career is worth that kind of price.

I like what motivational speaker and training consultant Jim Schaffer has to say. Jim recommends four practices for those days when you can barely hear yourself think (which for many of us means practically every day on the job):

1. *Be grateful.* Start your business day with an expression of gratitude, in whatever form it takes. Try this for a month or two, and you'll be floating on a cloud. Try it for a couple of years, and it will permanently transform your career and, indeed, your entire life.

2. *Be quiet.* Notice I didn't say "silent"—that might bring your career to a screeching halt. I mean internally quiet, with a deeply experienced sense of spaciousness and ability to listen and see things clearly as they are.

3. *Surrender.* Again, I'm not suggesting that you hide in your office re-reading old issues of *Rolling Stone* magazine. But most of us became successful by being good control freaks. Maybe it's time to loosen our grip and let go of our fears, judgments, ideas of how the world should be, and elaborate stories we weave about events that occur. It's time to stay in the present moment and remain open to what arises.

4. *This too shall pass.* Know that whether you're struggling with a particularly nagging problem or enjoying the adrenaline rush of success, the situation has already begun to change. You'll be much more effective if you can learn how to watch it evolve. The more you cling to pleasure and try to avoid pain, the less energy you'll have for acting skillfully as things unfold.

Jim's suggestions are some of the best I know for helping you stay on balance when the world is trying desperately to push you off-center.

Here is another. It comes from Bob Sherman, a legendary media manager and entrepreneur. When Bob was working in the Midwest, he found the sight of farmers ending their workdays in the evening deeply inspirational:

> Think about the farmer in his field, looking over the acreage he's just plowed with pride and surveying the beauty of a good day's work. After a few minutes he calls it a day to be with family and his passions. Every manager needs to have the same kind of wrap-up ritual for the end of the day. Look at your field. Reflect on what you've accomplished. Feel satisfied about your work. Then turn off the Blackberry for the night and move on to rest of life. Enjoy what you've worked so hard for.

There's wisdom in Bob's advice. The urgent always seems so important until it sits a few hours and settles into its rightful place. The key is knowing when it's time to disconnect.

Balance for the Long Haul

Understand that balance does not happen in any given hour, day, or week. It happens over longer periods. The balanced life doesn't mean that you never have crunch times or all-nighters or frenzied weekends in pursuit of a big account or an insane deadline. It does mean that you don't work to the exclusion of your life. Every weekend shouldn't be a working weekend; every vacation shouldn't be accompanied by cell phone appointments and marathon e-mail sessions. You should be able to schedule the things that matter to you and those you love—your kid's school play, a special dinner out—without having them cancelled for work (except on *very* rare occasions).

The same long-haul perspective applies to being happy with the work you do. Every job has its drudgery, and practically everyone has to do some things that he or she can't stand. Accepting a few such jobs with good grace is part of being mature. But when your work life is *dominated* by hateful chores, it's a sign of trouble.

Do you really enjoy your work or have you just gotten good at acting as if you like it—wearing the mask of happiness because you know that you need to put your best foot forward? Is it hard for you to remember the last time you felt *excited* about a project? Have you started counting the days until your next vacation and the months until you retire? If so, you shouldn't just swallow your unhappiness. Today's business world offers a broad enough range of managerial opportunities for anyone with leadership in his DNA to be reasonably fulfilled... not necessarily working at your dream job, but at least not *dreading* the daily sound of the alarm clock.

Periodically, apply the Turn-On Test to your job. While working on a project, do you ever feel energized? Do you begin to fantasize about the outcome? Do you get goose bumps about it? Is working on the project just plain *fun?* If you can answer yes, then you are turned on. If the answer is a consistent no, then you need to figure out why—and begin to connect more deeply with your own project portfolio or start looking for fresh opportunities elsewhere.

You won't feel turned on all the time. But you should feel turned on *sometimes.*

You Get More When You Give More

Finally, I have to say a word about giving back. Deliberately practicing generosity of spirit is one of the best ways to create and maintain a sense of balance and fulfillment in your life.

You don't need me to teach you what this is all about. If you have any questions, the great spiritual teachers of all time can answer them. So let me just offer a few reminders of things you already know you should do:

- Give to those who have nothing to give in return.
- Share everything you can.
- Be charitable with your time and energy.
- Be a mentor—coach, inspire, and listen to people.
- Commit to people. Try to take responsibility for their dreams—help make them come true.
- Do what you say you'll do.
- Don't knock people down—lift people up.

Here's an example that is silly, but very real. My wife was on her way to the dermatologist the other day when she got into the elevator with Richard Simmons. Yes, *that* Richard Simmons, the TV exercise and fitness guru—and no, he wasn't wearing dolphin shorts and a tank top. (I asked.)

Anyway, Richard took a look at my wife and immediately said, "Wow, look at you! Those arms, that waist! You must work out all the time."

Naturally, she was flattered, and she excitedly shared the story with me that evening. "How cool," I said, "What a compliment!"

And my wife replied, "Yeah, it made me feel great. You know what it is about him? He's a giver. He goes out of his way to make people feel good. We could all learn something from him."

Conclusion

Research tells us that managers are unhappy and stressed, and our interviews confirmed much of this. But there was a greater theme that we never lost track of. Today's managers are also hopeful, committed, and driven to find ways to contribute more. They want to get deeper into solutions and to take responsibility for success.

It's the dream of this manager that we can elevate our individual positions within companies and collectively change the business world. Changing the business world is a unique call to each of us. We are the ones on the fulcrum and the ones who must stand for the call of duty.

As for me, I'm not worried at all. I've seen your grace, your talent, and your energy. I know that together we will make this right. Together, we will be ignited!

INDEX

corporate legacies, updating,
190-193
Coulter, John, 49
courage, 234-239
Covery, Stephen, 84
criticism, offering, 159
customers
educating colleagues about,
171-173
turning into partners, 173-175
understanding, 169-171

D

Danly IEM, 97
decision-making, guiding with
corporate history, 216-219
defining problems, 257
Democratic leadership style, 83
demographic change, impact on
middle management, 8
departments, collaboration between,
128-132
designing personal project
portfolios, 31-33
direct communication, 67-69
Dixon, Lance, 178
doing versus knowing, 29-31
dot-coms, 209-210
Drake, Michael, 84, 87-88, 229-231
Drucker, Peter, 169
Dunn, Marcia, 240

E

E.Q. (emotional intelligence), 80-83
Edmondson, Brad, 148-150
emergent strategy, 187-190
emotional dynamics
consequences of ignoring,
239-243
emotional sensitivity, 231-234

feedback, giving, 232-234
insight and courage, 234-239
leading with the heart, 243
making positives out of
negatives, 231-234
motivation, 228-231
power of, 227-228
emotional intelligence, 80-83
*Emotional Intelligence: Why It Can
Matter More Than IQ*, 81
emotional sensitivity, 231-234
emotions, managing, 79-80
bad news, reacting to, 89-92
The Bigger Yes, 83-89
emotional intelligence, 80-83
maintaining balance between
company and team, 92-95
employees
employee satisfaction, 4
motivating, 72-75
empowerment
coercive power, 107
example of self-empowered
manager, 97-99
excuses for lack of
empowerment, 99-101
expert power, 107
information power, 107
legitimate power, 107
power of change, 109-111
power of righteousness, 112-113
referent power, 107
reward power, 106
seizing tools of empowerment,
101-104
sources of power, 106-109
Wagon Train Effect, 104-106
Engel, Dan, 52
Enthusian, 33
expert power, 107
explicit needs, 23-24

JOIN THE COMMUNITY OF IGNITED MANAGERS

For exclusive content, access to private events, and other valuable resources for managers, register for FREE at www.beignited.com.

GAIN ACCESS to extended content from the book:
- Worksheets and One-Sheets (The Manager's Universe, The Value Equation, and more)
- D. Karnedy's contract with new hires
- Valuable online resources for scanning your landscape

EXPLORE our Manager's Resources Center:
- CareerBuilder's salary tool
- Tips to write better emails
- Employment law information
- Tips for effective listening
- Funny workplace videos and websites

CONTRIBUTE to the conversation:
- Share your stories for Vince's next book
- Pose questions for and contribute to Vince's blog
- Spark dialogue with other managers

Join now for FREE at www.BeIgnited.com